THEORY AND INTERPRETATION OF NARRATIVE

James Phelan, Peter J. Rabinowitz, and Robyn Warhol, Series Editors

— 8 pages a day —

Ethics and the
Dynamic Observer Narrator

Reckoning with Past and Present in German Literature

Katra A. Byram

 THE OHIO STATE UNIVERSITY PRESS • COLUMBUS

Library of Congress Cataloging-in-Publication Data
Byram, Katra A., 1975– author.
  Ethics and the dynamic observer narrator : reckoning with past and present in German literature / Katra A. Byram.
       pages cm. — (Theory and interpretation of narrative) Includes bibliographical references
and index.
  ISBN 978-0-8142-1276-9 (hardback) — ISBN 978-0-8142-9381-2 (cd)
  1. German fiction—History and criticism—Theory, etc. 2. Narration (Rhetoric) 3. Literature
and history—Germany. I. Title.
  PT741.B97 2015
  833.009—dc23
                                    2014037182

Cover design by James A. Baumann
Text design by Juliet Williams
Type set in Adobe Minion Pro
Printed by Thomson-Shore, Inc.

9 8 7 6 5 4 3 2 1

For Todd, whose story is entwined with mine

contents

acknowledgments

In writing this book, I have enjoyed support, encouragement, and constructive criticism from many sources. The policies for junior faculty course and service release in the Ohio State University College of Arts and Sciences and Department of Germanic Languages and Literatures have given me the time I needed to write this book. Many friends and colleagues have read portions of the text at various stages and have provided valuable feedback. I thank them and look forward to continuing our writing exchanges in the future: Naomi Brenner, Sarah Copland, Jens Klenner, Bernhard and Marie Malkmus, May Mergenthaler, Kristin Rebien, Rob Schechtman, Megan Ward, and Chantelle Warner. Others gave valuable responses to presentations: Silke Horstkotte, Barbara Kosta, Erin McGlothlin, Leo Riegert, Johannes Türk, and James A. van Dyke. My dissertation committee members, Chana Kronfeld, Elaine Tennant, and Robert Holub, offered comments and advice that guided the first steps of my revisions and expansions. Robert Holub also read parts of the book manuscript and provided strategic advice about presenting the project; I am grateful for his ongoing mentorship. I owe deep thanks to the four readers who reviewed the manuscript for The Ohio State University Press, all of whom read it exceptionally carefully, and with an eye to helping me improve and better communicate my argument: James Phelan, Peter Rabinowitz, Irene Kacandes, and Scott Denham. James Phelan deserves particular recognition and gratitude for the encouragement he has offered since I first approached him about my project several years ago, and for his generosity with his time and advice during the revision process. The two acquisitions editors with whom I have worked at OSU Press, Sandy Crooms and Lindsay Martin, have been extremely responsive and helpful as I have prepared the manuscript for submission.

All of these people helped make the book better. A number of other people have made it possible. My parents, Will and Joan Byram, always told me I could go wherever I wanted to go and gave me everything they could to help me get there, from self-confidence to a warm sleeping bag to babysitting and dinners cooked after work. I could not have finished the book when I did (and maybe not at all) without the practical advice and daily encouragement I received from my online and on-site writing groups: Fiona, Sharon, TP, TB, MMFS, Lynn, Badia, profmaman, Adriana, Helen, Liza, Sylvia, Sophia, and Sarah, you know who you are. My children, Abram and Helena, have given me a reason to buckle down and write so I can go home and do other things. Finally, my husband, Todd, has challenged me whenever I didn't make sense or wasn't being clear; pushed me to trust my instincts and interpretations; shared the demands of the work/life balance; and, while being silly with me, always taken my work seriously.

introduction

How do people sometimes come to be in places where, when they stop to think, they wonder how they got there?
  —Wilhelm Raabe, *Stuffcake: A Tale of Murder and the High Seas*

How did we become what we are today?
  —Christa Wolf, *A Model Childhood*

Personal identity and personal history have been defining preoccupations—one might even say obsessions—of the modern age. Questions much like those asked by Wilhelm Raabe and Christa Wolf drive both fictional and nonfictional accounts, from confessional literature and Enlightenment autobiography, to the *Bildungsroman* and artist's self-portrait, to the memoirs crowding the shelves (or claiming the gigabytes) of today's bookstores. This book does not presume to explain this fascination or offer an exhaustive account of its exploration in writing, whether fictive or autobiographical. Instead, it investigates a peculiarity signaled by the similarity between Raabe's and Wolf's questions and the similar forms their answers take. The narrators' questions reveal a common struggle to understand their present identities in relation to their pasts, to make sense of the events and experiences that have led them to where they stand. The novels that answer these questions share a common form, in which a character narrator relates a story about another character's life. The shared questions and narrative forms suggest that these two works—separated from each other by nearly a century and straddling the line between the fictional and the factual—share a two-faceted conception of identity. First, identity relies on narrative. This narrative emerges from individuals' history and experiences, and from their

1

attempts to understand and explain who they are in the present by telling a story about the past. Second, identity is relational. The story one tells about the past doesn't have to be about oneself, at least not centrally. In fact, telling a story about someone else's past may be an extremely effective way to define who one is and has been—and who one is not.[1]

In other words, this book argues that the similarities between Raabe's and Wolf's novels are not peculiar at all; instead, they reflect fundamental aspects of the way many people have understood themselves for the last two hundred years. In Germany, the French Revolution and its aftermath crystallized the sense, already nascent in Enlightenment conceptions of subjectivity, of the relationship between the individual and a history unfolding its distinct eras through time. Within this new conception of history, the individual often understood himself as occupying a moment of historical flux and changing over time. This discovery of the "historicity of personal identity" informed a variety of the socially critical novel [*Zeitroman*] that combined the socially critical aspects of the genre with the focus on individual development characteristic of novels within the *Bildungsroman* tradition.[2] Twentieth-century modernity, and then again postmodernity, have offered competing models of understanding identity and its relationship to history: in both philosophical and narrative accounts, disjunction has often displaced development. Yet I argue that narratives in which one person tells a story about another's past represent a recurring effort to understand the self in terms of its relationship to its contemporaries and to its own past. In associating this narrative form with these challenges of modern identity, this book answers Ansgar Nünning's call to explore "the rich and messy domain of the history of narrative forms and the ways they are related to cultural history and the history of mentalities."[3] Modern lives and experiences are not continuous; they are punctuated by the myriad social, political, economic, and personal upheavals that separate what was from what is. The texts this book examines portray modern identity as being shaped by the need to negotiate these shifts and

---

1. The relationship between identity, self-narrative, and narrative about others has been discussed in two waves of autobiography studies. In the 1980s feminist scholars claimed a relational aspect to female identity based on the prominent role that narrative about others played in life-writing by women. See Mary G. Mason, "Other Voice"; Stanton, "Autogynography"; Susan Stanford Friedman, "Women's Autobiographical Selves." More recently, Nancy K. Miller and Paul John Eakin have made the case for relational identity and autobiography across gender lines. See Eakin, *Lives Become Stories,* chapter 2; Miller, *But Enough About Me*; Miller, "Representing Others."

2. Göttsche, *Zeit im Roman,* 9–26, quotation on 30. Göttsche's comprehensive history of the *Zeitroman* explains its genesis in terms of this new sense of time and history.

3. Ansgar Nünning, "Narratology and Cultural History," 171.

narrative as a common means for this negotiation. My book explains how telling a story about someone else can function in this way.

I do not claim that *all* texts in which a character narrator relates a story about another protagonist are concerned with the relationship of past and present identity. Nor do I mean to erase the line between fiction and nonfiction. In German-language literature alone, fictional and nonfictional variations of this form have been used over several centuries to address numerous issues: from Jean Paul's *Siebenkäs* (1797) to E. T. A. Hoffmann's *The Life and Opinions of the Tomcat Murr* (1822) [*Lebensansichten des Katers Murr*] and Heine's *Ideas: The Book of Le Grand* (1827) [*Ideen. Das Buch Le Grand*], to Adalbert Stifter's *Brigitta* (1844) and Theodor Storm's *The Dykemaster* (1888) [*Der Schimmelreiter*], to Hermann Hesse's *Der Steppenwolf* (1927), to Thomas Bernhard's *Frost* (1963) and Irmtraud Morgner's *The Life and Adventures of the Trobadora Beatrice as Chronicled by Her Minstrel Laura* (1974) [*Leben und Abenteuer der Trobadora Beatriz nach Zeugnissen ihrer Spielfrau*], to Monika Maron's *Pavel's Letters* (1999) [*Pawels Briefe*] and Uwe Timm's *The Friend and the Stranger* (2005) [*Der Freund und der Fremde*]. The striking differences between the textually playful *Book of Le Grand,* the classic frame novella *The Dykemaster,* and the memoir-like *The Friend and the Stranger* illustrate the difficulty, even the folly, of generalizing about all works with this narrative constellation. But the texts in the subset I examine, which I call dynamic observer narratives, resemble each other closely, both formally and thematically. While most of the texts I discuss are fictional, examples can be found in both spheres. All operate within a realist mode, where narrator and protagonist are clearly distinguishable figures with distinct historical and social identities.[4] Further, the narrator tells a story of past events during which both protagonist and narrator were present and, in many cases, participants. Yet for all the narrator's focus on the protagonist, he alone links the two temporal realms. While the narrator appears in both the narrated past and the narrating present, the protagonist is absent when (or where) the narrator tells his story, and the narrator's story encompasses an attempt to come to terms with his relationship with this now-absent protagonist. It is these kinds of texts that illustrate and explore an enduring tradition of using a story about someone else to attempt to come to terms with the past and its relationship to one's own present identity. In the wake of a historical or

---

4. I use the terms "realist" and "realistic" in a general sense, rather than a literary historical one. This usage follows Peter Rabinowitz's conception of the term in "Truth in Fiction" (131–33), where the degree of realism derives from the degree to which the fictional world resembles a historical one, or how many fictional elements (such as invented characters) readers must accept to enter the narrative world.

personal watershed, their narrators reinterpret the events of their protagonists' lives in an effort to reckon with their own past identities and their
present selves.

In the German tradition, the period since 1945 has produced a mul-
titude of such narratives addressing the National Socialist past: Thomas
Mann's *Doktor Faustus,* the entire genre of *Väterliteratur* [father literature],
Hans Peter Richter's young adult novel *Damals war es Friedrich,* and films
such as Helga Sanders-Brahm's *Germany, Pale Mother* [*Deutschland, bleiche
Mutter*].[5] Indeed, in German culture, individual and societal efforts to reckon
with the past are associated primarily with the post–World War II phenomenon of *Vergangenheitsbewältigung* [coming to terms with the past]. Yet the
need to address the relationship between past and present existed long before
National Socialism. Speaking of the years following the French Revolution,
Dirk Göttsche maintains that the "realistic hybrid of the individual and society novels" served a "reckoning [*Bewältigung*] with the failed revolution and
with middle-class self-assertion in the emerging Restoration period."[6] Uncertain attitudes toward past events and an uncertain identity in the present
produce attempts to make sense of both. Nor is this need restricted to German-speaking cultures. Although the analyses and claims of this book focus
on German texts and history, analogous developments and narratives appear
in other Western cultures and narratives, a point to which I return in the conclusion. The narrative constellation this study examines has been enmeshed
in processing the relationship between present identity and the past by way
of narratives about others since the turn of the nineteenth century—both in
using a story about someone else to work through the relationship between
past and present and in pondering that usage with a self-reflexive eye.

Reckoning with the Past in the Dynamic Observer Narrative

In the dynamic observer narratives I examine, the process of reckoning with
the relationship between past and present identity consists of four essential
components. First, it consists primarily of telling a story that reinterprets past
events and reassesses the behavior or character of the individuals who participated in them. This moment of reinterpretation is a key component of all
efforts to come to terms with one's past, whether they occur in fictional or

---

5. In this film, the daughter of the protagonist speaks in the first person in the voice-over,
approximating the role of a narrator. She also appears in the diegetic realm of the film where,
as a small child, she witnesses her mother's actions and suffering.

6. Göttsche, *Zeit im Roman,* 24.

nonfictional writing, in the negotiation of personal relationships, or in the symbolic gestures or reparations of the public sphere. After all, the need to come to terms with the past arises only when that past presents a difficulty to one's current view of or position in the world, a difficulty that requires one to try to make sense of or explain how one got from there to here. In cases of nostalgia, a world once despised may be transformed into a paradise, and a self once deemed "unlucky" suddenly mourned as having had everything a heart could desire. In cases of a critical judgment of the past, one may need to acknowledge the imperfections, even evil, of a society, people, and self that were once loved. And, of course, an engagement with the past often involves aspects of both dynamics. In the narratives under examination here, such reinterpretation is particularly crucial. For in these texts, as in many fictional and nonfictional narratives, such reinterpretation is the only method available for processing and coming to terms with past events. The protagonists are absent or inaccessible. Reunion, reconciliation, or restitution is impossible. Reinterpretation provides the only opportunity for achieving personal closure or for extending a gesture of goodwill, regret, or understanding toward others.

Second, this kind of reinterpretation occurs most readily in the wake of what I term a critical break. Such breaks are precipitated by periods of radical political or social change or by personal upheaval, and they invite reassessment of past events because of the changed vantage point from which they allow one to view those occurrences. As Werner Wertgen argues in his generalized theory of coming to terms with the past, "the possible historical interpretations also depend on the narrative possibilities at one's disposal," and in many cases, a critical break caused by a shift of great historical or personal consequence generates new narrative possibilities.[7] A military defeat or personal loss may be experienced as a tragedy when it occurs, for instance, but later happenings may cause it to appear fortuitous, as an event that cleared the way for positive developments. This propensity of historical discontinuities to bring about critical breaks helps to explain why the production of narratives like those discussed here surged in the nineteenth century; although the entire modern period is associated with social, political, and economic change, such shifts began to punctuate the social landscape with increasing frequency as the repercussions of the French Revolution spread throughout Europe and the industrial revolution began to gather speed. As borders and states were redefined, traditional economic structures and interest groups eroded, new relationships between religious and civic institutions legislated, colonies established, and gender roles destabilized, individuals

---

7. Wertgen, *Vergangenheitsbewältigung,* 64–65.

were forced to adjust their understanding of the world repeatedly—a process that continues today.

Finally, each shift in worldview, each reinterpretation of the past, requires the individual to revise not only his stories of past events but also his vision of the self that participated in or coexisted with those events. In other words, the values of a given worldview are inescapably linked to individual identity; a new understanding of the world entails a new understanding of the self. Moreover, the way one addresses past events and past identity carries consequences for one's identity in the present. Revising the story of how one arrived at one's present standpoint changes the way one evaluates and values that position, but it also stakes out this position anew. Declaring (or implying) one's relationship to the events and people of the past and present constructs a version of one's identity. Of course, this revised account of one's relationship to others also casts those others in new roles and redefines the relationships among all players. In all narratives that bear on the identities and relationships of the past and the present, then, stories are not merely constative descriptions of fact, to use J. L. Austin's terminology, but performative acts.[8]

In addition to depicting a reinterpretation of the past, the critical break that occasions it, and its impact on identity, all of the texts this project discusses share a fourth characteristic. While their *narrators* demonstrate varying degrees of consciousness about narrative's consequences for identity and relationships, all of the *texts* exhibit awareness of this power that narratives possess. The texts engage with specific historical events and individual identities, but they also address the general problem of the relationship between narrative and the identities and interpersonal relationships it represents and constitutes, or between poetics and ethics. Whether obliquely or explicitly, they contemplate what telling a story about someone else *does,* how it affects the identities of narrating and narrated subjects and constitutes or reconstitutes the relationship between them. In presenting narrative as praxis, these texts pose the question of its responsibility and open the act of narration to ethical examination.

Reckoning with the Past in German *Vergangenheitsbewältigung*

Those familiar with postwar German literature and culture will recognize these elements and concerns, because the salient features of these narratives accord closely with many fictional and nonfictional narratives of coming to

---

8. Austin, *How to Do Things.*

terms with the past in the post–World War II era (a process I designate with the historically specific term *Vergangenheitsbewältigung*). In his 1947 *The Question of German Guilt* [*Die Schuldfrage*], Karl Jaspers poses questions very similar to those asked by Raabe and Wolf: "We want to know where we stand. We seek to answer the question, what has led to our situation, then to see what we are and should be—what is really German—and finally to ask what we can still want."[9] The essential features of the process are similar, too. Reinterpretation, the critical break that spurs it, and its relationship to the identities of past and present feature prominently in philosophical, psychological, and social scientific accounts of *Vergangenheitsbewältigung*. In their influential *The Inability to Mourn: Principles of Collective Behavior* (1967) [*Die Unfähigkeit zu trauern: Grundlagen kollektiven Verhaltens*], Alexander and Margarete Mitscherlich define the process as a "sequence of steps in self-knowledge," and more recent studies, including those belonging to the international body of work on transitional justice, see reinterpretation as a key aim of the process.[10] A "break in continuity"[11] or "critical juncture"[12] has been called the condition of possibility for *Vergangenheitsbewältigung,* and the Mitscherlichs assert that the tendency to repeat the past is interrupted only "when historical events bring about a change in the level of consciousness."[13] In post-1989 accounts, this social and political sea change and a generational shift are seen as making a new approach to the National Socialist past possible.[14] Finally, writing about the German disillusionment following World War II, Jaspers maintains that "the very fact that honest consciousness and good-will were our initial guides is bound to deepen our later disillusionment and disappointment in ourselves. It leads us to question even our best faith."[15] And, one might say, our best selves. In attributing the German postwar failure to address the past to the continuing but unacknowledged entanglement of postwar identity with past

---

9. Jaspers, *Question of German Guilt,* 17.

10. Mitscherlich and Mitscherlich, *Inability to Mourn,* 14; Nolte, *Vergangenheitsbewältigung in Lateinamerika,* 20; Schaal and Wöll, *Vergangenheitsbewältigung,* 35–37; Eigler, *Gedächtnis und Geschichte,* 62; Fuchs, "Generational Memory Contests," 186; Holdenried, "Zum Aktuellen Familienroman"; Barkan and Karn, "Group Apology," 8; Teitel, "Transitional Justice," 10–12. For philosophical accounts that emphasize the role reinterpretation plays in an ethical remembrance of past wrongs, see Blustein, *Moral Demands of Memory,* 142–44; Margalit, *Ethics of Memory,* 199.

11. König et al., *Vergangenheitsbewältigung,* 11.

12. Teitel, "Transitional Justice," 7.

13. Mitscherlich and Mitscherlich, *Inability to Mourn,* 50. See also Adorno, "Coming to Terms," 129; Wertgen, *Vergangenheitsbewältigung,* 329–30, 54.

14. See Eigler, *Gedächtnis und Geschichte,* 62; Fuchs, "Generational Memory Contests," 186; Holdenried, "Zum Aktuellen Familienroman."

15. Jaspers, *Question of German Guilt,* 59–60.

identity, both Theodor Adorno and the Mitscherlichs underscore the inextricable relationship between the story of identity and the story of the past; in claiming that a confrontation with the past would help correct the Federal Republic of Germany's social and political malaise, they ascribe great performative power to the process.[16] Finally, Wertgen goes so far as to say that "the identity of individuals, of the perpetrators as well as of the victims, is thus the actual object of *Vergangenheitsbewältigung*."[17]

These postwar explanations of *Vergangenheitsbewältigung*, while historically specific, can help illuminate the phenomenon of coming to terms with the past more broadly. Many postwar narrative accounts, which often articulate the issues explicitly, do the same. Christa Wolf's *A Model Childhood* [*Kindheitsmuster*], with its narrator's extensive and pointedly agonizing self-reflection, is a canonical case.[18] Her narrator writes of the process of reinterpretation, of "the complete turnabout of your feelings. . . . It must have taken years of the greatest effort to accomplish this turnabout . . . free, unforced empathy for the 'others'" [vollständige Umkehr deiner Gefühle . . . , die hervorzubringen eine schwere jahrelange Angstrengung gewesen sein muß . . . : Gefühle, die sich jetzt frei und ungezwungen auf der Seite der einstmals "anderen" bewegen].[19] As she reports about how her protagonist's teacher prompts the girl's long-delayed renunciation of National Socialism, she illustrates that individuals need available alternative stories of the past before they can relinquish their old beliefs.[20] Most blatantly, the novel's narrative configuration dramatizes the tension that structures all of the texts I examine. The narrator writes about her childhood self *as if* about someone else, exposing the conflict between the narrator's past and present identities that lies at the heart of all these texts. Finally, Wolf's narrator is acutely aware

16. In their central thesis, the Mitscherlichs state this efficacy in the negative, attributing postwar Germany's social and political "sterility" to its failure to address the National Socialist past. Mitscherlich and Mitscherlich, *Inability to Mourn*, 26–27. Adorno maintains that if Germany is to have a healthy, democratic future, its citizens must process their continuing connections to the past and its authoritarian ideologies and strengthen their sense of self; only when they have done so will they be able to conceive of themselves as subjects of the political process. See Adorno, "Coming to Terms."

17. Wertgen, *Vergangenheitsbewältigung*, 163. With its talk of "perpetrators" and "victims," this statement is indicative of the way the particular experience of postwar Germany colors Wertgen's attempt to generalize the concept of *Vergangenheitsbewältigung* such that it can be applied to any kind of past event.

18. This book is offered as a canonical example even beyond the bounds of German-focused scholarship. Eakin, for instance, uses it in *Lives Become Stories* (93–98) to show how relational autobiography may negotiate the relationship between the discontinuous identities of past and present.

19. Wolf, *Model Childhood*, 315; Wolf, *Kindheitsmuster*, 399.

20. Wolf, *Model Childhood*, 388–92; Wolf, *Kindheitsmuster*, 493–99.

that in telling her story, she can manipulate events and her characters' identities to alleviate her own self-doubt and assuage her conscience; she fears the temptation to "exploit [the] helplessness" of the vulnerable figure Nelly and dislikes the idea that the people who fill her pages are "at [her] mercy" [[ihr] ausgeliefert].[21] The book returns again and again to the idea that the power of narration brings ethical challenges. Both the illustrative "as if" of this novel's narrative situation and its explicitness in discussing the process of coming to terms with the past make it an excellent illustrative example of the dynamics at work in the novels I discuss; they also ground my decision to omit it from the case studies, in favor of examining works that help show the pervasiveness of its approach.

Modern Identity as a Reckoning with the Past

Wolf's and Jaspers's questions clearly emanate from and are embedded within the specificities of the German postwar situation, and their responses to the questions are no less particular. Yet I contend that these postwar questions are related to questions that have driven similarly structured texts since the early nineteenth century, and that these texts have sought to answer those questions in similar ways. As another of Wilhelm Raabe's nineteenth-century narrators asks, "So, how is it then, really? Wasn't it different before, around you and inside you? How have you come to all this, and do you really belong here, and is everything that you're doing here and that you have to do serious, or is it a joke?" [Ja, wie ist denn das eigentlich? War das sonst nicht anders um dich her und in dir? Wie kommst du zu allem diesem, und gehörst du wirklich hierher, und ist das nun Ernst oder Spaß, was du jetzt hier treibst oder treiben mußt?].[22] The routes to the narrators' present locations are marked by their historical moments, but the procedure for tracing these routes is shared: the narrators tell a story about someone else's life to confront the trajectory of their own.

Chapter 1 presents more extended arguments about why coming to terms with the past has been a recurring process of modern identity. Here, I summarize the most important points. First, the need to come to terms with the past occurs when changing circumstances lead to a change in the individual's value system and sense of self. This need to reckon with the past is explained by the idea that one's values, identity, and sense of self are dependent on one's

---

21. Wolf, *Model Childhood,* 48, 200; Wolf, *Kindheitsmuster,* 65, 256.
22. Raabe, "Akten des Vogelsangs," in *Sämtliche Werke,* 19:334.

surroundings; that these surroundings change with history; and that identity changes as history does. Moderns have thus been concerned with "the historicity of personal identity" and with the troubling sense that they are not one with themselves over time.[23] "So great is the power of the conditions that surround us," laments the narrator of a novel from 1805, that "the person who had become a few years older had difficulty recognizing himself in the person of a few years ago."[24] While one trajectory of modern thinking has come to accept, or even celebrate, such disunity, it continues to disturb others. The narrators of these novels belong to this second group, and turn to narrative to try to reckon with it.

Second, modern identity depends heavily on the individual's relationships with others. These others populate the individual's historical surroundings, so that identity and a sense of self develop in their midst. But identity also depends on these relationships because one's sense of self is bound up with one's sense of morality, and for modern individuals, moral status turns largely on how one stands with respect to others. Charles Taylor maintains that the ideal of universal benevolence has been a pillar of Western modern identity and morality since the mid-nineteenth century. Combined with beliefs in the "significance of ordinary life" and the "free, self-determining subject," this ideal of universal benevolence has led to imperatives to reduce suffering for all and to establish universal justice and freedom. Taylor acknowledges that huge changes have taken place during this time. But he insists that underlying the surface changes, these ideals have remained constant.[25] An impulse to show benevolence toward the victims of past crimes, to do justice to them or to their memory, drives many efforts to come to terms with the past, from German reparation payments to wartime slave laborers to the narrative and symbolic reparations of the Truth and Reconciliation Commissions in countries from South Africa to El Salvador to Canada. In the texts about coming to terms with the past that I read, the narrators try to reckon with their changing identities by telling stories in which they show benevolence toward their protagonists.

Telling the story of how narratives construct a self that remains connected through time and that stands in a positive relationship to others is a potentially important task. That is not the story of this book, however. This book tells a story about narrators who desire such stories of self, but whose efforts to tell them fall short. The books' structure foregrounds their narrators' impulse to respond to the discontinuities of modern existence with stories: unsettled

---

23. Göttsche, *Zeit im Roman,* 29–30.

24. Weitzel, *Lindau,* 37–38.

25. Taylor, *Sources,* 394–96.

by a challenge to self-understanding, they reach to narrative to restore their equilibrium. It also foretells the impossibility of the enterprise. The divide that separates the narrator and his protagonist, the narrator's self-doubt, and the self-reflexivity of narrator and/or text all indicate a modern awareness of division, uncertainty, and self-questioning that calls the enterprise of telling a positive, unified story of self into question. As the narrators tell coherent, realistic narratives about their protagonists, their own stories appear piecemeal, in fragments around the edges of the central tale. Each of these novels is marked by the tension between stable identity grounded in coherent narrative, on the one hand, and the disruptions and self-reflexivity that undercut such stories of self, on the other.[26]

Book Overview

I first want to acknowledge three other studies that have investigated the same narrative situation. Each shares some concerns and claims with my approach, and each interprets the form with respect to changing historical contexts. Rachel Freudenburg traces changing conceptions of friendship in the twentieth century and provides psychoanalytic readings of the friendships depicted in four postwar German novels.[27] Freudenburg's work portrays the narrators of these novels as seeking a unified identity, much as I do. In her readings, all of the novels reveal the "coherent" identity achieved through friendship to be false; it is fictional, self-deceptive, and predicated on the end of the relationship. Employing psychoanalytical concepts such as narcissism, sadomasochism, and the mirror stage, she analyzes the psychological functions of narration in the novels and contextualizes them with respect to changing norms of friendship and of male gender identity in the twentieth century. Keith Ashley claims that the narrative form illustrates the changing epistemological ground of intersubjective relations since the eighteenth century.[28] His study also works from a body of German-language texts, but it spans a longer chronological period. In the course of his investigation, his attention to epistemological frameworks gradually cedes ground to a consideration of the social and historical circumstances that impinge on the narrator's ability to know

---

26. In this skepticism and resistance to closure, they differ from the "liberal narratives" that Ruti Teitel describes in "Transitional Justice" as underpinning processes of transitional judgment. On another instance of artistic resistance to the predominantly political liberal narrative, see also Rothberg, "Progress, Progression, Procession."

27. Freudenburg, "Fictions of Friendship."

28. Ashley, "Intersubjectivity in Narration."

the other figure, and to the ethical implications of various theories of knowledge. He reads the narrator of Jean Paul's *Siebenkäs* as a narrating intelligence; the narrator of Franz Grillparzer's *The Poor Fiddler* [*Der arme Spielmann*] as a representative of instrumental reason; and the narrator of Christa Wolf's *Quest for Christa T.* [*Nachdenken über Christa T.*] as a narrating subjectivity influenced and bound by the society in which she lives. In other words, he reads this final narrator as a representation of a person, rather than as a narrative function. Largely as a result of these shifting methods, Ashley asserts that ethically inferior nineteenth-century approaches to intersubjectivity are overcome in the approaches of the postwar twentieth century. As I discuss in the following section and in chapter 1, I, too, consider notions of ethical "progress" and trace the evolution of ethical principles in the novels. As much as possible, however, I apply the same methods to all of the readings and evaluate the novels' ethical frameworks within their own historical context.

Finally, Kenneth Bruffee's *Elegiac Romances* offers claims most similar to my own. This study, which focuses on English-language works but also includes a reading of Thomas Mann's *Doktor Faustus,* reads the form as a manifestation of the twentieth-century attempt to come to terms with loss and change and to overcome nineteenth-century ideals. Bruffee argues that in the genre of "elegiac romance," "the [narrator] expresses an unavoidable fact of modern life—the experience of catastrophic loss and rapid cultural change, and the need to come to terms with loss and change in order to survive."[29] While his characterization of the form coincides closely with my own, it is not identical. Bruffee construes the elegiac romance as a specifically modernist form in which its narrators seek to overcome nineteenth-century attitudes and thought, whereas I draw attention to its realist impulses and see it as covering similar terrain in both the nineteenth and twentieth centuries. Perhaps as a result of his focus on modernism, Bruffee's analyses focus on internal epistemological and psychological processes, even though he cites cultural change as a driving force of the narrator's storytelling; in his interpretations, the relationship with the "hero" figure becomes symbolic, so that the hero appears as little more than a projection screen for the narrator.

Two features distinguish my account from these three. First, where the others emphasize historical discontinuity, my study draws out the commonalities that inform even very disparate texts from the late eighteenth through the early twenty-first centuries. Second, where the other analyses tend to focus on "internal" aspects of self, such as epistemology and psychoanalysis, my analyses treat the protagonist as distinct from the narrator and target "external" aspects, such as social, historical, and linguistic context. This

---

29. Bruffee, *Elegiac Romance*, 15.

approach corresponds to a concept of identity in which subjectivity and one's internal sense of self are bound up with others' view of who one is, with external markers of social identity.[30] In particular, I analyze the texts' use of historically and socially marked language and the narrators' orchestration of voice within their stories. The tensions between the narrators' languages and those of their protagonists often illuminate the historical conflicts being negotiated in the texts.[31] The narrators' treatment of these voices holds key importance because it bears on their effort to reckon with the past by doing justice to the protagonist. The analyses focus on the social, historical, and ethical dimensions of the form and reflect on how it has evolved as successive generations of authors have used it to represent the process of coming to terms with the past. They suggest that, over time, the narrators' effort to do justice to the protagonist increasingly entails letting that protagonist's "voice" be heard in the text.

The idea that the individual should be able to speak for himself has been central to Western society since the Enlightenment. Implied in the principle of self-determination and enshrined in the right to free speech of all modern democratic constitutions, this ideal proclaims that humans have the right not only to decide how they live but also to articulate who they are and what their lives mean. When combined with the ideals of benevolence and universal justice, this right implies a duty to secure the freedom of speech and self-determination for others. Taylor claims that these ideals have remained constant since the late nineteenth century, but that the moral demands they generate have escalated as new groups have won these rights and as standards of benevolence have become more stringent.[32] He does not claim a teleological progression toward universal justice and the elimination of human suffering; instead, he argues that the historical record of the West shows a development largely according to these principles.[33] The history of Western social movements over the last two centuries, for instance, has been a history of campaigns to extend the rights of freedom and self-determination to ever new groups of people: abolitionism, female suffrage, the normalization of national self-determination, the civil rights movement, and the current trend toward legalization of same-sex marriage all operate with these ideals and standards.

---

30. Alan Palmer calls this dualistic concept of identity "situated identity." See *Social Minds*, 14–15.

31. See Lanser, *Fictions of Authority*, on the development of a narratological concept of voice that attends to social identity and ideology.

32. Taylor, *Sources of the Self*, 397.

33. Ibid., 394–96.

This book argues that, in the novels I read, these expanding obligations manifest themselves in the narrators' treatment of voice. While in the earlier novels the narrator tries to do justice to the protagonist by representing him positively, increasingly the aim for justice entails letting the protagonist speak for herself. Taylor believes that "notions of the good are interwoven with modes of narrative," and his book traces the historical development of overarching narrative modes.[34] My book historicizes the form in which a character narrator tells a story about another protagonist and argues that, within that form, changing strategies of marshaling and managing voice correspond to the evolving moral ideals of universal benevolence and freedom.

I make my argument in three parts. The first, theoretical section links the problem of coming to terms with the past with modern identity more broadly and with the narrative form. As suggested by the sources I use in this section (philosophers, narrative theorists, scholars of life-writing, and theorists of coming to terms with the past), my claims here derive from studies of literature and of the "real world," and many of them pertain to both fictional and nonfictional writing. Chapter 1 shows that theories of coming to terms with the past share important assumptions and features with many contemporary theories of modern identity. Both see identity as dependent on its historical context. Both view it as narrative and relational. Finally, both assume that it is inseparable from one's ethical stature. I begin by showing how Taylor's concept of identity resembles the assumptions that theories of *Vergangenheitsbewältigung* make about the historicity of identity, its inherent ethical dimension, and its reliance on narrative. I then discuss Paul Ricoeur's treatment of narrative, which explains how stories can help people navigate historical and personal change by integrating their experience into a coherent whole. Finally, I summarize Adriana Cavarero's view of narratives as acts that possess ethical status, not only as articulations of particular ethical frameworks but also in their own right. Such approaches, which emphasize how narrative can recognize and do justice to another person, resemble theories of *Vergangenheitsbewältigung* that emphasize the key role narrative plays in the (often impossible) attempt to compensate victims of past crimes. I also highlight the resonances between these theories and the fictional texts I examine. At the same time, I suggest that the texts cast doubt on these assumptions, anticipating and echoing antinarrativist approaches to identity such as those of Galen Strawson and Judith Butler. As the texts portray a reckoning with past and present, they dramatize a negotiation between a faith in and mistrust of narrative—a tension that might also be seen as characteristic of the modern era.

---

34. Ibid., 396.

Chapter 2 defines the dynamic observer narrative narratologically and asserts that its prominent structural features focus the reader's attention on crucial issues in the process of reckoning with past and present identity. In realistic texts, character narration draws attention to the narrator's historical identity and encourages readers to evaluate his or her reliability. The central position of the protagonist's story encourages readers to assess the relationship between the narrator and the protagonist, both its historical and its ethical dimensions. Finally, the dramatization of and reflection on the narrative process invite ethical inquiry about narrative itself and raise questions about narrative's efficacy for reckoning with past and present identity. As do the theoretical treatments discussed in chapter 1, the narrative form presents individual identity, interpersonal relationships, and ethical stature as intertwined. In the process of linking structural features to the process of coming to terms with the past, I argue that in realist texts, narrator reliability has a text-internal historical dimension deriving from text-internal tensions. In such texts, narrator unreliability may be used precisely to draw attention to these historical tensions. The tensions between past and present, narrator and protagonist, and narrative movement and metanarrative commentary signal the dynamic observer narrative's status as a hybrid form whose combination of textual modes is uniquely suited to representing the effort to come to terms with the past.

Parts II and III contain the textual analyses from which the claims of the introduction and first two chapters are derived. These chapters follow the narrators' efforts to come to terms with the past by telling "good" stories about their protagonists. In the perennial modern attempt to reckon with past and present identity by telling another person's story, a "good" story is one that provides acceptable identities for both the self (narrator) and the other person (protagonist). To analyze how the narrators attempt to tell such a "good" story—and how successful they are in their attempts—I conduct three mutually supporting kinds of investigation: (1) I elucidate the historical forces and positions in the book and consider what "acceptable" identities for narrator and protagonist are in this context; (2) I examine the narrative strategies, especially the manipulation of voice, that the narrator uses to construct, negotiate, maintain, or assert these identities; and (3) I assess how fruitful these strategies are, and how the text signals their success or failure. Together, these investigations yield "descriptions which take into account both thematic and formal features of texts and the ways in which the epistemological, ethical, and social problems are articulated in the form of narrative representations."[35]

---

35. Ansgar Nünning, "Narratology and Cultural History," 170–71.

While most of the texts I discuss are fictional, not all are; chapter 6 examines three autobiographically based narratives that span the transitional space between fiction and nonfiction, demonstrating the relevance of the dynamic observer narrative and its concerns in both spheres. My primary aim, however, is to investigate how fictional texts have used the form to stage the historical, ethical, and narrative conflicts at the heart of modern identity.

Part II comprises two chapters explicating nineteenth-century texts. Chapter 3 treats the emergence of the narrative form by discussing two texts with relatively reliable narrators. In Friedrich Ludwig Textor's *The Life, Adventures, and Heroic Death of Paul Roderich the Democrat,* hereafter referred to as *Paul Roderich* (1794) [*Leben, Abentheuer und Heldentod Paul Roderichs, des Democraten*],[36] the narrator tells the story of a friend whose enthusiasm for freedom led him to support the French Revolution into its violent, anarchic phase. As he does, he both valorizes his own past belief in democratic ideals and clearly establishes an antirevolutionary identity in the present. In this early example of the narrative form, no discord undercuts this self-positioning with respect to historical events. In Theodor Storm's *A Double,* hereafter *Doppelgänger* (1886) [*Ein Doppelgänger*],[37] both historical and narrative tensions begin to appear. As the narrator graciously rehabilitates a convict's character, he both absolves himself of guilt for his past condescension toward the man and solidifies his middle-class self-understanding. Self-positioning is achieved through benevolent narration. I contend that the text suggests the narrator's continuing condescension toward the protagonist, however, and I end the chapter by exploring how Storm's novella both exposes and discourages judgment of this condescension. Chapter 4 discusses a very different narrative strategy for suspending reader judgment. In Wilhelm Raabe's novel *Stuffcake: A Tale of Murder and the High Seas,* hereafter *Stuffcake* (1890) [*Stopfkuchen: Eine See- und Mordgeschichte*],[38] no single, coherent story of the past dominates. In fact, the novel is grounded in the narrator's realization that his story of the past must compete with alternative accounts, and that the voice that dominates the tale holds great power over identities, interpersonal relationships, and social structures. Against the backdrop of colonialism, the novel dramatizes the conflict between different stories of the past; the chapter argues that the undecidability these conflicting stories generate is a common characteristic of the narrative form and the process of reckoning with the past.

---

36. Translations from Textor are my own.

37. Translations from Storm are my own.

38. Translations from *Stopfkuchen* refer to Raabe, *Tubby Schaumann,* trans. Barker Fairley, unless otherwise noted. German citations refer to *Stopfkuchen,* in Raabe, *Sämtliche Werke,* 18:6–207.

The three chapters of Part III investigate texts from the fifty-year period following World War II. Chapter 5 focuses on Günter Grass's *Cat and Mouse* (1961) [*Katz und Maus*].[39] The analysis shows how the narrator's reckoning with the past falters as he lapses into the comfortable rhythms of long-familiar litany, rather than offering a confession in the new, untainted language sought by post–World War II German authors. The prominent place that litany holds in both Grass's fiction and his nonfiction prose up through his 2006 autobiography, *Peeling the Onion* [*Beim Häuten der Zwiebel*],[40] suggests an enduring autobiographical awareness of the comforts and dangers that such language holds. In a sense, this chapter tells the classic story of *Vergangenheitsbewältigung,* and of its (misplaced?) faith in the power of narrative to heal the rifts of the past. In its focus on the narrator's voice alone, it also interrupts my story of a historically increasing obligation to allow others to speak with their own voices. It serves, then, as an important reminder that this trend is neither necessary nor universal. Chapter 6 examines a heretofore unexamined collection of books about mothers: Peter Handke's *A Sorrow beyond Dreams,* hereafter *Sorrow* (1972) [*Wunschloses Unglück*], Verena Stefan's *It Was a Rich Life: Report on My Mother's Dying,* hereafter *Rich Life* (1993) [*Es ist reich gewesen: Bericht vom Sterben meiner Mutter*], and Hanns Josef Ortheil's *Hedge* (1983) [*Hecke*].[41] Competing ethical demands dog the narrators of these mother books. Wishing both to recognize mothers who were victims of patriarchy, poverty, and provincialism and to reject the narrow and tainted beliefs those mothers espoused, the narrators seek a mode of narration that both gives the mothers voice and distances themselves from that maternal vocabulary. In their empathetic treatment of their mothers' positions during the National Socialist era, the narratives trouble common characterizations of generational writing in the era of *Väterliteratur,* and in their highlighting of historical voice they give explicit attention to an element long present in narratives of this form. Finally, chapter 7 examines a high-profile text of this century, Sebald's *Austerlitz* (2001).[42] This novel is often celebrated for its ethical narration, because the German narrator appears to allow the Jewish protagonist to speak for himself and, in so doing, to redefine his identity. Yet as the narrator blends his voice into his protagonist's,

---

39. Translations refer to Grass, *Cat and Mouse,* trans. Ralph Manheim, unless otherwise noted. German citations refer to *Katz und Maus* in Grass, *Werke,* 4:5–150.

40. Translations refer to Grass, *Peeling the Onion,* trans. Michael Henry Heim, unless otherwise noted. German citations refer to *Beim Häuten der Zwiebel* in Grass, *Werke,* 10:206–638.

41. Translations refer to Handke, *Sorrow beyond Dreams,* trans. Ralph Manheim, unless otherwise noted. Translations of Stefan and Ortheil are my own.

42. Translations of *Austerlitz* refer to Sebald, *Austerlitz,* trans. Anthea Bell, unless otherwise noted.

he disappears into that figure. This blending and disappearance render the ethical triumph questionable; indeed, I argue that the text presents the protagonist's Jewish story as repressing the narrator's German one. My reading thus both interrogates the adequacy or viability of the strict divisions often made between "narratable" and "unnarratable" identity and experience in the Holocaust and aligns itself with the more skeptical body of readings of "second-wave" Sebald criticism.

Untangling the books' discursive levels and webs of interlocking voices is complicated. Tracing their historical, social, and cultural resonances from a chronological and geographical remove is difficult. Linking changes in narrative form to changing historical and social circumstances is more so. But the claims that these efforts yield offer a point of departure for continued argument and insight about the narrative forms associated with modern identity. I enter, then, the "rich and messy domain" where history and narrative form intersect.

PART I

Contexts of Dynamic Observer Narrative

Philosophy and Narrative Theory

one

Modern Identity
Historical, Relational—and Narrative?

> In order to have a sense of who we are, we have to have a notion of how we
> have become, and of where we are going.
>   —Charles Taylor, *Sources of the Self*

> Vainly I ask, "Who are you?" and then, more soberly, "What have I become
> here?"
>   —Judith Butler, "Giving an Account of Oneself"

> What is it about the other person that makes me what I am?
>   —Nancy K. Miller, *But Enough about Me*

> The self does not plan her destiny, nor does she follow it; rather, she finds it in
> the tale of others, recognizing with surprise the acts of her life.
>   —Adriana Cavarero, *Relating Narratives*

The authors of this chapter's epigraphs belong to two distinct groups.
Charles Taylor and Adriana Cavarero are emphatic proponents of a
narrativist approach to identity, pegging both selfhood and the good to the
ability to tell stories about oneself and others. In contrast, Judith Butler represents an antinarrativist approach that views narrative as repressive, deceptive,
and inhibitive of change. In this chapter I argue that the narratives I discuss
combine elements of these two approaches. While they depart from narrativist assumptions, much as many accounts of the process of coming to terms
with the past do, their structure and dramatization of the narrative act reveal
antinarrativist skepticism about narrative's adequacy for providing either an
ontological account of or an ethical approach to identity. In this way, they are

examples of what Claudia Breger calls "narrative performances." Breger contends that while narrative and (antinarrative) performance have often been polemically theorized in opposition to each other, aesthetic productions often combine elements of each. As narrative performances, the narratives I discuss both combine narrative and performative approaches to modern identity and its challenges and call attention to the narrative mediation of identity.[1]

My argument in this chapter is not merely that these narrative performances combine two unlike views. Rather, the texts lead me to draw out three assumptions about modern identity that underlie both approaches: that identity is historically contingent; that it must account for the individual's "becoming" over time, for change; and that the relationship to other people is part of that becoming. These shared assumptions explain the similarity between the philosophical statements in this chapter's epigraphs and the fictional narratives' central questions. Both narrativist and antinarrativist accounts also see the narratives that intervene in this process as having ontological and ethical status. One views narrative as descriptively and ethically valuable, while the other decries it as insufficient, but both are concerned with its functioning. The narratives are not literary arguments for one set of theories over the other. When I say that they depart from narrativist assumptions but reveal doubts about narratives' ontological and ethical adequacy, I am not arguing that they arrive happily at a superior antinarrativist position. Rather, they share important impulses with both views of narrative, so that in them, an unresolved tension persists between a desire for and belief in narrative, on the one hand, and doubts about its value, on the other.

Identity as Historical, Ethical, and Narrative

I begin my exploration of the relationship between the two approaches by explicating the shared assumptions that underlie theories of *Vergangenheitsbewältigung*, the novels I discuss, and Charles Taylor's account of modern identity in *Sources of the Self: The Making of Modern Identity*. The core belief of these assumptions is the idea that identity is impinged upon from without. It is historical, relational, and influenced by the linguistic environment in which it develops. The title of the first novel I discuss foregrounds these external factors as it identifies its protagonist and narrator: *Life, Adventures, and Heroic*

---

1. Breger, *Narrative Performance,* 9–10. Breger contends that narrative performance is the dominant aesthetic mode of contemporary literature, film, and theater, but she also stipulates that art has produced combinations of performance and narrative for centuries (10–12, 23).

Death of Paul Roderich the Democrat: A History from the Present-Day War Written by His Aristocratic Cousin. As it signals the social positions of both cousins, the title foreshadows the linked differences of station and opinion that drive the two figures' reactions to the French Revolution. It shows that the narrator defines both his cousin and himself with respect to the groups to which they belong. This conception of individual identity as strongly dependent on group identity belongs to Taylor's central convictions: "One is a self only among other selves," he writes. "A self can never be described without reference to those who surround it" (35). The self always answers the question "who are you?" with reference to her position within her human community.

Because individuals understand themselves with respect to the historical groups to which they belong, individual identity depends on one's relationships with others. And within such a relational understanding of identity, stories about others can be integral to the story of the self. In the dynamic observer narratives I read, the narrators achieve whatever self-understanding they do by narrating or reflecting on their relationships with their protagonists. Such novels have long recognized and played through a dynamic that has recently gained attention in studies of nonfictional life-writing, as well. Paul John Eakin and Nancy K. Miller seek to expand the definition of self-narrative beyond Philippe Lejeune's canonical definition of autobiography as the "retrospective prose narrative written by a real person concerning his *own* existence, where the focus is *his individual life,* in particular the story of *his personality.*"[2] Self-narrative, they contend, is often centrally concerned with the existence, lives, and personalities of the people one has known.

In the texts I examine, these narratives often lend particular weight to the narrator's conversations with her protagonist. The narrator of Sebald's novel, for instance, recounts very little beyond his conversations with Jacques Austerlitz. Language and linguistic interactions constitute key sites of the exchange between and reciprocal definition of the individual and the people who surround her. Language and conversation play a similarly central role in Taylor's account of identity. In fact, he maintains that is impossible to arrive at a sense of self that does not develop in conversation with others: "I am a self only in relation to certain interlocutors. . . . A self exists only within what I call 'webs of interlocution'" (36).[3] One might say that people can only really understand themselves and what they believe by understanding the conversations they have had with others. Moreover, the language in which these conversations take place is of crucial importance, because it bears within it what

---

2. Lejeune, *On Autobiography,* 4 (my italics). See Eakin, *Lives Become Stories;* Miller, *But Enough about Me;* Miller, "Representing Others."

3. For additional discussion, see Taylor, *Sources of the Self,* 35–40.

Taylor calls a moral framework. For Taylor, being a person *means* having a moral framework that allows one to make judgments about right and wrong, or at least better and worse. Knowing who one is means knowing what this framework is: "my identity is defined by the commitments and identifications which provide the frame or horizon . . . within which I am capable of taking a stand" (27).[4] This knowledge resides in the languages one speaks, in their designations of what is given, what is possible, and what we are as human beings. Expressing the belief in the constitutive nature of language that has become common in recent decades (including in performative approaches to identity), Taylor thus asserts that "to study persons is to study beings who only exist in, or are partly constituted by, a certain language" (34–35).[5]

The narrators of the books I read seek to solidify their identities by establishing a new understanding of the languages and relationships within which they have developed. Ortheil's narrator understands his own antipathy toward the past and achieves a new approach to it only after tracing his family's linguistic history; he first revisits his enchantment and disenchantment with his mother's language and then traces the development of that language through her experiences of National Socialism, World War II, and the postwar period. My analyses assess the narrators' historical and ethical positions by focusing on their linguistic relationships and exchanges with their protagonists. I show, for instance, how the narrator and protagonist of Textor's *Paul Roderich* share the vocabulary of Enlightenment thinking, while the narrator rejects the emotional excesses that the protagonist attaches to these terms. In chapter 6 the children of National Socialist mothers present themselves both as heirs to and as resisters of their mothers' conservative, provincial language. As the novels' and memoirs' narrators revisit and reinterpret conversations with key figures from their pasts, they find themselves confronting and negotiating linguistic differences, and these differences force them both to reevaluate their past identities and moral stances and to reflect on or adjust their present selves and moral principles.

---

4. The intimate link between identity and morality is Taylor's central theoretical assertion, and the opening claim of his book: "Selfhood and the good, or in another way selfhood and morality, turn out to be inextricably intertwined themes" (3). He contends that humans necessarily operate within moral frameworks or horizons, and that these frameworks are "constitutive of human agency, that stepping outside these limits would be tantamount to stepping outside what we would recognize as integral, that is, undamaged human personhood" (27).

5. Taylor emphasizes the linguistic framework within which the self takes shape, but he refuses the poststructuralist move in which the subject dissolves into language and anonymous discourse, insisting on the integrity, coherence, and responsibility of the self. See Taylor, *Sources of the Self,* 35, n. 8.

The simultaneous presence of a moral reorientation and a reconsideration of one's identity is not coincidental. Reckoning with the past entails reevaluations of both. In the wake of National Socialism and the Holocaust, for instance, Jaspers's questions about what it means to be German are predicated on the assumption that this national identity entails a particular moral quandary: "We want to know where we stand. We seek to answer the question, what has led to our situation, then to see what we are and should be—what is really German—and finally to ask what we can still want."[6] Knowing what is really German means acknowledging Germans' postwar moral position and facing the question of what their moral and ethical responsibilities are. This conflation of morality and identity also informs more contemporary accounts of coming to terms with the past: "A human lives in an historical structure that cannot be suspended and that contains all the elements shaping his identity and interactions (or capability for interaction)—and with them, also his moral quality and his responsibility."[7] Finally, it is implicit in the notion of "the grace of belated birth" [*Gnade der späten Geburt*], the idea that Germans too young to have fought in the war or committed its crimes enjoy an inherent moral advantage over members of the war generation. The narrators of the fictional texts share this sense of entwined identity and morality, too. The question that the narrator asks at the beginning of Raabe's *Stuffcake* does not necessarily include moral overtones: "How do people sometimes come to be in places where, when they stop to think, they wonder how they got there?" (157) [Wie kommen Menschen dahin, wo sie sich, sich besinnend, zu eigener Verwunderung dann und wann finden? (7)]. But as the novel progresses, readers come to see that the narrator's disorientation is moral, as well. As the protagonist attacks him for his boyhood cruelty and his present, shallow dedication to conventional mores, both the narrator's sense of self and his sense of what is good are shaken. This kind of disorientation is precisely what provokes the effort to come to terms with the past. The moral crisis is also a crisis of self; the narrator no longer stands where he thought he stood.

Both in efforts to come to terms with the past and in Taylor's account, however, this moral crisis is cause for hope rather than despair. Reckoning with the past occurs when people understand themselves to have improved as individuals or as a society; Germans must reckon with National Socialism because they now condemn its actions and moral framework. Taylor's view of the way humans understand themselves through time assumes a similar sense of movement in a positive direction. He stipulates that the communities and

6. Jaspers, *Question of German Guilt*, 17.
7. Wertgen, *Vergangenheitsbewältigung*, 183.

the webs of interlocution to which people belong can change; the language that initially formed their sense of self may yield to, or be confronted with, other languages and the moral frameworks and identities they communicate (34–38). People understand themselves as being in motion, so that where they are today is not where they will be tomorrow. This sense of movement invests narrative with a crucial importance for self-understanding: the account of how people have moved in the past and intend to move in the future is an "unfolding story" (47). In a statement that resonates with the questions of Jaspers, Raabe, and Wolf, Taylor claims that "in order to have a sense of who we are, we have to have a notion of how we have become, and of where we are going" (47). The stories that capture this idea of self do so not only by recounting events but also by explaining the links between them and giving them meaning. In other words, stories about our lives give us a sense of who we are by giving our lives sense. Consciously or not, we use them to relate our history to underlying moral frameworks. And because we need to understand ourselves as being oriented toward what is good, stories of change tend to be stories of movement toward that good, in which inferior moral frameworks are discarded for new, superior ones (46–52, 64–65).

This view of identity as relying on a coherent narrative that characterizes the self as on the path to good is problematic for at least two reasons. While Taylor contends that a belief in moral progress and improvement has suffused morality and identity since the nineteenth century (393–94), nostalgia and the vision of modernity as moral decline have been powerful currents of thought, as well. In addition, as I discuss in the next two sections, antinarrativists object to the idea that stories can or should create a sense of continuous identity and maintain that a desire to cast the self in these terms—and especially as "on track" toward good—tends to yield self-deception, rather than self-knowledge.[8] Whatever the problems with this view may be, however, such a story of self and of good clearly motivates the process of coming to terms with a difficult past and informs common understandings of it. Wertgen writes, for instance, that "people need a (positive) qualitative-diachronic identity to be able to act. They need it to construct a self-conception that guarantees the individual's consistency as well as his social competence."[9] As the title of her book summary indicates, Ruti Teitel conceives of "transitional justice *as* liberal narrative," a narrative of progress toward knowledge and social unity.[10] And, I argue, the desire to construct such a story of self drives the narrators of all the dynamic observer narratives—

8. See Strawson, "Against Narrativity," 443; Butler, "Account of Oneself," 35.
9. Wertgen, *Vergangenheitsbewältigung,* 175.
10. Teitel, "Transitional Justice" (my emphasis).

whether or not their stories are convincing in the end. Even the texts that show the inadequacy or ethical failings of such narratives use the figure of the narrator to acknowledge the *desire* for this kind of self-story. Such desire prompts the narrator of *Cat and Mouse* to cast himself as an innocent bystander in the past who works for social good in the present, and, I argue, leads the narrator of *Austerlitz* to identify with Jewish trauma. The narrators' desire for a narrative of moral progress belongs to the novels' diagnosis of society and the individuals who people it. The novels register the same persistent desire that Taylor's historically based philosophy does.

A desire for moral progress does not necessarily produce it, however, nor are narratives of progress always convincing. The dynamic observer narratives are frequently skeptical about the "good" of this mode of self-understanding, and they question both the efficacy and the ethical ramifications of such a narrative enterprise. Taylor, too, is careful to point out that, although individuals believe they have exchanged a bad moral framework for a good one (or, at least, a lesser good for a better one), this transaction is never neat. Inevitably, the new good fails to displace the old good entirely. Remnants of old frameworks and old moral languages remain, or are consciously preserved (64–66). This persistence of past values animates one line of critique of the postwar German term *Vergangenheitsbewältigung*. While I translated it in the introduction as "coming to terms with the past," "overcoming the past" is a more literal rendering. The primary critique of the term insists on the impossibility of ever overcoming the destruction wrought by National Socialism.[11] In Adorno's analysis, the inability to overcome the past is also rooted in the failure to escape the mental, social, and political structures that caused the disaster in the first place. Not coincidentally, he writes of the "reprocessing" [*Aufarbeitung*] of the past, rather than of its overcoming.[12] In the narrative texts, this continuing entanglement manifests itself in the persistence of old moral languages, along with the implicit assumptions and ways of understanding that they support. The narrator of *Cat and Mouse* continues to use a ritualistic language reminiscent of National Socialism, even as he tries to atone for his youthful culpability during the war years; this circular language allows him to avoid an image of himself as a perpetrator, though his postwar social work and his story testify to his unspoken guilt. As Taylor writes, a shift in morality is "not necessarily a once-for-all affair. The older condemned

---

11. See, for instance, Mitscherlich and Mitscherlich, *Inability to Mourn*, 14: "It is obvious that the murder of millions of people cannot be 'mastered.' . . . Rather, by 'mastering' we mean a sequence of steps in self-knowledge. Freud called these 'remembering, repeating, working through.'"

12. See Adorno, "Coming to Terms," 124.

goods remain; they resist; some seem ineradicable from the human heart. So that the struggle and tension continues" (65). In fact, as the readings in chapters 3–7 show, this struggle and tension drive the narrators' need to tell their protagonists' stories. Morals and frameworks that have been completely abandoned hardly need to be discussed.

The assumptions about identity and morality that occupy the core of theories of *Vergangenheitsbewältigung* and the texts I analyze also underpin Taylor's narrativist account of identity. For this reason, Taylor's thought is an important resource in explaining how the political, social, and personal shifts in the dynamic observer narratives both destabilize the narrators' sense of self and animate their need to reckon with the past. The new moral horizons and languages associated with these shifts force the narrators to confront their past and present identities in new terms. The "webs of interlocution" that bind them to the protagonists take on new meaning, so that these linguistic and narrative encounters unsettle their self-understanding (36). Some of these crises arise when the narrator suddenly "sees" for the first time a language and perspective that challenges his own. Such is the case in Storm's and Raabe's nineteenth-century texts. In *Doppelgänger* the middle-class narrator comes to see his earlier self as unfeeling when he confronts the privation, helplessness, and desire that drove the protagonist's tragedy. The crises of self suffered by the post–World War II narrators, on the other hand, tend to occur because a historical shift remains incomplete; the confrontation with the protagonist symptomizes an incomplete break with a society, language, or morality tainted by National Socialism. In listening to Austerlitz's story of Jewish suffering and loss of identity, Sebald's narrator is returned to the historical site of atrocity and reminded of his ineradicable ties to its perpetrators.

Narrative as the Ground of Coherent Identity?

The dynamic observer narratives, theories of *Vergangenheitsbewältigung,* and Taylor all see narrative as offering a mechanism for coping with breaks in self-understanding. Antinarrativist accounts, too, acknowledge that narrative often functions in this way; they simply deny that it is adequate or appropriate to the task. While Taylor asserts *that* life stories help individuals make sense of critical breaks in identity and morality, he does not explain *how* narrative helps people withstand such disorientation and reinterpret their lives or *why* it can serve this function. Paul Ricoeur's account of identity, especially in *Oneself as Another,* does. Although his metaphysical reasoning is far from my own methods, his explanation of how narratives construct a continuous sense of identity through time and across breaks and discontinuities strongly resembles the picture of narrative and identity that emerges from the texts I read. Other aspects of these same texts threaten to fracture that picture, however, conjuring antinarrativist doubts about narrative's value as a producer of coherent individual identities. Galen Strawson's rejection of narrative as a ground of identity denies that a continuous sense of identity is desirable and pleads, instead, for a view of identity that accepts unreconciled breaks. In the terms of my project, Ricoeur explains why narrative is productive for coming to terms with past and present, and Strawson why it should be cast off.

Ricoeur contends that narratives provide such a continuous understanding of self by mediating between two different facets of identity: *idem*-identity, or identity as sameness, and *ipse*-identity, or identity as a sense of selfhood.[13] According to Ricoeur, these two different conceptions of identity come into conflict precisely when one considers the problem of the self's permanence in time. He names two possible anchors for this permanence: character and the ability to keep one's word. A belief in character makes it possible to answer the question "who are you?" with a description of one's lasting characteristics, or to describe "what" one is (119–22). It allows the narrator of *Hedge* to characterize himself as an architect and music lover, uninterested in women, and detached from the relationships and gossip of his home village (7, 14, 16).[14] Such self-descriptions resemble the responses that Taylor's self offers to the same question, containing information not only about one's disposition but also about one's position within both the human community and a particular moral horizon. In fact, Ricoeur's definition of character resonates with Taylor's insistence on the self as defined through the web of interlocutions and moral framework of one's given historical community; Ricoeur casts it "as a finite, unchosen perspective through which we accede to values and to the use of our powers" (119).

Ricoeur writes that in character, the sense of sameness (*idem*-identity) and the sense of selfhood (*ipse*-identity) can coalesce; the sense of *what* one is may be very closely allied to one's sense of selfhood. In contrast, the ability to keep one's word relies entirely on the idea of selfhood, on the existence of a self who can accept responsibility. Crucially, that ability persists even when the self's characteristics change dramatically, when the self is no longer "the same." In

---

13. Ricoeur introduces this key distinction in *Oneself as Another* (2–3), then returns to a substantial discussion of it in his section on narrative and selfhood over time (115–25)—a sign of the crucial importance of narrative in his conception of self.

14. Parenthetical citations referencing plot points or examples (but not direct quotations) refer to the English translation, when available, or to the German original for texts with no published translation.

such moments, *ipse*-identity and the ability to keep one's word constitute the only guarantors of identity (118–24, 147–50). In *Doppelgänger,* for instance, the central conundrum is how to connect two seemingly opposite characters in one man: the gentle father a daughter remembers and the violent husband who killed his wife. Initially, they are connected only by the idea of selfhood and by the responsibilities that persist beyond the break of the mother's death: his responsibility for his daughter, and his ineradicable record as a legally convicted criminal. Both the sense of self and that of enduring responsibility can create a need to come to terms with the past. The continuous sense of self propels the effort to link different "characters," and the sense of responsibility that attaches to it drives the frequent effort to repair or atone for past deficiencies or crimes.

Moments of character change often lead to a reckoning with past and present identity because they jolt one's "finite, unchosen perspective" and, with it, one's language, moral framework, and story of self. For Ricoeur, the purpose of narrative is precisely to bridge these moments of disruption when *ipse*-identity alone guarantees permanence and to fold them into a cohesive story and character. A story constructs this *idem*-identity through a dialectical movement that transforms moments of disruption and departure into necessary moments of development. It produces a character that "draws his or her singularity from the unity of a life considered a temporal totality," even as that unity is shaken by "the disruptive effect of the unforeseeable events that punctuate it (encounters, accidents, etc.)" (147). In looking back to tell the story of a life, people make its accidents into necessary developments in the character the story as a whole produces. Contingency becomes part of the character of the life, so that "chance is transmuted into fate" (147). By imaginatively recreating his protagonist's experience, *Doppelgänger*'s narrator's story bridges the two parts of the man's life and identity. The narrator of Handke's *Sorrow* sees the era in which his mother's economic and familial independence and National Socialism coincided both as exceptional in her life and as central to her character (15).[15] In equating character with narrative, Ricoeur makes a general understanding of narrative productive for an understanding of identity. If narrative in general subsumes and repairs moments of disruption,[16] the story of a life produces the "discordant concordance" of an individual's character (148).

---

15. I discuss the significance of this statement for Handke's handling of National Socialism in chapter 6.

16. See Bruner, *Acts of Meaning,* 47–50; Todorov, *Poetics of Prose,* 111; Kafalenos, *Narrative Causalities,* 1–9.

The process of coming to terms with the past does not generate a seamless coherence between past and present; it links past and present because its reinterpretation of the past has ramifications for the identities of the present. Similarly, Ricoeur's vision of character is not that it remains constant over time. In the end, character seems to be stable, and the characteristics that persist contribute to the self's permanence in time. But many other characteristics change. Character evolves. The impetus for change may come from within; the self does something new, and continues doing it, until what was new has become part of the stable, reliable aspect of character. The impetus for change may also come from without; the self encounters, and then internalizes, "otherness." (Or, as I will argue in the next section, it may "disidentify" with the difference it encounters.) A life story provides an account of the internally and externally driven changes that have produced a seemingly stable character: "character has a history which it has contracted. . . . What sedimentation has contracted, narration can redeploy" (122).[17] Nearly all of the texts I discuss show their narrators explaining their protagonists by relating the accidents of their lives. Unjust privilege and arbitrary exercise of power bring Paul Roderich to hate traditional social structures and make him a democrat (*Paul Roderich*); discrimination, poverty, and helplessness make John Glückstadt violent (*Doppelgänger*); Heinrich Schaumann's childhood defense of a persecuted girl makes him a self-satisfied land baron (*Stuffcake*); an early arrest by National Socialists makes Katharina fearful (*Hedge*); and the inclusion on a Jewish children's transport from Prague to England determines Jacques Austerlitz's life trajectory and character (*Austerlitz*). All the stories create clearly defined characters who are memorable for their strong character traits. But in each story, these identifying traits are the product of far-reaching change. In the stories the narrators tell about the protagonists, change contributes to the "discordant concordance" of the narrative and the character, and "chance is transmuted into fate."

All of my examples of how narratives subsume change into lasting character come from their stories of the protagonists' lives, because all of the narrators fail to provide a stable account of themselves. Instead, their "stories" must be gleaned from the (relatively) brief and isolated passages of their explicit self-reference and from the texts' linguistic, formal, and structural cues. Theirs are what Ricoeur might call "unsettling cases of narrativity" (149); advocates of performance might say that they are cases where narrative breaks down in the face of an experience incommensurable with narrative's capacity to make meaning of it. The end of *Sorrow* dramatically depicts this movement

---

17. Ricoeur discusses character in *Oneself* (118–23).

that leads both into and away from narrative. Returning to his hometown for his mother's burial, the narrator struggles to gain his footing in the face of the contrast between life and civilization, on the one hand, and death and a threatening nature, on the other (64–66). The coffin in the ground and the surrounding forest menacing him, he suddenly sees human life as "an episodic jumble of shapes" (66) [ein episodisches Getümmel von Gestalten (98)]. At that moment, he resolves to write his mother's story, the coherent account that the reader has just finished. But the text the reader encounters from this point forward no longer tells a coherent story. It dissolves into "unsettling" snippets about the narrator, where the lack of any narrative connection is highlighted by the blank lines that separate each snippet from the next. The same moment that produced the linear, coherent biography of the mother prompts narrative degeneration when the narrator himself is the subject. He cannot—or will not—construct a coherent narrative of himself.

This failure of or resistance to narrative recalls the antinarrativist mistrust of coherent life narratives. While Ricoeur values narrative for its capability to subsume difference, this unifying function serves as the point of attack for approaches like those of Galen Strawson and Judith Butler.[18] Both Strawson and Butler challenge the body of thinking on "narrative identity" that has developed over the past decades[19] and reject the normative demands for coherence and sameness over time that they see in such thinking. Strawson's challenge merits closer discussion here, because it shares its point of departure with the fictional narratives I discuss: his argument, like the narrators' stories, departs from a sense of disjuncture between the self of the present and the self of the past. Strawson maintains that many people experience no sense of relationship between their present selves and the selves associated with their physical bodies at other points in time. He dubs such people Episodics and asserts that they do not understand themselves through narrative. In contrast, Diachronics see themselves as connected to the selves of their pasts and futures and often use narrative to explain and understand the relationship between these selves. Strawson deplores the dominance of the narrative approach to identity not only because it describes identity incorrectly, by extending a Diachronic's view of identity to all people, but also because it valorizes this narrative understanding of self. According to Strawson, many adherents of narrative identity insist that identity *should* be

---

18. The pieces I discuss here are Strawson, "Against Narrativity," and Butler, "Account of Oneself."

19. In addition to Taylor and Ricoeur, see, for example, MacIntyre, *After Virtue*; Bruner, "Life as Narrative"; Bruner, *Acts of Meaning*; Schechtman, *Constitution of Selves*; Cavarero, *Relating Narratives*.

narrative, that "a richly Narrative outlook is essential to a well-lived life, to true or full personhood."[20] Strawson begins by arguing for a neutral view of the ethics of narrative and nonnarrative selves, but in the course of his article, the nonnarrative self emerges as the ethically preferable option: he shares Sartre's judgment that "narrativity is essentially a matter of bad faith, of radical . . . inauthenticity," so that "it is in the sphere of ethics more of an affliction or a bad habit than a prerequisite of a good life."[21] In a similar vein, Butler opposes "the seamlessness of the story to something we might tentatively call the truth of the person."[22] In this view, Handke's narrator does not fail to construct a stable story; he resists the temptation to do so.

As I have shown, the texts I examine exhibit a tension between these two views. On the one hand, they exhibit a distinct narrativist and "Diachronic" slant. Disoriented by a clash or gap between past and present identity, the narrators tell stories to recover a coherent sense of self, as Ricoeur might predict. In these moments, which "expos[e] selfhood by taking away the support of sameness," the oscillation between sameness and selfhood swings toward the pole where the only indicator of a self or identity is the sense of selfhood itself (149). Character, beset by change, is no longer a reliable source of identity at all. In *Stuffcake* Eduard writes because he suddenly finds himself regarded—and begins to regard himself—as a narrow-minded, conformist, cruel philistine, rather than a bold and successful adventurer. He, like the other narrators, tries to "repair" or negotiate discontinuity by providing a coherent account of the protagonist's life. These efforts yield the largely cohesive, linear stories that earn the texts the label of "realist," or, at the least, the reputation of working with realist traditions. The narrators' own life stories remain disjointed, however—even though it was this sense of disjointed identity that had prompted their tales.

Narrative, Identity, and the (Ethical) Relationship to Others

The narrators' fractured self-presentation points, perhaps, to narrative's inability to capture the essence of an identity, the experience of a life. But there are other possible explanations. Their splintered self-portrayals may also be a product of their unwillingness to reckon with the relationships between their past and present selves; they may resist linking the episodes of their lives

20. Strawson, "Against Narrativity," 428.
21. Ibid., 435, 50.
22. Butler, "Account of Oneself," 35.

to evade the guilt or shame that all of them feel in some measure as they face their pasts. In either case, the contrast between their stories about their protagonists and the form of their self-representations raises questions about the ethics of telling life stories; the asymmetry leads to questions about the role narrative plays in the relationship between self and others.

Up to now, I have reconstructed the narrativist and antinarrativist positions on the relationship between narrative and identity by focusing on their treatment of the relationship between narrative and the self. In the books I investigate, however, narrative also plays a key role in mediating the intertwined identities of the narrating self and his protagonist. These protagonists play important roles, not only as conversation partners in the narrators' stories but also as the stars of their own life histories, which the narrators tell to try to come to terms with the past. As the narrators relate these tales, they display a fascination—and struggle—with the other person's story. This fraught relationship to another person's story again resonates with both theories of coming to terms with the past and contemporary theories of identity; in all three arenas, stories about other people carry a heavy ethical load. While Taylor insists on the historical and social origins of the subject and Ricoeur derives the self through its relationship with others, an understanding of the self remains the central goal in both accounts. In the last section of this chapter, I attend to theories that place the relationship between self and other at the heart of their investigation of narrative, identity, and ethics. Here as in the previous sections, the similarities between theoretical explorations of these relationships and fictional representations of them suggest that the forces driving the fiction also operate in the extraliterary world.

Narrative as the Ground of Ethical Relationships: Adriana Cavarero

Because a reinterpretation of past events stands at the heart of a reckoning with the past, the narratives that reconstruct those events often take on significant ethical importance. These narratives can yield a variety of effects. Looking forward, participants may alter their beliefs and their actions because they understand the past and themselves in a new way. In Taylor's terms, they may change course to aim toward a newly perceived good (and away from a newly perceived evil or folly). In the postwar German context, accounts like those of Adorno or the Mitscherlichs emphasize this benefit of reckoning with the past; they advocate for Germans to come to a new understanding of their responsibility for and entanglement in totalitarian and fascist National Socialism, so that they can achieve a healthier psychological state and a strongly democratic society.[23] Looking back, participants may try to make amends for acts now perceived as evil or inadequate, or to make reparations to others now perceived as victims of such actions. Cases of actual reparations, such as German payments for the slave labor extracted in its concentration camps, garner great attention. But, in many cases, the narrative reinterpretations themselves and the symbolic acts they produce (such as memorials or apologies) bear significance because they are the only means available for trying to do justice to the past and its victims, or to atone for it: those who perished in the German camps can receive no reparation. Narratives and symbolic acts based on reinterpretations of the past, especially apology, recognize the experience and point of view of those who have suffered. Although some contest the value of such symbolic measures, others hold them to be essential elements of any reckoning with the past.[24] A story in the present may extend belated recognition to those who had previously been denied it. In the contexts of crimes of genocide or religious persecution, for instance, the apology that emerges from the reinterpretation of another's story serves "the victim's need for acknowledgement," of his humanity and of his suffering.[25] Similarly, the narrator of *Doppelgänger* offers John Glückstadt a posthumous acknowledgment of his human status; he is no longer only a convict, a wife batterer, or a ghostly voice on the moors, but a human with a history, loyalties, and passions. The narrators of both Handke's and Stefan's texts write their mothers' stories to acknowledge the vital, human hopes and suffering that passed unnoticed and unappreciated during their oppressed lives.

This potential for narrative to grant human recognition also stands at the center of Adriana Cavarero's account of the positive ethical value of narrative. Cavarero envisions the narration of a life story as the fundamental ethical act in the relationship between individuals. In her understanding, people fulfill their ethical responsibility to others by recognizing them, and they recognize them by acknowledging and telling their unique life stories. Caverero's take on the relationship between narrative and identity is somewhat different than in other accounts because, rather than seeing narrative as constructing identity or giving it meaning, she sees narrative as registering the specific events of a physical life (42, 35–36). Moreover, rather than being a means of individual self-understanding, narrative here is the fundamental element in relationships

---

23. Mitscherlich and Mitscherlich, *Inability to Mourn;* Adorno, "Coming to Terms."

24. The literature on transitional justice treats such symbolic measures extensively. See Teitel, "Transitional Justice"; Barkan and Karn, "Group Apology," and many of the essays in Thompson and Rotberg, *Truth vs. Justice.* For a philosophical account, see Blustein, *Moral Demands of Memory,* 143–44.

25. Barkan and Karn, "Group Apology," 5.

between people. For Cavarero, a human's identity depends on being recognized as human; people are human because others see them that way (20–22). Further, selfhood resides in the sense that the self is narratable, and that one's life has a singular story defined by the singular details of one's physical and social existence (33–34, 38–40). Recognition, therefore—not the identification as a biological human, but the recognition of one's humanity—occurs through the recognition that one is "a narratable self with a unique story" (34). Despite the importance she places on the life story for the individual's sense of self, Cavarero insists that no one can tell a complete story of her own life. This necessary incompleteness begins in the simple facts of human existence: no one can tell the story of her own birth or childhood (38–39). Yet people still *desire* a complete life story, one that generates a "unity" of their identity. So they look to others to provide the information they cannot; the stories that other people tell fill the gaps in their own (37–41). The stories told by others complete the self's own story and "unity." Cavarero is careful to note that this unity is constructed; all narrative relies on selection, and the character of the "unified" life is determined by the selection of events included in its story. Yet she insists that the events and circumstances of the story, and the desire for the story, exist beyond the narrative itself (42). Providing sympathetic narration for another fulfills a fundamental human desire. It recognizes the individual's humanity and gives her a story of self, so that "there is an ethic of the gift in the pleasure of the narrator" (3–4). In Stefan's book about her mother, the dedication is not merely formulaic but an acknowledgement of the mother's desperate desire for the story Stefan gives her: "for my mother / who wrote for her life" [für meine Mutter / die um ihr Leben geschrieben hat].

Narrative and the Ethics of Disidentification

Many recent discussions of reckoning with the past and of narrative ethics have emphasized, however, that such narratives are only gifts when they refrain from colonizing the other person's story with one's own needs, desires, or self-understanding. Cavarero, for instance, maintains that to be a true gift (or to enact real recognition), a story must affirm the singularity of the self it narrates, its character as "this and not another." It cannot confuse or conflate the selves of narrator and protagonist. Cavarero calls this principle an "altruistic ethics of relation. . . . No matter how much you are similar and consonant, says this ethic, your story is never my story. . . . I do not dissolve both into a common identity, nor do I digest your tale in order to construct the meaning of mine" (92). Nancy K. Miller contends that autobiography and memoir are valuable precisely because they can promote "an ethics of disidentification."[26] In disidentification, authors and readers may come to see what they share with a figure in the story, but they also realize their fundamental difference from that figure. Similarity prompts human recognition, but difference prohibits identification. Dorothy Hale sees a similar trend in reflections about the ethical status of novels. She contends that, from Martha Nussbaum and Gayatri Spivak to J. Hillis Miller and Butler, scholars have recently posited an "ethical value of the readerly self." This ethical value resides in the reader's decision to acknowledge the alterity encountered in the novel and to submit to that alterity for the duration of the reading experience.[27] Reading novels encourages people to recognize, in Cavarero's sense, people who are very different from themselves.

Important differences mark the thinking of these scholars. In Nussbaum and Butler, for instance, the purpose for recognizing alterity is very different. Nussbaum wants readers to recognize different people's experience so that they can empathize with otherwise incomprehensible others, becoming better citizens in the process.[28] Butler, on the other hand, writes that recognizing alterity must sometimes mean acknowledging the impossibility of ever understanding another's experience, or translating it into one's own terms.[29] In Nussbaum, it seems, recognizing difference is to reduce the distance between different people; in Butler, it is to remind them that they do really stand apart. Still, they share with Miller and Cavarero the imperative of acknowledging another person's position: that the other *is* a person; that the other has a particular experience, story, and identity; and that that other position is truly different from one's own. This kind of recognition of others, so prevalent in theories of recent decades, seems to me to relate closely to the ideals of universal concern and universal justice that Taylor observes developing in modern conceptions of morality and identity (394–96). Ultimately, the goal, or responsibility, is to affirm the equal value of other individuals, with their very different life stories. Having recognized that equal but different value, one is to be moved to support others' rights and improve their quality of life (as

---

26. Miller, *But Enough about Me,* 120. Similar notions of empathic but self-reflexive relations to others appear in several other fields, as well. Kaja Silverman's *Threshold of the Visual World* provides a psychoanalytic model of "heteropathic identification" (2, 23–24); Eve Kosofky Sedgwick's *Epistemology of the Closet* considers the problems and opportunities of "identification as" and "identification with" in the context of feminism and queer studies (59–63); and, in the field of trauma and Holocaust studies, Dominic LaCapra's *Writing History, Writing Trauma* advocates an empathy that recognizes the other's alterity (40).

27. Hale, "Fiction as Restriction," 188–89.

28. Nussbaum, *Poetic Justice.*

29. Butler, "Values of Difficulty," 205–9.

Taylor holds, 393–96); or to advocate for social justice (as Nussbaum hopes readers will after reading Dickens's *Hard Times*);[30] or to grant them freedom of self-determination (as Butler's plea not to redefine others in one's own terms seeks to do).

This tension between empathy and the recognition of absolute difference pervades attempts to reckon with the past, too. It exists, for instance, within the memorial culture focused on the Holocaust. One approach to memorializing Holocaust victims is to engage audiences in learning about the victims' world and experience and, in so doing, to encourage empathy with the victims. This is the approach taken by the U.S. Holocaust Museum, where visitors receive an identification card that encourages them to follow the experience of one individual as they move through the historically organized permanent exhibit. It is also the approach taken in many films; Roman Polanski's *The Pianist*, for instance, repeatedly encourages viewers to look with its protagonist's eyes (as in the many scenes framed by windows) or hear with his ears (as when a bomb hits his apartment building and momentarily deafens him). The other approach is to emphasize the complete unintelligibility or untranslatability of the victims' experience. The epitome of this approach appears in the concept of the *Muselmann*, the walking dead whose experience is inaccessible because it occurs outside the framework of normal human existence.[31] Many (even most) self-reflexive and critical accounts assert or reveal such an unbridgeable divide at one point or another, however. In Art Spiegelman's *Maus*, the survivor father's Polish-inflected English continually marks his experience and identity as foreign to his New York–born son and chronicler. In chapter 7 I highlight the tension between empathy for victims and a recognition of their difference in *Austerlitz*.

Despite the contrast between these approaches—and the vitriol that sometimes accompanies their responses to each other—both are predicated on the recognition of another person's experience and identity. In both cases the audience is asked to confront, recognize, and affirm the validity of a foreign experience, and to acknowledge a story of the past that is different from its own. In the end, the goal of a reckoning with the past is often to achieve consensus on a shared story of the past by recognizing and incorporating different, "foreign" positions.[32] Yet even those who advocate constructing such shared narratives insist that, sometimes, the perspectives, frameworks, and languages of the parties may differ so fundamentally that they cannot be

30. Nussbaum, *Poetic Justice.*

31. See Levi, *Survival in Auschwitz*, 87–100; Agamben, *Remnants of Auschwitz*, 41–86.

32. See Nolte, *Vergangenheitsbewältigung in Lateinamerika*, 20; Barkan and Karn, "Group Apology," 5; Teitel, "Transitional Justice," 11.

integrated; in such cases, the shared story must emerge from a "bridging discourse" that draws from common concerns without violating the principles of either position.[33] The search for a balance between difference and empathy also animates the "memory contests" in which post-1990 German-language writers acknowledge their families' experiences of the National Socialist past, even as they pursue buried, conflicting accounts.[34] The authors and narrators of these recent texts seem to seek a language and story that can encompass and maintain a critical distance from both understandings of the past.

Disidentification might be seen as the precondition for a narrative reckoning with the past; empathy opens the door to interpretation within a new, "foreign" moral framework, while the recognition of difference assures that the reinterpretation remains anchored in one's own identity and historical experience. That same kind of disidentification prompts the narrative reckoning undertaken by the narrators discussed in this book. Ricoeur writes that either internal or external events may initiate character change; the self may innovate, changing what it does, or it may confront "otherness" and then internalize it (121–22). All the narrators I examine experience external challenges to their notions of self, challenges brought by the protagonist's "otherness." But while Ricoeur says that character changes when the self identifies with the other person, I contend that many of these narrators' self-understanding changes because they *disidentify* with their protagonists. The narrators recognize the protagonists' similarity as humans with stories of their own, but as they reinterpret those stories, they realize the difference that separates them from their narrative subjects. The narrator of *Stuffcake* learns to see his protagonist not as a comic figure but as a man with a history lived from the inside. Recognizing this other perspective causes him to question his previous interpretive framework, and to see himself, at least momentarily, in a new and uncomfortable way: as a narrow-minded man of convention and veiled violence, rather than as an adventurous colonial hero. The relationships in Stefan's mother book move in the opposite direction. Since her youth, the daughter has defined herself against her mother and her mother's brand of womanhood, but after her mother's death, she writes her mother's story to feel her way into her experience. The book ends with a reaffirmation of the two women's difference, however; relating her process of writing, the daughter reports that when she tried to adopt her mother's perspective and words, she became physically ill (152–53). To write the book successfully, she had

---

33. Barkan and Karn, "Group Apology," 14.

34. See Fuchs, "Generational Memory Contests." For similar descriptions of post-1990 literature, see also Eigler, *Gedächtnis und Geschichte,* 24–33, 61–62; Holdenried, "Zum Aktuellen Familienroman."

to disidentify: to describe her mother's beliefs and language, hopes and suffering, but to do so from her own, external (and still critical) perspective. For the narrators in these books, reckoning with the past and with their own past and present identities begins with an experience of disidentification, and continues as they try to tell new stories about the past that acknowledge or incorporate the stories the protagonists might have told about themselves. In fact, the later narrators increasingly tell their stories so as to allow the protagonists to tell their own stories, in their own voices. Rather than trying to adopt their protagonists' perspectives, the narrators reproduce the protagonists' own, "foreign" language.

The Dangers of Narrative

From an antinarrativist perspective, however, this effort to identify and give voice to the other person's language bears significant ethical dangers. I have suggested that dynamic observer narrators' disjointed self-narration may reveal narrative's insufficiency for capturing identity over time, much as Strawson objects to the (false) coherence that narrative imposes. Narrative, he suggests, is an ethically inferior mode of understanding oneself. For similar reasons, Butler insists that, while we cannot live entirely without narrative, it is an ethically suspect approach to others. Cavarero sees the narration of another person's story as a gift. Butler sees it as a cage. While Butler shares Cavarero's conviction that an ethical approach to others requires acknowledging them as subjects or selves, in "Giving an Account of Oneself," she resists the idea that stories can provide such acknowledgment. Narrative may be a tool for making oneself "recognizable and understandable," but a story can never give a full account of the self (26). First, like Taylor, Butler sees self-understanding as reliant on a framework of language and norms that we do not choose, but which predate us and to which we have to accede, so that a narrative is always "disoriented by what is not mine, or what is not mine alone" (26).[35] A narrator does not reproduce her protagonist's language, but the language within which the protagonist has been forced to define herself. I discuss this problem of narration in chapter 6, where the conventions of language and narrative trouble Handke's and Stefan's narrators' efforts to recognize their mothers' individual identities. More problematic for Butler is the necessary lack of self-knowledge and the resulting incompleteness of narrative that Cavarero also asserts. Instead of turning to others for one's story, as

---

35. Here, Butler's suggestion that the true account of myself would be "mine and mine alone" indicates a commitment to the uniqueness of the self that is similar to Cavarero's.

Cavarero's self does, Butler's self reflects that the self-knowledge impossible for the self is also impossible for others (27–28). The ethical stance is to recognize others' selfhood *despite* their imperfect self-knowledge; it "consists in asking the question, 'Who are you?', and continuing to ask the question without any expectation of a full or final answer" (28). One should not try to provide a complete and coherent story about "who" someone else is. Above all, Butler's ethical self does not demand that others provide definitive accounts of who they are. Definitive accounts are closed, and closure precludes desire, and desire is the essence of what it means to be human and alive (28–30). Butler distrusts narrative precisely because of its tendency to coherence, precisely for its ability to mediate "permanence over time," as it does in Ricoeur, or to provide a sense of "unity" for the life as a whole, as it does in Cavarero.

In reading the dynamic observer narratives, one might posit that the narrators insist on generating coherent stories for others while evading clear stories of self. As I discussed earlier, their fragmentary, inconclusive self-accounts contrast sharply with the chronological, cohesive stories they often tell about their protagonists. In telling these stories, they both "answer" and interrupt their initial implicit or explicit questions about how they came to be where they are. In this reading, the narrators grant themselves the indeterminacy brought about by a critical break, while erasing the traces of such open possibility from their protagonists' stories. Butler distrusts narrative largely because she suspects that even if people allow themselves to be inconsistent and changeable, they tend to want other people's stories to be coherent and stable. It is, in fact, in the context of talking about someone *else* that she writes, "It may be that we prefer the seamlessness of the story to something we might tentatively call the truth of the person, a truth which, to a certain degree, and for reasons we have already suggested, is indicated more radically as an interruption" (35). Stories are dangerous because they tempt people into denying others their moments of interruptive truth, and for Butler, these moments are indispensable to individual freedom and development: "the encounters I undergo . . . are those by which I am invariably transformed; recognition becomes the process by which I become other than what I was and, therefore, also, the process by which I cease to be able to return to what I was" (24). The encounters between the narrators and their protagonists are asymmetric. Read through Butler's lens, one could interpret the narratives as moments of living change for the narrators, and of foreclosing definition for the protagonists.

Fundamentally, the disagreement between narrativist and antinarrativist positions is not *whether* narrative plays a role in identity.[36] The question

---

36. In response to Strawson's polemical article, Eakin's "Response to Galen Strawson"

is what kind of role it plays, or should play. Both the antinarrativist positions and the fictional works cast doubt on the narrativist faith expressed by thinkers like Taylor and Cavarero and by theorists of reckoning with the past. The books question the adequacy of stories as a foundation for identity or a truly generous gift to others. But they do not jettison narrative, either. In fact, many of them turn precisely on their narrators' or protagonists' problematic lack of a satisfactory story of self.

---

argues forcefully that humans cannot live entirely outside of narrative. See also Battersby, "Narrativity, Self, and Self-Representation"; Phelan, "Who's Here?"

Structural and Historical Tensions in the Dynamic Observer Narrative

> [Storytelling] does not aim to convey the pure essence of the thing, like infor-
> mation or a report. It sinks the thing into the life of the storyteller, in order to
> bring it out of him again. Thus traces of the storyteller cling to the story the
> way the handprints of the potter cling to the clay vessel.
>
> —Walter Benjamin, "The Storyteller"

B *oth theoretical accounts* of the process of coming to terms with the past and the dynamic observer narratives I discuss work from a conception of identity as historical and relational. In this view, identity emerges from the relationship between different frameworks of morality, language, and experience: between one's changing frameworks over time, on the one hand, and the relationship between one's own frameworks and other people's, on the other. Negotiating identity, in other words, entails negotiating between these differing frameworks. So, too, does coming to terms with the past. In fact, to come to terms with the past *is* to reckon with the clashes between shifting frameworks, and with their implications for the individual's self-understanding in past and present. In many accounts, this reckoning takes place through narrative, as participants of the process construct a new story about the past that reconciles the stories told within various frameworks. This view of the process invites a rhetorical approach to narrative, in which narrative is understood to be "not just story but also action, the telling of a story by someone to someone on some occasion for some purpose."[1] In a reckoning with the past, the purpose of narrative is to align, or at least mitigate or explain the differences between, different understandings of past events.

---

1. Phelan, *Narrative as Rhetoric*, 8.

In this chapter, I argue that the dynamic observer form has often been used to explore the problem of coming to terms with the past because its structure highlights conflicting frameworks of meaning and the interactions between them. This function makes it an important narrative form, despite its seemingly hybrid structure. I claim that the three major formal features of the dynamic observer narrative—its character narration, focus on a separate protagonist's story, and metanarrative passages—highlight the narrators' efforts to use stories to reconcile the antagonistic interpretive frameworks belonging to their protagonists and to their own past and present. In most cases, the narratives resist resolving all the tensions, thus questioning the possibility of reconciling those frameworks—or casting a questionable light on the story or narrator that would claim to do so. In other words, dynamic observer narratives are defined by the correspondence between their structural tensions and the conflicts that drive their stories.

These interlocking tensions operate on two levels. First, each text offers historical or social commentary by distinguishing between the frameworks present during the period of German history that it treats and commenting on the relationships and conflicts between these frameworks. Second, all reflect on narrative's role as a mediator between frameworks by associating these frameworks with the narrative's structural features and figures—with characters, narrators, and authors. Both the realistic historical representations and the narrative reflections encourage readers to recognize something about the world and the interpretive frameworks and stories that give it meaning. At the same time, they invite readers to judge the relative value of the interpretive frameworks and to consider the ethical implications of telling stories. Finally, the analytical chapters will show that the body of dynamic observer narratives as a whole reveals a connection between these two levels: different frameworks of interpretation contain different valuations of narrative and different criteria for assessing narratives' ethical status. But here I am getting ahead of myself. I turn now to a narratological definition of the dynamic observer narrative and to my explication of the relationship between its structure and the problem of coming to terms with the past.

Narratological Definition of Dynamic Observer Narrative

From New Critics to structuralists, narrative theorists of all stripes have recognized the case of the character narrator telling another's story as a distinct variety of character narrative.[2] My term of dynamic observer narrator derives

---

2. Cleanth Brooks and Robert Penn Warren's New Critical matrix of narrative situations in *Understanding Fiction* (589) includes a scenario described as "minor character tells

from the rhetorical tradition, where James Phelan has characterized observer narration as "narration by a character narrator who is not a protagonist."[3] I have adopted this terminology because much of it is more intuitive than structuralist terminology, and because my interpretive approach aims to bring historical and cultural interpretation of narrative form into dialogue with the rhetorical tradition, particularly Phelan's work on character narration. But I have adapted the terminology because the description that Phelan offers of the observer narrator shortchanges the critical role that dynamic observer narrators play. It suggests that the narrator who is not the "hero" of his story plays only a subordinate role in the story's events, and that the observer narrator functions merely to inflect the story about the protagonist.[4] In contrast, the narrators I examine are key to the concerns that the texts address. Indeed, one could argue that they are protagonists in their own right. The word "dynamic" in my term signals this active function.

Dynamic observer narrators' centrality emerges clearly in the structures of the texts where they appear, and in the roles they play in the texts' narrative progression—the reciprocal development of the textual construction of the narrative, on the one hand, and of readers' experience, interpretation, and judgment of it, on the other.[5] First, the narrators alone connect the various narrative tracks. Not only do they give readers a glimpse of the worlds and identities they occupy as they narrate, but they also figure in the stories they tell. They inhabit both the narrative present, which usually appears as a frame story, and the story they tell about the past. When multiple narrative layers are present, as in *Stuffcake* or *Austerlitz*, the narrator appears in each (although, as I discuss in chapter 7, the scenario in *Austerlitz* differs somewhat from the other texts). Even in cases where the narrator repeats a story the protagonist has told him, his connection to the story extends beyond

---

main character's story." Norman Friedman distinguishes between "I-protagonists" and "I-witnesses" in *Form and Meaning*, 150–52. Franz Stanzel's *Narrative Situations* (62–65) places this configuration on the continuum between the authorial narrative situation, in which a perceptible narrator speaks from a position outside the fictional world, and the first-person narrative situation. Even when structuralist narratologists such as Gérard Genette and Mieke Bal abandon the category of first-person narrator, their typologies specify the case of the narrator as "witness." Bal calls this figure a character-bound narrator who also acts as focalizor, but who is "probably not important from the point of view of action. It stands apart, observes the events, and relates the story according to its point of view." *Narratology*, 28. In Genette's terms, the "witness" is an example of an extradiegetic-homodiegetic narrator: a first-degree narrator (one who addresses the audience of readers) who is also a character in the story he tells. Within this category, Genette distinguishes the "secondary" witness narrator from the autodiegetic narrator who is the hero of his own story. *Narrative Discourse*, 27–31, 43–48.

3. Phelan, *Living to Tell*, 198.

4. Ibid., 99.

5. Phelan, *Experiencing Fiction*, 3.

the acts of listening and narration. In fact, all of the narrators are associated with the central instability of the narratives about the past: the protagonists' problematic relationships to themselves, other characters, or their social environments. Thus, although the narrative track dealing with the protagonist is always in the past tense, preceding the time of narration, there are no "historians" among the narrators here, like those of Adalbert Stifter's *Brigitta* or Nathaniel Hawthorne's *The Scarlet Letter;* none relates a story whose events and players he knows solely through hearsay, or unearths a story in old letters or manuscripts. The narrators have connections to both worlds. The supposed protagonists, on the other hand, are absent from the narrative present.

Although the narrator is merely associated with the instability that drives the protagonist's story in the narrative track about the past, the progression of the present-tense track centers on the narrator and on an instability in her present character or situation.[6] This instability can emerge at any point, although most of the texts I read begin by exposing it. Invariably linked to the instability in the past-tense narrative, it prompts readers to expect some development or resolution: in other words, some dynamism. Either the narrator and his situation will change, or readers' understanding or judgment of him will. Nor does this expectation disappoint. All of the narrators punctuate their past-tense stories with periodic returns to the present, so that the instabilities of both narrative tracks develop in interlocking, reciprocal progressions. The central event of the present-tense progression, the narrator's telling of her story, affects readers' understanding and judgment of both protagonist's and narrator's actions in the past, while the events of the past provide context for understanding and judging the narration of the present. All of the texts I read end with the conclusion of the present-tense progression, whether this conclusion be the resolution of the present instability or the signal that it cannot be resolved; the present-tense progression could conclude before the text's conclusion, however. Wolf's *Model Childhood* is exemplary in the way its progression highlights the narrating figure's centrality to the novel as a whole. While the child, Nelly, is the star of the embedded past-tense story, the adult narrator's feelings about Nelly are the book's central conflict. The novel begins with the narrator's unwillingness to associate her present self with her past self (Nelly), and ends only when the narrator overcomes her distaste for Nelly's beliefs and actions and acknowledges the child's presence "in me."[7] It is this resolution that allows the reader to interpret and judge the book as a whole.

---

6. On the role of instabilities in narrative progressions, see ibid., 15–16.

7. Wolf, *Model Childhood,* 406; Wolf, *Kindheitsmuster,* 519.

In fact, Wolf's (autobiographically inspired) novel provides a paradigmatic example of the narrative reckoning with the past that takes place in dynamic observer narratives of all varieties. Whereas Wolf is explicit about that reckoning and about the primary importance of the frame's narrative progression, however, the relative weight of the two progressions is much less clear-cut in the texts that I examine. The protagonists' stories dominate their page count. Most of their narrators contend that their object is to tell those protagonists' stories. The narrator of *Cat and Mouse,* for instance, avers that "this is not the place to tell my story. . . . Here I am speaking only of you [protagonist]" (529) [es soll ja nicht meine Geschichte . . . abgespult werden— vielmehr darf hier nur von Dir [protagonist] die Rede sein (4:106)]. In some cases, generations of readers have accepted these claims. And yet, the works' progressions point toward the narrators' centrality: the progressions begin and end with these characters, and also intersect there. The present progression depicts the narrative act that aims to resolve the past instability. The narrators alone register the tension between the narrative tracks of past and present.

The narrator's structural position in these texts creates two fundamental tensions. First, it generates uncertainty regarding the relative importance of protagonist and narrator. Although the narrator claims primacy for the protagonist's role—and the protagonist dominates the reported action—the narrator's status as the sole connection between and his role in the progression of the two narrative tracks belie this claim. This tension accounts for the qualifiers and confusions contained in many theoretical descriptions of the "I-witness" narrative situation: Norman Friedman's designation of cases in which the narrator threatens to overshadow the protagonist as technically deficient; Wayne Booth's distinction between "observers" and the "narrative agents" who "produce *some measurable effect* on the course of events"; Franz Stanzel's characterization of it as an "intermediary form" in which the narrator is a "*relatively* uninvolved witness to the outskirts of the action"; Mieke Bal's definition of the witness narrator as one who is "*probably not important* from the point of view of action"; and Phelan's list of the widely varying degrees to which observer narrators may participate in the story's action.[8] The tension between the present and the past is just as fundamental. The past-tense story contains all the action, while the present-tense track consists almost entirely of the narrator's reflections and his account of his writing.

8. See Friedman, *Form and Meaning,* 160; Booth, *Rhetoric of Fiction,* 153–54; Stanzel, *Narrative Situations,* 62; Bal, *Narratology,* 28; Phelan, *Living to Tell,* 198 (my emphases). Stanzel specifically refutes the notion that such intermediary forms are inferior (62); indeed, his entire project argues for the equal value and potential of the entire spectrum of narrative situations.

But it is far from clear that the former is more important to the text's overall progression.

The group of texts I examine is defined by the correspondence between these structural tensions and the conflicts in the stories the narrator tells. The embedded, past-tense story shows a conflict between the protagonist and the narrator's youthful self. As the narrator recollects and relates the events of the embedded narrative, however, he struggles not only with the protagonist—who, after all, is no longer present—but also with himself. From the vantage point of the narrating present, the dominant tension is between the narrator's youthful and present selves. His narration as an adult betrays unease with the shape of his youthful relationship to the protagonist. As a result, the narrator must confront his own youthful character. In the end, this confrontation between the narrator's past and present selves shapes his narration of his troubled relationship to the protagonist. The problems may have begun with the relationship between narrator and protagonist, but the narrator's problematic relationship to himself over time drives the progression of the present-tense narrative: "How was it? Where do you come from? Where do I come from?" [Wie ist es gewesen? Wo kommst du her? Wo komme ich her? (*Rich Life* 42)].

This correspondence between the tensions of form and content also manifests itself in tensions between narrative modes. Phelan identifies three major narrative modes: narrativity, lyricality, and portraiture. "If narrativity can be reduced to somebody telling that something happened," Phelan asserts, "and lyricality can be reduced to somebody telling that something is, portraiture can be reduced to somebody telling that someone is."[9] In other words, narrative is concerned with events and change, often in the past; lyricality with states of being, usually in the present; and portraiture with identities. "How was it? Where do you come from? Where do I come from?" Stefan asks, posing lyrical questions about the states of the past. Wolf and Raabe ask questions about the states and identities of the present: "How do people sometimes come to be in places where, when they stop to think, they wonder how they got there?"; "How did we become what we are today?" As the concern with movement in all three quotations suggests, however, the dominant mode of dynamic observer narratives is narrativity. Fundamentally, these narratives investigate how states and identities change over time and explore how people use narrative to comprehend, instigate, or influence that change.

Dynamic observer narratives are a hybrid form, then, a type of *synthetic metanarrative* that combines lyricality, portraiture, and narrativity in order

---

9. Phelan, *Experiencing Fiction*, 153.

to reflect on the relationships between them. The narrative mode predominates both in the past-tense narrative track and in the progression established between the two tracks, but both tracks still incorporate significant components from the other two modes. The present-tense progressions always include passages that evoke the narrator's thoughts, emotions, or state of being during the time of narration. Much of the present-tense narration in *Hedge,* for instance, conjures the obsessive fever with which the narrator pursues his mother's wartime story, and his allusions to the isolated, often sterile life he has led since his emotional estrangement from her serve to illuminate his desperate situation. Such focus on the narrator's present state establishes a lyric mode, where "the text focuses on revealing the dimensions of the character narrator's current situation" and "revelations about 'what happened' are made not for their own sake but in the service of explaining 'what is.'"[10] Portraiture plays an important role in the past-tense narrative tracks, where the narrators often construct rich and detailed explanations of their protagonists. In *Austerlitz,* for instance, the narrator devotes extended discourse to characterizing Austerlitz by describing his appearance, habits, and intellectual pursuits. Individual dynamic observer narratives use lyricality and portraiture to represent and elucidate the historically specific states and identities that they seek to capture; they provide a portrait of the married woman in rural Austria in the 1960s or recreate the experience of a once self-confident colonialist who begins to doubt himself. Still, they are more interested in the evolution of these states than in their static existence. As a class, too, dynamic observer narratives are invested primarily in change. They incorporate lyricality and portraiture because they are interested in the way that narrative drives and affects changes in state and identity—or how people try to use it to effect such change. Dynamic observer narratives make tangible and visible the function of narrative as Ricoeur understands it: mediation between change and constancy.

Form Follows Function:
Dynamic Observer Narrative and Reckoning with the Past

The dynamic observer narrative's structure reproduces the historical tensions the text addresses: that between narrator and protagonist in the past, and that between the narrator past and present. In the remainder of the chapter, I explain how the three major formal features of dynamic observer narra-

---

10. Phelan, *Living to Tell,* 158.

tives—character narration, narration by one character about another, and metanarration—encourage readers to attend to the issues at stake in a reckoning with the past. David Herman writes that in postclassical narratologies, the focus has been on the "interplay between the way stories are designed and the processing strategies promoted by their design."[11] This focus unites very disparate approaches to narrative theory—from cognitivist to feminist to postcolonial to rhetorical—and it underlies my own efforts to understanding the dynamic observer narrative. At root, my approach is rhetorical, analyzing the "recursive relationships among authorial agency, textual phenomena, and reader response" that shape the texts' effects and meanings.[12] In this chapter I argue that, because these texts are narrated by a character, and because the narrator presents himself as telling a story about someone else, readers process the story and judge its figures differently than they would if an extradiegetic narrator told the protagonist's story or if a character narrator told his own. Yet while rhetorical theorists do sometimes account for the historically specific frameworks of interpretation and understanding that shape texts and readers' responses to them, these frameworks of interpretation do not (generally) stand at the heart of their analytical enterprise. They are at the heart of mine—not only because I think they are crucial, although I do, but also because I argue that contending with these frameworks is the core concern of dynamic observer narratives themselves. These stories are about interpretive frameworks and about the role narrative plays in mediating them.

My discussions of the three defining features of the form draw out the convergence of rhetorical and historical concerns. I contend that the character narrator encourages readers to wonder about who that narrator is and whether she can be trusted, but specify that in realistic texts, where the fictional world closely resembles a historical one, the answer to that question always possesses a historical component.[13] Further, when that answer changes over time, as it does in these texts, character narration emphasizes the historicity of identity. Similarly, I maintain that any character narrator's story about another character draws attention to the relationship between the two figures and, insofar as it affects both figures, raises the question of narrative's ethical dimension. But, again, when narrator and protagonist represent differing interpretive frameworks, as they do in these texts, the narrative configuration also points to ideological, social, or other historical tensions *and* to the role narrative plays in negotiating them. Finally, the metanarration, the

---

11. David Herman, "Introduction," 8.

12. Phelan, *Narrative as Rhetoric*, 19.

13. My use of this term is general, rather than literary historical. See the introduction, n. 4.

dramatization of and reflection on the story the narrator tells, draws attention to the ethics of narrative. At the same time, it also necessarily reveals, or at least provides clues to, the interpretive framework(s) within which narrative itself is understood. That is, even in making the most universal of claims—or perhaps especially then—metanarrative reveals the historical specificity of the frameworks that color narrators', authors', and readers' understanding of what narratives can and should do. Taken together, these three features encourage reader attention to two key elements of the process of coming to terms with the past: the historical identities and interpretive frameworks that it attempts to address, and the crucial function attributed to narrative in that process. Because the structural features and historical issues converge in this way, defining the formal features of dynamic observer narration is not merely a theoretical exercise in sharpening narratological terminology. In contexts such as postwar Germany, disentangling the relationship between "protagonists" (or actors) and "observers" (or bystanders), or understanding when and why people trust others' accounts of the past, are projects with far-reaching cultural and ethical consequences.

Character Narration, Historical Identity, and Voice

I begin by explaining the character narrator's function in highlighting both historically specific interpretive frameworks and voices and the interpretive tensions that these frameworks generate. Simply put, character narrators draw attention to themselves and their foibles of perception, understanding, and judgment. Narrative theorists of all schools concur on this point.[14] As soon as readers perceive such a figure, as soon as they realize that its views will affect their understanding of the story, they begin to try to deduce who it is and what its views are. They want to know the degree to which those views can be trusted and in what ways those views may skew the narrator's, and readers', understanding. In other words, they begin to assess the narrator's reliability. By presenting a narrator as unreliable—or putting his reliability into

---

14. The structuralist Bal writes that the narrator's use of the first-person pronoun makes the figure "perceptible," and that the focalizing narrator reveals something about himself with every seemingly "objective" picture he paints. *Narratology,* 48. Similarly, the cognitivist Ansgar Nünning maintains that a narrator's judgments allow readers to draw conclusions about his horizon of understanding and of belief, and the rhetoricist Booth asserts that as soon as an "I" appears, "we [as readers] are conscious of an experiencing mind whose views of the experience will come between us and the event." Nünning, *"Unreliable Narration* zur Einführung," 18; Booth, *Rhetoric of Fiction,* 151–52. See also Stanzel, *Narrative Situations,* 24.

question—the text invites readers to pay attention to the narrating figure, even making it the element of primary interest in the text.[15]

My goal in the next pages is to establish the historical component of narrator reliability, and to explain why narrator unreliability should be seen not only as a symptom of history but also as a means of illuminating it. Since different standards are usually applied in assessing nonfictional reliability, the discussion in this section is relevant primarily to fictional texts—although, as I discuss in chapter 6, fictionalized life-writing often employs tactics used by authors of fiction. Cognitive theorists like Ansgar Nünning have read unreliability in the symptom mode. Unreliability, they argue, cannot be judged based on text-internal factors. Instead, it emerges as a product of the reader's processing strategies: a reader deems a narrator unreliable to naturalize the discrepancies or irritations between textual features and the reader's frameworks of (textual and/or extratextual) understanding and expectations.[16] In other words, Nünning claims that readers perceive narrators as unreliable when their narration violates readers' sense of what is normal, either in the world or in a text. Reliability has a historical dimension because readers' sense of what is normal varies across time and place, as do literary conventions and the reader expectations they encourage. Vera Nünning uses the reception history of *The Vicar of Wakefield* to demonstrate this historical dimension, arguing that the novel's first readers perceived its narrator as reliable because they shared his values, while today's readers see him as unreliable because their values and assumptions no longer align with his Victorian views.[17] As I discuss in chapter 4, reception of Raabe's *Stuffcake* shows a similar pattern. Bruno Zerweck shows that the phenomenon of the unreliable narrator has a literary historical dimension, too; the unreliable narrator as understood today did not emerge until the end of the eighteenth century, and it has been far more prominent in some literary movements than others.[18] In the cognitive model, unreliable narration is the product of an interpretive gap between narrator and reader, and this gap may itself be the symptom of history, of the distinct interpretive frameworks associated with specific times and places.

The perception of unreliability may be symptomatic of the historical gap between text and reader, but I believe that unreliability can also reside in the

---

15. See Ansgar Nünning, "*Unreliable Narration* zur Einführung," 19; Hansen, "Reconsidering the Unreliable Narrator," 230.

16. Ansgar Nünning, "*Unreliable Narration* zur Einführung," 26. In *Structuralist Poetics,* Jonathan Culler develops the idea of reading as naturalization, or understanding a text within a framework that "is already, in some sense, natural and legible" (138).

17. Vera Nünning, "Unreliable Narration."

18. Zerweck, "Historicizing Unreliable Narration."

historical gaps that exist *within* the text, and serve to clarify those gaps. To examine the functioning of these text-internal relationships, I turn to rhetorical accounts. In Booth's original conception of reliability, a narrator is reliable when the facts he reports and the values he espouses correspond to those of the implied author, the author's "created 'second self'" whose "norms and choices" determine the form and meaning of the text as a whole.[19] In further refining the concept, Phelan adds another axis of reliability to those of Booth's reporting and evaluating; he maintains that narrators' reliability also depends on what they know and how they interpret or "read" events.[20] Reporting, evaluating, and interpreting all take place within an interpretive framework, however. Character narrators' reliability is historically inflected, then, when the gaps between narrators' and implied authors' interpretive frameworks consist (at least partly) of the gaps between the values and assumptions associated with particular social and historical positions. In fact, character narrators can be used to highlight these social and historical gaps. In realist and in socially critical writing that concerns itself with social and historical conditions and positions, gauging the reliability of a narrator's reporting, interpretation, and evaluation requires considering the social and historical position he inhabits with respect to the other frameworks contained within the text.[21]

An unreliable narrator may be cast precisely to characterize that historical position. Mikhail Bakhtin emphasizes the historical self-disclosure that takes place as narrators tell their stories. Because Bakhtin sees characters as linguistic manifestations of particular ideological and historical perspectives, he contends that the narrator indexes his social position with each sentence he utters or writes. In fact, Bakhtin holds that character narrators (or, as he terms them, posited authors or narrators) are useful precisely because they present "specific and limited verbal ideological points of view, belief systems, opposed to the literary expectations and points of view that constitute the background needed to perceive them."[22] Character narrators are

---

19. Booth, *Rhetoric of Fiction*, 158–59, 71–76.

20. Phelan, *Living to Tell*, 49–51. Viewing unreliability as a product of a gap between narrator and implied author does not preclude attention to the readers who interpret these features. Rhetorical readers may try to understand how readers' interpretive frameworks inflect their understanding of textual features, but they never abandon their focus on the textual features themselves. See ibid., 48–49; Hansen, "Reconsidering the Unreliable Narrator," 234–36. Nünning's list of textual features that signal unreliable narration itself suggests a textual foundation in "*Unreliable Narration* zur Einführung" (27–32).

21. Zerweck contends in "Historicizing Unreliable Narration" that narrator unreliability is almost universally a phenomenon of realist writing because it depends on a comparison with the "real" network of assumptions, values, and conditions that the text aims to reproduce (159–60).

22. Bakhtin, *Dialogic Imagination*, 313.

always unreliable to a degree, and this unreliability has a historical dimension *within* the text. It is no stretch, I think, to associate the contrast Bakhtin draws between this "specific and limited verbal ideological" perspective and the "literary expectations and points of view" that make it visible, on the one hand, with the contrast between the narrator and the implied author, or the text's "core of norms and choices,"[23] that determines narrator reliability in rhetorical approaches. For Bakhtin, the very point of a character narrator is to be unreliable—unreliable in the sense that readers see him as limited by a particular social and historical perspective. Or, as Phelan puts it, the figure of the character narrator allows the implied author to communicate indirectly with readers[24]—specifically, as Bakhtin would have it, about the narrator's historical viewpoint. The reader is invited to puzzle out the language, beliefs, and interpretive capacities that restrict the story the narrator tells.

Viewing the representation of this restrictive historical framework as a central goal of the text suggests the need for revising another rhetorical account of reliability: Peter Rabinowitz's typology of audiences. Specifically, a historical approach requires resurrecting Rabinowitz's concept of the ideal narrative audience. Rabinowitz originally claimed that readers of fictional texts may function as members of four different audiences: (1) the actual audience of flesh-and-blood readers; (2) the authorial audience, the audience envisioned by the implied author; (3) the narrative audience, which reads and judges as if it were an inhabitant of the storyworld; and (4) the ideal narrative audience, which inhabits the storyworld *and* interprets the narrator as he wishes to be understood.[25] When the narrative and ideal narrative audiences converge, the narrator appears reliable; unreliability ensues as they move apart.[26] Later, he and others dropped the ideal narrative audience, locating the interpretive gap between narrative and authorial audiences. I agree that disregarding the ideal narrative audience is defensible if its interpretive framework is an idiosyncratic one, characterized, for instance, by gullibility. In that case, readers' interpretations and judgments do rely on the interpretive frameworks of the narrative and authorial audiences. But if, as in many realist texts, the ideal narrative audience is ideal not only *because* it believes but because it believes something *in particular*—if the ideal narrative audience represents a historically particular interpretive framework—and if the authorial audience is meant to reflect on the relationship between this interpretive framework and that of the narrative audience, then appreciating the

---

23. Booth, *Rhetoric of Fiction,* 74.
24. Phelan, *Living to Tell,* 1.
25. Rabinowitz, "Truth in Fiction," 126–28.
26. Ibid., 133–35.

identity and beliefs of the ideal narrative audience is crucial to understanding the work.[27] One cannot judge the reliability of the narrator in *Doppelgänger*, for instance, or the implied author's presentation of him, without appreciating the ideal narrative audience's belief in Enlightenment ideals. Likewise, *Austerlitz*'s ideal narrative audience has a historically distinct set of beliefs about the Holocaust and about appropriate ways of representing it.

Revealing the ideal narrative audience's views as deluded can be a central tactic of trenchant social critique. Rabinowitz claims that the distance between authorial and narrative audiences is usually one of fact; the authorial audience knows that Austerlitz and his narrator are fictional characters, while the narrative audience believes that they exist. In contrast, he maintains that "the distance between the narrative audience and the ideal narrative audience tends to lie along an axis of ethics or interpretation."[28] To expose an ideal narrative audience is not merely to reveal that it believes what is false; it is to reveal it as having false beliefs. This kind of exposure may be especially rhetorically effective—and maximally uncomfortable—when the ideal narrative audience shares its interpretive framework with flesh-and-blood readers, a dynamic I explore in chapters 6 and 7.

Of course, that discomfort pertains only if flesh-and-blood readers succeed in stepping into the authorial audience. Here, I want to acknowledge the difficulties involved in taking this historical step, and in assessing reliability on text-internal grounds. Distinguishing between the interpretive frameworks of a fictive (but realistic) sociohistorical world, and judging them from within that context (rather than one's own), is tricky. On the one hand, large removes of time and place make assuming foreign frameworks or evaluating them on their own terms difficult;[29] from the vantage point of a historically distant reader, the text's interpretive frameworks may be hard to recognize and to disentangle, or even to distinguish from one another. On the other, being party to one of the frameworks involved may blind readers to the commentary being offered. Additionally, as Phelan maintains, character narration relies on the "art of indirection,"[30] and indirect communication is prone to ambiguity and failure. Still, a good-faith attempt to read historically may protect readers from the kind of readings that cognitivists decry, in which judgments of a narrator's reliability are based only on an unacknowledged "subjectively tinged

---

27. Considering the historical aspects of the text shows that one does not have to appeal to the unusual case of second-person narration to revive the category of ideal narrative audience, as Phelan does in *Narrative as Rhetoric* (142–45).

28. Rabinowitz, "Truth in Fiction," 135.

29. Ibid., 130–31.

30. Phelan, *Living to Tell*, 1.

value-judgment or projection governed by the normative presuppositions and moral conviction of the critic."[31] And, difficult as it is, it is the only way readers can try to reconstruct the message intended by the author, whether the implied one or the historical figure.

In addition to these historical factors, dynamic observer narratives complicate judgments about reliability because of the amalgamation of estranging and bonding reliability they tend to generate.[32] Most of the narrators are highly ambivalent figures. These characters tell their stories to affect relationships and identities, and, often, the reciprocal progressions of the two narrative tracks bring readers to suspect their motives and to judge them for their unreliability—their lapses in judgment, perception, and reporting. Yet most of the narrators' stories are also motivated by their desire to do justice to the protagonist in the present, as they had not in the past. This desire encourages a readerly experience of bonding unreliability because of the narrators' "progression toward the norm" and the "optimistic comparison" readers make between their former and current selves.[33] Finally, the lyrical facet of the narratives also supports a bonding dynamic, what might be called *lyric bonding*. Phelan maintains that lyric narrators invite a sympathetic effort at understanding, as readers try to assess "the underlying value structure of the lyric narrative," and to move "toward deeper understanding of and participation in what is revealed."[34] In all of the texts from *Doppelgänger* forward, doubt about the narrators' motives interrupts and restricts this participation. Still, to the degree that dynamic observer narratives are about the present, they are about the implied author's attempt to illuminate the narrator's historically specific state, and the narrator's to make it understood. In my examination of *Doppelgänger,* I link lyricality to bonding unreliability and to a special status for unreliability along the axis of perception and understanding.

I have treated narrator reliability and its historicity at such length because unreliability emerges from the conflicts between differing interpretive frameworks, just as a reckoning with the past does. In fact, in reading dynamic observer narratives, the reader who tries to read historically struggles with the same set of conflicting interpretive frameworks as does the narrator. The reader compares and judges these conflicting frameworks to assess the

---

31. Ansgar Nünning, "Unreliable, Compared to What?" 60.

32. For an introduction to the concepts of bonding and estranging unreliability, see Phelan, "Bonding and Estranging."

33. Ibid., 231–32.

34. Phelan, *Living to Tell,* 158. See also Phelan, "Rhetorical Literary Ethics," 635. Phelan's discussion of the types of unreliability and the "ethics of reading" in *Living to Tell* assume that, in general, the reader's assessment of the narrator entails judgment (49–60). Nünning, too, emphasizes in "*Unreliable Narration* zur Einführung" that readers judge unreliable narrators (19).

narrator's reliability and the text's meaning, while the narrator confronts the differences between her present framework and those of the protagonist and her past self as part of her effort to come to terms with her changing identity. Both narrator and readers of *Austerlitz*, for instance, grapple with the contrasts and coincidences between wartime and postwar German and Jewish frameworks of understanding. Dynamic observer narrators wrestle with the gap between the interpretive framework that guides their present perception, values, and reporting, and that which shaped their assumptions, beliefs, and actions in the past. In effect, this gap reveals their own past unreliability when they confront the inadequacy of their previous understanding of the protagonist's story.

Telling Another Person's Story and Narrative Ethics

Character narration focuses attention on the character narrator's historical identity, and potentially unreliable character narration on the conflicts between historically specific interpretive frameworks. In all of the texts I discuss, these contrasting frameworks raise the question of what it is good to be and to believe in a particular place and time. To be clear, I claim neither that all texts with character narrators are concerned with historical identity and the conflicts between interpretive frameworks, nor that character narration is the only technique for concretizing such historical struggle in a narrative text. Rather, I maintain that character narration provides a technical strategy for illuminating and reflecting on the negotiations between interpretive frameworks over time. In this section I analyze the effects of the second defining structural feature of these texts: their narrator's focus on another character's story. I argue that this focus supports an exploration of the ethical import of stories that serve a reckoning with the past, and of narrative in general.

Although my object of investigation here is the narrators' focus on other characters' stories, my aim in this section is not to ascertain whether or not the texts are really "about" those other protagonists—in other words, whether or not they are observer narratives. Rather, I want to investigate the impact that the choice to have a character narrator tell a story about a separate protagonist has on the story the text tells. The narrator tells the story *as if* it is a story about someone else, and this intervention changes both the texture and the import of the protagonist's story.[35] While Stanzel emphasizes the

---

35. See Booth, *Rhetoric of Fiction*, 345–46. Booth also maintains, however, that readers always want to know whether the narrator's version of the story is actually "right" (or, in other words, how reliable the narrator is).

importance of the relationship between the narrating and experiencing selves
in the first-person narrative situation, in the case of the authorial novel, he
declares that the "structure of meaning" resides primarily in the "references
and relationships between the fictional world and the figure of the authorial
narrator and from the resulting tensions in values, judgments, and kinds of
experience."[36] In the intermediary form of the dynamic observer narrative, the
character narrators assume strongly authorial stances toward their protagonists' stories, distancing themselves from those stories and providing frequent
evaluative commentary on them.[37] Indeed, they often present themselves as
inhabiting different "worlds" from those their narratives represent; most have
left their childhood homes in the province to live in the city or abroad. Thus,
the structure of meaning in the dynamic observer narrator shifts. While the
relationship between experiencing and narrating self remains important, illuminating the individual's change over time, the narrator's focus on the protagonist's life means that the "references and relationships" between narrator
and protagonist also play a key role in the text's overall meaning. The effect
of the form is to emphasize that the individual's relationship to others is as
important as that to himself over time.

In Bakhtinian or Taylorian terms, the protagonist provides a "language"
and "horizon" against which the dynamic observer narrator comes to realize
his own interpretive framework. As they tell stories about their protagonists,
the narrator concretizes the goal of the novel as Bakhtin conceives it: "what
is realized in the novel is the process of coming to know one's own language
as it is perceived in someone else's language, coming to know one's own horizon within someone else's horizon."[38] The process Bakhtin sees at the heart
of the novel is, fundamentally, the same as the process of reckoning with
past and present identity as it appears in the texts I examine. Facing their
past selves and their protagonists from across a social, political, or personal
divide, the narrators of the frame stories are forced to confront the different
historical voices and interpretive frameworks that these figures represent. In
narratological terms, the contrasting narrator and protagonist figures draw
attention to voice and its functioning in narrative. Genette's structuralist narratology uses the term *voice* solely to designate the narrative instance that
speaks, but, as I have already argued, a character narrator encourages readers to wonder about the figure who mediates the story: what she believes and
understands, and where she comes from. In other words, character narrators encourage readers to think about voice in terms akin to Susan Lanser's

---

36. Stanzel, *Narrative Situations*, 86–89, 28.
37. For a succinct summary of Stanzel's authorial type, see ibid., 23–24.
38. Bakhtin, *Dialogic Imagination*, 365.

definition of it, where "narrative voice . . . embodies the social, economic, and literary conditions under which it has been produced."[39] The narrator's relation of the protagonist's story emphasizes this social dimension of voice. As they present a narrator who tells a story about the protagonist's life, the texts all raise questions about the relationship between the distinct social and historical voices and identities that the two figures represent. With varying degrees of explicitness, they all use the narrative configuration to highlight who can speak and narrate, and under what conditions. The narrator who tells another protagonist's story thus allows insight into both the interpretive frameworks being negotiated and changing ideas about the ethical importance of voice—in particular, about whether the individual ought to be able to tell her own story. They inquire into the same relationships of power and voice that Lanser's groundbreaking study does, only from a different direction. While Lanser concentrates on how narrators use textual strategies to establish their own authority to speak,[40] these texts use a pair of textual voices to question whether narrators might have the obligation to grant that authority to others. While the assumptions about the ethics of voice change from Textor in 1794 to Sebald in 2001, the following chapters show that all of the narrators have an awareness of the relationship between their own voice and their protagonist's.

While the narrators may learn to see their own voices with respect to others' voices, however, the books all show that they cannot escape their individual languages and interpretive frameworks. The narrator of *Stuffcake,* for instance, is forced to recognize himself as having been a conformist bully who ostracized his overweight classmate, but he continues to use the boy's derogatory nickname. In fact, it is the book's title. As they tell their protagonists' stories, the narrators come to recognize the historical and social interpretive frameworks that have shaped them. The implied authors show that those frameworks still constrain them. Readers, too, come to understand the narrator through his engagement with the other person's story. The text's meaning resides largely in this revelation about "the speaker's situation and perspective."[41] In the individual texts, this revelation leads to readers' judgments about the narrator, as well as about the historical interpretive frameworks embodied by the various characters. Individual texts call for individual, historically specific judgments. In the body of texts as a whole, the focus on another person's story highlights the degree to which the narrators understand their identities in relation to others' identities, by both relating to and

---

39. Lanser, *Fictions of Authority,* 5.

40. Ibid., 6–8.

41. Phelan, "Rhetorical Literary Ethics," 635.

disidentifying with them.[42] Although a critical break between past and present enables the narrators to reinterpret their past identities, the break itself does not force reinterpretation in any of these texts. The provincial boy becomes an urbane lawyer (*Doppelgänger*), the war ends (*Cat and Mouse*), the feminist revolution occurs (*Rich Life*). Reinterpretation occurs only when the narrators confront their protagonists' stories and are forced to see them, and themselves, in a new light: when the lawyer meets an ex-convict's daughter (*Doppelgänger*), the postwar social worker remembers his war-hero "friend" (*Cat and Mouse*), the feminist unearths her mother's unheard story (*Rich Life*). The narration of a separate protagonist's story underscores the degree to which the narrators' self-understanding relies on how they understand their contemporaries, and how those contemporaries understand them. It underscores the interplay of historical identities over time. In their presentation of identity as relational, these fictional (or fictionalized) texts are counterparts to what Irene Kacandes has called "autobiography once removed."[43] They are autobiographical texts in which, as Paul John Eakin maintains, "the focus is, paradoxically, on someone else's story."[44]

Metanarration and Narrative Ethics

Their focus is not only on someone *else's* story, but also, as in the autobiographies Eakin discusses or in Kacandes's "paramemoir" about her father, on someone else's *story*.[45] That is, as my discussion of voice has already suggested, they all have a metanarrative component; the "stories of getting the stories" play important roles, and the "narrator reflects on the process of narration."[46] All of the texts depict, dramatize, or discuss the narrator telling his story. Readers see the narrators sitting down to write or hear their thoughts about that writing and about the story it tells. While metanarrative can take many forms and fulfill a wide variety of functions,[47] the metanarrative in the texts

---

42. On disidentification, see chapter 1.

43. Kacandes, "When Facts Are Scarce." Kacandes's book *Daddy's War* discusses, and is itself an example of, the related genre that she terms "paramemoir."

44. Eakin, *Lives Become Stories*, 56.

45. In *Lives Become Stories* Eakin maintains that "the story of the story plays a determining role" in the corpus of relational autobiographies he examines (58). In *Daddy's War* Kacandes defines paramemoir as an account that encompasses "analytical components" and "the stories of getting the stories" as well as the personal narratives of traditional memoir (51).

46. Kacandes, *Daddy's* War, 51; Ansgar Nünning, "On Metanarration," 19.

47. For a discussion of the types and functions of metanarrative, see Ansgar Nünning, "On Metanarration"; Monika Fludernik, "Metanarrative and Metafictional Commentary."

I examine often raises questions about the ethical implications of the stories the narrators tell, and about the ethics of narration more generally. As it draws attention to the narrative present and the ethical import of the story told there, it also emphasizes the texts' lyric dimension. By presenting a narrator who claims to tell a story about someone else, the texts highlight the narrativity that is central to their enterprise, but by having the narrator *reflect* on that story, they shift their narrative balance back toward a synthetic form that emphasizes the relationships between the three narrative modes.

The metanarrative elements highlight the ethical dimension of narrative in two ways. First, the dramatization of the narrator and his writing presents the story he tells as an act in the relationship between himself and the protagonist. By emphasizing the rhetorical nature of the narration—its status as an act committed "for some purpose"[48]—the texts encourage inquiry into the ethical ramifications of the narrator's storytelling. Readers are invited to think about what the story does, and why the narrator tells it. They are invited to assess how the story affects the two figures and their relational identities. Readers may ask, for instance, why the narrating sons of *Sorrow* and *Hedge* tell their mothers' stories, and how these stories affect the mothers and sons and their relationships to each other. At times, the narrators explicitly state their intention to manipulate identities and relationships through their stories. The first sentence of *Stuffcake,* for instance, stipulates the self-image the narrator hopes to convince his readers to share: "Before I proceed with the setting down of this narrative, I would like it understood that I still consider myself an educated man" (157) [Es liegt mir daran, gleich in den ersten Zeilen dieser Niederschrift zu beweisen oder darzutun, daß ich noch zu den Gebildeten mich zählen darf (7)]. In *Hedge* the narrator's commentary reveals the dynamics of his relationship with his mother, and his hope to free himself from her narratively: "Yes, that is how my mother tells stories, and I stop here so as not to repeat them" [Ja, so erzählt meine Mutter, und ich breche hier ab, um ihre Geschichten nicht zu wiederholen (22)]. Studies of nonfiction narration have examined how stories about others intervene in "the web of interpersonal and intertextual relationships in which the story and experience are entwined" and have outlined the ethical implications of stories based on the positive and negative effects they can have for the real people they portray.[49] I contend that the figures in the fictional texts are created to direct attention to such effects, and to their consequences for particular historical relationships.

---

48. Phelan, *Narrative as Rhetoric*, 8.

49. Shuman, *Other People's Stories*, 23–24. For a collection of reflections on ethics within biography and autobiography, see Eakin, *Ethics of Life Writing*.

Thus, my readings attend to the repercussions the stories have on their fictional characters, and my analysis of these repercussions undergirds the historical aspect of my textual interpretations. I elucidate how the narrators use stories to attempt to redefine the specific social and historical identities and interpretive frameworks at stake in the texts, and how readers might judge these attempts. The texts' metanarrative dimension shows that stories affect identities and relationships, and encourages readers to ponder, and perhaps to judge, their ethical value.

The metanarrative elements also communicate the texts' assumptions about and commentary on the ethics of narrative in general, and of particular narrative strategies. Some of this communication is direct, as narrators ruminate explicitly about the ethical status of their own stories and, by extension, of the process of narration. Handke's narrator, for instance, articulates an ethical imperative not to subsume his mother's experience in the formulations of (male) literary language, not to make her mere fodder for "a chain reaction of phrases and sentences like images in a dream, a literary ritual in which an individual life ceases to be anything more than a pretext" (28) [eine Kettenreaktion von Wendungen und Sätzen wie Bilder im Traum, ein Literatur-Ritual, in dem ein individuelles Leben nur noch als Anlaß funktioniert (44)].[50] Other narrators, however, apprehend the power of narration only vaguely, or fail to appreciate how decisively their narrative choices define the relationships and identities they claim only to represent. Narrators like that in *Doppelgänger* simply do not see the full effects of their stories. They remain unaware for the same reason that they are necessarily unreliable: their interpretive framework remains historically limited, and this limitation remains largely invisible to them. Confronting the protagonists' differing languages makes them aware of *some* of the assumptions their frameworks propagate, but they can never recognize their full reach. Of course, no one can. But these narrators are staged within texts that expose these implications. The narrator of *Doppelgänger* explicitly acknowledges stories' power to tame the past, but the staging of his narration exposes the social inequalities that power can serve. Even when the narrators and their ideal audiences remain unaware, the implied author and narrative and authorial audiences reflect on the relationship between narrative, identity, and ethics; the combination of metanarrative staging and commentary communicate indirectly what the narrator cannot, or will not, see.

---

50. Manheim's translation altered.

A Speculative Conclusion

In this chapter I have argued that the structure of dynamic observer narration focuses attention on the conflicts between interpretive frameworks and on the ethical import of the narratives that negotiate these conflicts. It highlights key elements of the process of coming to terms with the past. Before I explore how the texts display these narrative negotiations, I want to speculate about one last interpretive effect of the dynamic observer narrative: the way it encourages conjecture about the authorial act and what I call the historical author. I believe that dynamic observer narratives encourage readers' tendency to equate narrator and author—that is, to blur the distinction between fact and fiction. Paul Dawson has recently argued that actual readers perceive fictional narratives as a kind of public statement made by their actual authors; not only do these readers view actual authors as responsible for the narratives, then, but they also tend to conflate narrator and actual author unless the text clearly signals their difference.[51] Not only do many dynamic observer narratives fail to signal this difference clearly, but they actively highlight the narrator's and author's similarity. From Storm to Sebald, many of the authors employ narrators who share striking characteristics with the historical author, playing with what Philippe Lejeune has termed the autobiographical pact: the coincidence of the author, implied author, and narrator.[52] With varying degrees of playfulness, the texts thus invite speculation about the historical author. Such a stance is familiar from "autobiographical" character narratives, from Karl Philipp Moritz's *Anton Reiser* (1786) to Joyce's *Portrait of the Artist as a Young Man* (1916) and Sylvia Plath's *The Bell Jar* (1963). In making the narrator someone who insists he is telling a story about someone else, however, the historical author makes the narrator conspicuously like himself in a functional way, as well. As these texts' metanarrative components question what telling a story about someone else does, both to the protagonist and for the narrator, they may gesture toward what fiction writing does for its author. In reading, I have often wondered whether they invite their readers to judge that historical figure—or, in a lyric mode, to try to understand his perspective and situation.

---

51. Dawson, "Real Authors," 111. Dawson proposes omniscient narrative as a form that often permits such conflation. He cites Lanser, *Narrative Act* as arguing for readers' tendency to equate narrator and actual author, but the passage he cites actually refers to the "extrafictional voice or 'implied author'" (151). Lanser does stipulate, however, that this "textually encoded, historically authoritative voice [is] kin to but not identical with the biographical person who wrote the text" (152).

52. Lejeune, *On Autobiography*.

Bringing the historical author into the analysis harbors a number of potential dangers, of course. It can yield facile equations. In an area where very few textual clues exist, it may rely too much on the inappropriate imposition of readers' interpretive frameworks, on text-external factors, or on insupportable generalizations. It can devolve into remote psychological analysis of the historical figures. And yet, in the chapters that follow, I find that I have to ask questions about the historical author again and again. In the complex of overlapping and conflicting interpretive frameworks that these texts set up, these figures seem important. If the texts aim to question the value or ethics of telling a story about another person's past, to interrogate what that storytelling does for and to the teller and the protagonist, and to critique the relationship between particular pasts and presents—then their goal is to question authorial activity. And not, as I shall argue in several cases, without grounds. Unreliable narration has been said to give the impression of "unintentional self-recrimination."[53] Many of these texts may harbor an element of authorial self-recrimination, whether intentional or not.

In raising the possibility of authorial self-recrimination or pleas for understanding, I once again return to the nexus of lyric, portraiture, and narrative. In a sense, my argument in this chapter has been that the dynamic observer form allows authors and readers to explore the nature of narrative reckoning with the past because it occupies the space between these three categories. This hybrid is more than an in-between phenomenon, a spot on a continuum between three ideal types. It corresponds to a central aspect of modern experience. The three modes intersect where the events of the past exert a hold on the present, even as the narrator uses a story to distance himself from them (narrative). They intersect where who the narrator is can only be explained in relation to whom she has known and has been (portraiture). They intersect where the interpretive frameworks of narrator, characters, and text can be understood only in relation to each other (lyric).[54] They intersect where the confrontation of these value structures may leave questions of judgment unanswered, or where the very desirability or possibility of judgment may be challenged. They intersect where narrative represents the hope of self-mastery and self-understanding, but where that hope often remains futile. In other words, they intersect in a place that inhabitants of the modern world know very well.

---

53. Zerweck, "Historicizing Unreliable Narration," 156; Ansgar Nünning, "*Unreliable Narration zur Einführung*," 6.

54. See also Phelan's reading of Frost's "Home Burial," where the distance between the interpretive frameworks becomes more important than the content of the frameworks themselves. *Experiencing Fiction*, 211.

PART II

Nineteenth-Century Pasts

three

On the Right Side of History

Emerging Dynamic Observer Narration in
Friedrich Ludwig Textor and Theodor Storm

> Our circumstances make more of us than does nature; and we can never pass
> correct judgment, either on the worth of the individual or on that of entire
> peoples, if we cannot step from our own circumstances into theirs.
> —Johann Weitzel, *Lindau, or the Invisible Alliance*

> No one can endure being silent forever.
> —Theodor Storm, *Doppelgänger*

T̶he heart of the dynamic observer novel is the narrator's effort to "step
into the circumstances" of the protagonist and her own past self in order
to be able to "pass correct judgment" on both. Yet dynamic observer narratives emphasize that no one can entirely adopt another's interpretive framework or disappear behind another's story: the narrator is always audible. To
tell the story of the dynamic observer narrative's development, I begin by discussing two texts from the long nineteenth century whose narrators' distinct
ways of making themselves heard show the emergence of the form: Textor's
Paul Roderich (1794) and Storm's *Doppelgänger* (1886). These two texts are
models of successful narrative reckoning with the past; they reconcile divergent interpretations of events, as the accounts of protagonist, narrator, and
implied author converge. At the end, a stable story emerges. As models of
a successful reckoning, however, they represent the beginning point of the
dynamic observer narrative. The hallmark of this narrative configuration is
interpretive instability between the narrative positions—protagonist, narrator, and implied author—but the narrators of both these texts maintain a clear

ethical and rhetorical superiority over their protagonists, tightly controlling the protagonists' stories and their significance. From Textor to Storm, the first hints of tension between narrator and implied author begin to appear, however, and the first doubts begin to arise about the use to which people put narrative as they try to tame history.

Emergence of the Dynamic Observer Narrative: Textor

Friedrich Karl Ludwig Textor (1775–1851) was a jurist from Frankfurt, whose youthful forays into literary writing are today highly obscure. He published one play, written in the dialect of Frankfurt, and the novel *Paul Roderich*. This novel begins as a hybrid of popular eighteenth-century forms and develops a dynamic of tension of voices only at its end.[1] The first thirteen chapters follow established narrative conventions borrowed from sentimental, epistolary, and satirical Enlightenment novels to tell the story of the protagonist, Paul Roderich. The preface sets this pattern. In it, the narrator forecasts Paul's fate of a vain death for freedom in the War of the First Coalition following the French Revolution; he refers to himself only incidentally, in his desire to plant rosemary on Paul's grave. The chapters then detail the many coincidences, tragedies, and twists of fate that dominate Paul's pre-Revolution life, illustrating his lifelong commitment to freedom and satirizing the social and political structures that frustrate him.[2] As a schoolboy, for instance, he wants his classmates to elect a worthy "king," prompting his father to fear that he will end on the gallows. The narrator rarely appears in these chapters, and most of his self-reference consists of conventional explanations for his knowledge of the story: he has family records, Paul's letters and journals, and a copy of an acquaintance's autobiographical manuscript. His few more substantial appearances establish his affinity with Paul and his Enlightenment principles, rather than revealing his role in Paul's life, as is the case in the other texts I discuss. He offers occasional supportive commentary on Paul's trials and tribulations, for instance, as when he laments the detrimental effects of public appointments determined by social standing and absolutist power. In his most extended appearance in the past-tense narrative, he and Paul are kindred university students who, in contrast to their hedonistic and corrupted classmates, devote themselves to their studies and to the pleasures of virtuous

---

1. Dirk Göttsche classifies it in *Zeit im Roman* (240–41, 244) as a combination between a satirical Enlightenment novel that employs the conventions of the adventure novel and an eighteenth-century *Individualroman*.

2. See ibid., 241–42.

sociability. He describes Paul in glowing terms that affirm the Enlightened principles they share:

> He was passionate and fiery about everything beautiful—he had the intellect to grasp the grand scheme of things and an appreciation of nature; his genius was freer and had a reach that was beyond the everyday intellects of the rest of the student body. Freed of the thousand chains, the tyrants of the earth, superstition and prejudice . . . we took an isolated path and understood each other when no one else understood us.

> Er war warm und feurig für alles Schöne—er hatte Geist für das Grose [sic] und Sinn für die Natur; sein Genie war freier, und nahm einen Schwung, den die Alltagsköpfe der übrigen Studentenzunft nicht kannten. Losgerissen von den tausend Ketten, die Tirannen der Erde Aberglaube und Vorurtheil . . . giengen wir einen isolirten Pfad und verstanden uns, wenn uns, sonst niemand verstand. (68)

In short, the first thirteen chapters establish Paul's virtues and character, and the narrator is important primarily insofar as his affinity with Paul corroborates these ideals.

Even in those thirteen chapters, however, the narrator's comments on Paul's eccentricities and excesses foreshadow the consequences of his friend's idealistic enthusiasm. When they come to fruition in the French Revolution, the narrative approach changes radically, and characteristics of the dynamic observer form begin to emerge. From this point on, the body of the text consists largely of Paul's enthusiastic letters about revolutionary developments; readers receive accounts of the events in his unmediated voice. At the same time, the narrator refutes Paul's views both in short passages in the main text and in extensive footnotes that sometimes completely overwhelm it. These changes signal a shift both in the relative importance of the two figures and in the novel's adherence to narrative conventions. The epistolary form, like other forms of sentimentalism [Empfindsamkeit], has been read as a symptom of the middle class's withdrawal from political life,[3] but, here, it takes a political turn. This adoption of the form for a political object is particularly visible in the novel's use of the term Schwärmer [fanatic or enthusiast]. Schwärmerei was usually discussed as a weakness in which religious or sensual feeling, enthusiasm, and imagination overwhelmed clear perception and thought; it,

---

3. Richards, "Era of Sensibility," 223.

too, has been read as compensatory for the political situation.[4] The passion in Paul's "rapturous letters" [schwärmerisch[e] Brief[e] (332–33)], however, is directed toward a political object.[5]

Even as the narrator allows Paul to "speak" through his letters, however, he now clearly distinguishes his opposing views and stipulates that his report is not an apology for Paul's opinions. Paul's description of the 1790 celebration of the first Bastille Day, for instance, rejoices in the energy and enthusiasm of the crowds. The narrator responds almost angrily:

> Now, that's too much, I exclaimed. . . . It is a terrible shame that my good cousin is losing his reason in that awful Paris! He was never dumb, but he easily exaggerated good and evil. . . . You [Paul] have not considered that the advantages of violent political revolution can perhaps never outweigh the disadvantages of the temporary anarchy that always follows revolutions.

> Nun, das ist zu arg, rief ich . . . es ist doch jammerschade, das der gute Vetter in dem heillosen Paris seinen Verstand verliert! Dumm war er gerade nie; aber er übertrieb leicht das Gute und das Böse. . . . Du [Paul] hast nicht überlegt, daß die Vortheile gewaltsamer Staatsrevolutionen vielleicht niemals die Nachtheile der einstweiligen Anarchie überwiegen, die jedesmal den Revolutionen folget. (334)

When Paul revels in a new appreciation of "how majestic and glorious humanity can be" [wie majestätisch und herrlich die Menschheit sein kann (331)], the narrator insists on the dangerous energy of the mob, and a footnote that consumes half of the page denounces the wild violence that engulfed Paris and the defeated German cities (332–33). Similar dynamics appear as Paul describes the injustices done to the French people, and the footnotes detail the injustice done to Louis XVI (325–28); or as Paul celebrates the glory of dying for freedom, while the footnotes condemn the dishonorable behavior of the French army (335–38). Examples abound: more than five pages of the twenty-six pages in chapter 14 consist of footnotes (and fourteen of the book's last eighty-five). Although the narrator has defended the ideals of free-

---

4. Sauder, *Empfindsamkeit*, 1:140–43. In their combination of subjective response and political commentary, they might be seen as a forerunner to the epistolary, democratic *feuilleton* writing in texts such as Ludwig Börne's *Letters from Paris* [*Briefe aus Paris*] (1834) and Heinrich Heine's *Letters from Berlin* [*Briefe aus Berlin*] (1822). On the relationship of the *feuilleton* to epistolary literary traditions, see Kernmayer, "Gattungspoetologische Überlegungen."

5. The narrator calls Paul a *Schwärmer* several times (335, 338, 399).

dom, justice, and equality through most of the book, the events in France and Germany compel him to establish himself as condemning revolutionary action. The last section of the novel, then, emphasizes not only the relationship between individual self-understanding and historical horizon[6] but also the conflicts between the protagonist's and narrator's moral frameworks. Crucially, however, that conflict dissipates and resolves in the book's conclusion. Disillusioned himself, Paul eventually renounces the French attempt to establish democracy, even as he emphasizes the personal cost of this move and affirms the principles of freedom: "I have lost everything, my peace, my happiness, and the idol most deserving of love [freedom], which I will eternally honor in my heart, I will never again seek in vain in reality" [ich habe alles verlohren, meine Ruhe, meine Glückseligkeit, und das liebenswürdigste Idol [Freiheit], das ich ewig in meinem Herzen verehre, werd' ich nimmer in der Wirklichkeit vergebens suchen (371)]. The cousins' positions have converged, and their final meeting is warm and friendly.

This schematic discussion highlights the presence of the historical forces and narrative tensions that drive the dynamic observer form. The French Revolution—an event often seen as the beginning of modern Europe—appears as a crucial critical break in the continent's political makeup and in the convictions and self-understanding of its citizens. In its wake, the narrator reevaluates and reinterprets prerevolutionary events. He first defends the democratic principles that have fallen into disrepute and emphasizes the noble impulses that animate them. Then, perhaps recognizing that this defense could make him appear a dangerous political radical, he dramatically reverses his narrative strategies to establish a respectable antirevolutionary stance. A footnote offers a compressed story of this transformation:

> I was enamored with France's first constitution—I considered it to be the most beautiful fruit of culture up to this point, a child of refined morals and the highest justice. There, politics was no longer separated from a love of humanity and from the right. What is right and good in itself was also so with respect to the state. All hail the French nation—all hail its constitution! I thought, it alone is worthy of our time. . . . How greatly have I changed my opinion!

> Ich war eingenommen für Frankreichs erste Konstitution—ich hielte sie für die schönste Blüthe der bis hieher möglichen Cultur, für ein Kind der verfeinerten Sittlichkeit und der höchsten Gerechtigkeit. Da war nicht

---

6. Göttsche, *Zeit im Roman*, 240.

mehr Politik von der Menschenliebe und von dem Recht getrennt. Das an sich recht und Gute war es auch in Rüksicht des Staatsintresse. Heil der französischen Nation—Heil ihrer Konstitution! dachte ich, sie allein ist unsrer Zeit würdig. . . . Wie sehr habe ich meine Meinung geändert! (331)

Textor's novel thus shows a narrator wrestling with the prototypical dynamic observer conflict: that between the need to show his adaptation to new conditions, on the one hand, and his unwillingness or inability to abandon his past views entirely, on the other. In this novel, both narrator and protagonist show themselves to be "subject[s] of (hi)story [*Geschichte*] in the dual sense of the word, where the life stories of the characters [*Lebensgeschichten*] are marked by contemporary history [*Zeitgeschichte*] and, at the same time, the characters develop their self-understanding from their relationship to history [*Geschichte*]."[7]

Still, important differences distinguish this novel from later examples of dynamic observer narratives—primarily, differences in the narrator's function and his relationship to the protagonist and implied author. For the majority of the book, its progression centers entirely on Paul and the revelation of the beliefs he represents. The narrator's concern with his own position manifests itself only at the end, when he enters the dangerous terrain of the Revolution. In contrast, all of the later narrators show a palpable, driving self-concern from the first. Susanne Knaller writes that in the nineteenth century, the epistolary novel fell into disuse, because explorations of expressive subjectivity moved into poetry, while the question of the individual and its moral standing was dominated by the third-person, "objective" novels of realism.[8] In his dual incarnation as a subjective participant and authorial observer, the narrator of this partially epistolary novel still combines the lyric and narrative modes—or, conversely, augurs the tension between lyricality and narrativity that characterizes all of the dynamic observer narratives.

The clearly authorial stance that the narrator assumes throughout much of the book correlates with a second difference: this narrator is entirely reliable. There is nothing to suggest that the implied author invents him to comment on the limitations of his historical position, as Bakhtin asserts is the function of "posited" narrators.[9] On the contrary, many features signal the proximity, even identity, of narrator and implied author. The narrator shows self-awareness about his relationship to Paul, as when he pokes fun at the "pedantic tone" [Hofmeisterton (206)] with which he lectures his hot-headed

---

7. Ibid. As Göttsche observes, Paul's self-understanding also develops with his historical experience (243).

8. Knaller, "Der italienische Briefroman," 291–92.

9. Bakhtin, *Dialogic Imagination,* 313. See also the discussion in chapter 2.

cousin. Textual conventions corroborate this sense of a narrator equal to his creator. The same narrative voice is heard in the preface and the story, and, as I have already discussed, the opinions the narrator expresses in the body of the text align with those in the footnotes.[10] The narrator's views on Enlightenment ideals and contemporary realities are also the implied author's; readers are to understand the narrator's commentary, Paul's eventual disillusionment with revolution, and the two figures' final *rapprochement* as a hopeful view toward Enlightenment-inspired reform in Germany.[11] In this book, then, past and present value structures are not only reconciled successfully on the level of the story. The narrative stance itself allows for a univocal resolution of the conflict. In the later dynamic observer narratives, stable resolution remains elusive, as the gap grows between the narrators' accounts of events and those that the implied authors suggest.

Finally, although the narrator writes to affirm Paul's moral character, his *self*-positioning does not rely on that positive characterization. If anything, the opposite is true. It is, perhaps, because he praises Paul and shares his convictions that he insists so vociferously on his moderate, antirevolutionary stance. This narrator's moral self-positioning depends on his standing with respect to historical philosophical and political movements; his benevolent treatment of Paul only symbolizes that standing. Similarly, his extensive quotations of Paul's revolutionary letters document the movement of history and the corruption of intellectual ideals; they do not resurrect a historical voice that has otherwise gone unheard. Whereas the narrators in the texts from Storm onward tell benevolent stories about their protagonists at least in part to establish an ethically sound position for themselves, this narrator tells Paul's story to illustrate his own relationship to history.

Emerging Tensions in the Dynamic Observer Narrative: Storm

The conflict between Enlightenment ideals and existing political and social conditions did not end with the French Revolution. From its immediate aftermath to the failed revolutions of 1848 to the establishment of the German Empire in 1871, the divide between the universal, liberal ideology championed by the middle classes and the realities of life in the German Empire plagued middle-class self-understanding.[12] As the early cultural historian

---

10. Cf. Sophie von La Roche, *Geschichte des Fräuleins von Sternheim*, (1771; repr. Stuttgart: Reclam, 1983), where the original editor (Christoph Martin Wieland) consistently signals his superior understanding.

11. Göttsche, *Zeit im Roman*, 243.

12. See Gall, "Selbstverständnis des deutschen Bürgertums."

Wilhelm Riehl wrote in 1851, the *Bürgertum* had represented "the universal-ism of modern social life" since the Revolution,[13] yet the ideals of political, economic, intellectual, and moral independence for all were far from realized in the German Empire as governed by Otto von Bismarck from 1871 to 1890. From religious discrimination against Catholics in Chancellor Bismarck's *Kulturkampf* [cultural fight], to the Prussian electoral system that weighted votes according to the amount of taxes that individuals paid, to the laws that forbade socialist organizations and publications, inequalities and restrictions on independence persisted.[14]

The narrator of the novella *Doppelgänger* deals with this long-lasting contradiction between ideals and realities.[15] One of the last novellas pub-lished by the canonical poetic realist Theodor Storm (1817–1888), this text runs counter to his reputation (shared with many German realist writers) as a provincial, middle-class writer who ignored or remained blind to the politi-cal and social tensions of his day. My close reading of the text in this chapter shows that Storm's narrator suffers an amorphous feeling of guilt when he realizes that his own childhood behavior toward a working-class ex-convict, John Hansen, participated in this contradiction. Following this realization, he tells John's story to extend an enlightened, universal respect for human-ity across class lines. Riehl asserted that the "social question," the problem of intractable class conflict, was the dominating tension in German society: "A ceasefire in our political battles is possible, today or tomorrow; in the social [battle], no ceasefire, not to mention peace, will be able to assert itself until the grass has long grown on our graves, and on our grandchildren's."[16] Storm's

---

13. Riehl, *Die bürgerliche Gesellschaft*, 246.

14. As part of the effort to solidify Protestant Prussia's reign over Catholic areas after German unification in 1871, Bismarck introduced policies (collectively referred to as the *Kulturkampf*) to reduce the Church's influence and to cement the state's control. Measures included a ban on Jesuits, the designation of civil union as the path to legal marriage, and in Prussia, as in other states, the state's assumption of school operation and oversight. In the three-tiered Prussian electoral system, which regulated elections to the state parliament until 1918, voters were assigned to one of three voting divisions depending on the amount of taxes they paid; while the number of voters in an electoral district's top tier was numerically far smaller (sometimes having a single member), the group carried the same electoral weight as the third tier, to which the majority of voters often belonged. The *Sozialistengesetze* [socialist laws], in force from 1878 to 1890, were intended to prevent working-class challenges to the government and to quash the widely feared threat of social and political revolution. Begin-ning in 1883, conciliatory laws granting benefits, such as sick leave, workers' compensation, and pensions, represented a new strategy for defusing the perceived socialist threat.

15. Portions of the analysis of *Doppelgänger* were originally published in Byram, "German Realism's Proximal Others," and are published with the permission of Cambridge Scholars Publishing.

16. Riehl, *Die bürgerliche Gesellschaft*, 4.

middle-class narrator attempts to resolve this "social question" by telling an empathetic and respectful story of the working-class John. Still, this chapter shows that, while he tells his story to affirm the man's equal humanity, he continues to distinguish himself from this other "class" of men.

Dynamic observer narratives address the predicament that arises when changing identity and shifting moral frameworks cause individuals to see their past relationships in a new light, a light that illuminates what now appears as their past failings. Storm's novellas have long given the impression that they are driven by a complicated guilt, one that is entwined with the identities and self-conception of those who bear it. Reviewing Storm's *oeuvre* in 1887, Alfred Biese maintained that using the terms "guilt" and "penance" to characterize Storm's novellas invokes too much of a sense of the criminal justice system; instead, he ruminated, Storm's narratives show that "much more often, we atone for the guilt of the general body of which we are a part, for that of humanity, of the age in which we live, . . . of the estate/class in which or with which we live."[17] A century later, Eckart Pastor prefaced his investigation of Storm's novellas with the observation that the first-person narrators of his many frame novellas often tell their stories to overcome their own "guilty entanglement" in them; readers' sympathy for those narrators encourages them to overlook this personal entanglement, but the novellas reveal that "someone has reinterpreted his earlier life in order to be able to endure it and to survive."[18] Yet Pastor's analyses concentrate primarily on what befalls the novellas' protagonists, rather than on what motivates and influences the narrator in his storytelling. In this chapter I pursue this uninvestigated relationship between past guilt, present identity, and the narration that attempts to reformulate this closely intertwined complex.

Doppelgänger lends itself to this exploration because, although it is lesser known than Storm's last published work, *The Dykemaster,* its narrator is particularly prominent, and his struggle with his own past and identity commands an unusual amount of attention; the frame story of *Doppelgänger* makes up approximately one-third of the novella's total pages, more than in any of Storm's other novellas. The text opens with its narrator, an attorney, recalling a past journey. Having stopped at an inn, he strikes up a conversation with a forester, who eventually invites the narrator to visit him and his wife at their home. The narrator accepts, and before leaving the inn, he learns that he and the forester's wife, Christine, are both natives of the same distant town. When he arrives at their home the next day, he finds both of his hosts to be sensitive about Christine's origins; Christine's memories of her father are

17. Biese, "Theodor Storm," 226. See also Pizer, *Ego–Alter Ego,* 96.
18. Pastor, *Sprache der Erinnerung,* 9.

confusing and troubled, and the forester reveals that she does not know that her father, John Hansen, was an ex-convict who was called John Glückstadt after the prison in which he had been incarcerated.

After retreating to his room for the evening, the narrator reconstructs John's life story from a combination of memories and trancelike vision. The narrator relates that, after being released from prison, John married Christine's mother, the fiery Hanna. The two were happy for some time, despite the continuing prejudices of the townspeople; eventually, however, economic hardships exacerbated by discrimination ignited arguments that led to domestic violence and Hanna's death. This tragedy cured John of his temper, and he spent his last years providing and tenderly caring for his young daughter. But a chance encounter with his former partner in crime tarnished his image with the townspeople yet again, and John found himself unable to feed and shelter Christine adequately. Wandering in a field at night as he searched for potatoes to steal, he fell into a well and died; the townspeople and his daughter knew only that he disappeared.

The narrator wakes from his reverie and goes to bed, and the next morning he tells his host the history he has conjured. At first the forester resists telling Christine this story of her father, but after the narrator has left, he decides to share it. An initial reaction of stormy tears gives way to a new affection for her father, whose confusing "doubleness" she now understands. The narrator becomes a cherished family friend, and the text ends as he anticipates visiting them again after many years. John's Jekyll-and-Hyde history and Christine's shadowy childhood are difficult pasts that demand reckoning and resolution in this novella. As the narrator tells the story, however, it is his own past that most strongly influences his tale. His own fraught relationship to Christine's family motivates his narrative efforts to mitigate the tension between himself and them and, by extension, between the middle and lower classes to which they belong. As a result, *Doppelgänger* highlights the way narratives about the past can intervene in present social identity and the relationships it shapes. In particular, it shows that guilt about past behavior can be transformed into a guarantor of present identity when it allows the "reformed" individual to "do justice" to the wronged person through narrative—when it prompts a narrative reckoning with the past.

The Narrator's Identity and the Poetics of Social Critique

In explaining how the narrator's class-inflected identity influences his story about the Hansens, I integrate analysis of the two issues around which scholarly interpretations have clustered, but which they never have joined: the novella's social critique and its reflection on narrative poetics. The question of its social critique dominated the first century of discussion, from its appearance in 1886 until 1985. Biese initially compared the novella's achievement of a "gripping fidelity to reality" in its depiction of the miserable poor to that Zolá attained in *Germinal*.[19] In 1888 Johannes Wedde claimed that it depicted "the value and the ability of the so-called 'simple folk' [*kleinen Leute*] . . . on whose foundation the future must be built. At the same time, the *Doppelgänger* contains a—perhaps unconscious—cutting protest against the conditions that condemn such a noble human force to such heartrending destruction."[20] But for nearly the next century, the majority of critics refuted Wedde's suspiciously socialist reading. Apparently overlooking Wedde's suggestion that the critique may have been unconscious, many insisted that Storm's firm conviction in the existing social order precluded his artistic attack on it; instead, his merciless representation of John's misery addressed the "human" and "ethical" dimensions of the problem.[21]

The 1980s saw a shift in scholarly interpretations of the novella. On the one hand, the turn toward politically engaged literary criticism brought a chorus of voices affirming Storm's critical attitude toward society and the criminal justice system. Wolfgang Tschorn, for instance, reads Storm's texts as exposing the increasing pressure that political and economic forces placed on the sanctuary of the family.[22] Harro Segeberg holds that the novella expresses Storm's preference for the new juridical and legal system developing within the Prussian state over the older moral regulation of conduct.[23] At the same time, many criticize the ambiguous elements that soften the text's social criticism. The frame story draws the heaviest fire in this regard, as it seems to solve the working classes' economic and social hardships by whisking its progeny (Christine) into the middle class.[24] At the same time, other scholars began to read the novella as a statement of Storm's poetics. Manfred Schunicht holds that the frame story presents "poetry," including the narrator's embedded story, as a "sought-for alternative to a negatively judged reality." Fundamentally, the text is concerned with the poetics that can redeem that reality,

19. Biese, "Theodor Storm," 224.

20. Wedde, *Theodor Storm*, 26, quoted in Laage, "Ein Doppelgänger," 1011.

21. Stuckert, *Theodor Storm*, 390–93; Goldammer, "Einführung," 92–93. See also Böttger, *Storm in seiner Zeit*, 345–47; Frank X. Braun, "Theodor Storm's 'Doppelgänger,'" 269–70; Niewerth, "Theodor Storm," 317.

22. Tschorn, "Verfall der Familie."

23. Segeberg, "Storm als 'Dichter-Jurist.'"

24. See Neumann, "Text und sein Doppelgänger," 56–57; Burns, "'Vorbestraft,'" 438–39, 47–49; Schuster, "Eine Gegenüberstellung," 205–6.

rather than with reality itself.[25] Brigitte Leuschner concentrates on the role of interpretation and imagination in the relationship between poetry and reality.[26] Others argue that the text rejects purely "objective" approaches to representing reality—scientific discourse, naturalist writing, and photography—in favor of a poetry or narration that can enrich human experience and create text and world as balanced wholes.[27]

The text's social critique and its poetics cannot be separated, however, and I analyze the largely unexplored link between the narrator's actions as a middle-class child in the embedded story and his narration as a middle-class adult in the frame. While Pastor and Renate Bürner-Kotzam consider how class tensions relate to the form and purpose of the narrator's story, neither examines extensively enough the way he represents himself as an individual actor in the past nor weighs the personal motivations he may have for telling his story in the present.[28] In these interpretations, the crucial relationship between social identity, individual responsibility, and the narratives that surface when conceptions about these shift—the relationship that characterizes the effort to come to terms with a problematic past—disappears.

The frame story has often been discussed as an idyllic fairy tale of middle-class complacency. Yet its middle classes are not as monolithic, and its narrator is not as self-assured, as some would have it. Instead, it subtly evokes the hairline cracks that threatened middle-class cohesion and identity at the end of the nineteenth century.[29] A dispute between the narrator and the forester about the proper place of poetry, for instance, evokes a conflict regarding the role culture played in middle-class self-understanding. Among the upper reaches of the middle classes, made up largely of the *Bildungsbürgertum*, self-definition relied heavily on a shared culture and *habitus*.[30] Pursuits that demonstrated its members' symbolic possession of the "time and leisure" of economic independence, such as literature, music, and theater, assumed particularly prominent positions in this culture, and also helped propagate its values.[31] In their conversation about poetry, Storm's narrator, an attorney, and the forester, the son of a rural pastor, demonstrate their participation

---

25. Schunicht, "Theodor Storm: *Ein Doppelgänger*," 82–83.

26. Leuschner, "Erfinden und Erzählen."

27. See Ladenthin, "Erinnerndes Erzählen"; Ladenthin, *Gerechtes Erzählen;* Plumpe, "Gedächtnis und Erzählung."

28. Pastor, *Sprache der Erinnerung;* Bürner-Kotzam, *Vertraute Gäste.*

29. Byram, "German Realism's Proximal Others."

30. See Gall, "Selbstverständnis des deutschen Bürgertums," 608–9, 19; Linke, *Sprachkultur und Bürgertum,* 19–26; Kocka, "Bürgertum und bürgerliche Gesellschaft," 26–33.

31. Kocka, "Bürgertum und bürgerliche Gesellschaft," 31. See also Linke, *Sprachkultur und Bürgertum,* ch. 9; Sheehan, *German History,* 801.

in this culture. The forester's reminiscences about Ludwig Uhland's poetry, which he associates with his courtship of his wife, suggest that it even colors his personal history. The forester still finds poetry suspect, however, a pursuit of the impractical or unproductive "dreamer" (517). For those segments of the middle class that earned their living through commerce or trade, as for the forester, "practical independence" took precedence over the ideals of "intellectual and moral" autonomy, and self-definition did not depend on education or the culture it imparted.[32]

The novella also highlights the tensions that attended the middle classes' transition from numerous regional or communally based identities to a shared national identity. On one hand, references to the "hometown" that the narrator shares with Christine abound, as do general remarks about the value of *Heimat* [homeland]. When Christine tells him when she left their hometown, for instance, he exclaims, "Oh, at that time I was still in our homeland, before so many of us had to go into exile" [O, damals war ich noch in unserer Heimat, bevor wir, so viele, in die Fremde mußten (525)].[33] Storm might well have uttered such a plaint himself, as the many biographical descriptions of his suffering under his exile from his native Schleswig-Holstein attest.[34] Attachments to or a yearning for local and regional communities, perceived to be more organic than the society of Bismarck's state, continued to suffuse the discourse on state and society in the late nineteenth century. The narrator's repeated assertions of his friendship with the working-class members of his hometown also suggest a fond remembrance—or retrospective construction—of a "community of place" [Gemeinschaft des Orts] that bridged the barriers of economic and social difference (525–26, 575).[35]

---

32. Gall, "Selbstverständnis des deutschen Bürgertums," 612.

33. The text contains other expressions of yearning for *Heimat,* as well (524, 530), although it begins with the narrator's report that he was living in his birth city at the time of the events (517). This discrepancy can perhaps be attributed to the novella's original serial publication and the time pressure Storm was under as he wrote it. See Laage, "Ein Doppelgänger," 1002–5. The text certainly suggests that the narrator and Christine share a bond because of their common geographical origins, as the usage of kinship terms and variations on the term "countryman" ("Landsmann") shows (525, 526, 528, 530).

34. See Segeberg, "Kritischer Regionalismus," 127; Stuckert, *Theodor Storm.*

35. The "community of place" belongs to Ferdinand Tönnies's analysis of the transition from a traditional to a modern society in *Community and Society [Gemeinschaft und Gesellschaft],* which was first published in 1887, the year after *Doppelgänger.* Tönnies and Storm were personal friends, maintaining a correspondence until Storm's death, and Tönnies published a memoir of Storm in 1917. I do not claim that Tönnies's ideas directly influenced Storm's work but rather suggest that both were operating within the development of the broad nineteenth-century discourse on community and society/state. On this discourse, see Walker, *German Home Towns,* 421–27. For discussions of the relationship between Storm, Tönnies, and their work, see Bartoleit, "Verhältnis"; Segeberg, "Spiegelung eines Epochenumbruchs"; Fechner, *Dichter und der Soziologe.*

Language was an important symbol of this regional belonging. The narrator first becomes acquainted with the forester because the forester finds his speech oddly familiar; the narrator then learns that he is from the same town as the forester's wife and concludes that traces of their common dialect must have attracted the man. He is surprised, however, that it is still perceptible: "Does the sound of home lie so deeply as to be indestructible?" [Liegt der Heimatklang so tief und darum auch so unverwüstlich? (520)], he exclaims. Despite his emphasis on the importance of *Heimat,* the narrator's reaction to the dialect's presence betrays conflicted feelings about its persistence. Listening for traces of it in Christine's speech, he notes few: "Only a few times did I think I perceived the sharp S before another consonant, which I myself believed I had long ago forsaken" [nur ein paar Mal meinte ich das scharfe S vor einem anderen Konsonanten zu vernehmen, dessen ich selbst freilich mich längst entwöhnt glaubte (523)]. The three qualifiers in the short second phrase (selbst, freilich, längst) suggest an ambivalence that could lie in the meaning that dialect, or its absence, took on for middle-class identity. Riehl identifies a departure from dialect as an achievement of the middle-class's "universal spirit" and the goal of all educated people.[36] Angelika Linke's study of the linguistic *habitus* of the nineteenth-century *Bürgertum* suggests that this view is quite representative. Members of the middle class denigrated regional dialect as they attempted to develop a national and class identity that would supersede local loyalties, so that, in the social sphere, locally colored language gave way to a standard language characterized by its faithful reproduction of written discourse.[37] In his uncertain linguistic position and his longing for a homeland that no longer exists, the narrator appears as a man no longer at "home" in an intact community, but also not fully absorbed in or committed to the national middle class that he, a traveling attorney, represents. Although the frame appears to present the picture of a perfect middle-class world, it registers the divisions in the middle classes of the 1880s.

The fairy-tale impression that it yields derives largely from the stark contrast between the lives of the narrator and his middle-class hosts, on the one hand, and the ex-convict John and his family, on the other. This gaping divide deflects attention from the much subtler divisions within the world of the frame story, and to the threats they hold for the narrator's middle-class self-understanding. The narrator needs this distance, and underlines it subtly in his discussions of the role language plays in middle- and working-class lives. At the same time, however, he tells John's story to reduce the distance between them. By recognizing John as a man who loved and cared for his

36. Riehl, *Die bürgerliche Gesellschaft,* 250.
37. Linke, *Sprachkultur und Bürgertum,* 233–63.

family under difficult circumstances, he acknowledges John's belonging to a universal humanity. This human recognition assuages his vague sense of guilt about his childhood interactions with John and Hanna and symbolically defuses class conflict. As a middle-class child, the narrator judged and looked down on John and his family, but as an adult, he uses his story to distance himself from John's tormenters and to imagine himself as a friend of the working class.

His narrative recasting of the past corresponds to the tension between the Enlightenment dictate to universal benevolence and the desire to maintain class identity and distance. Philosophically, members of the enlightened middle class were obliged to work toward a world in which the working class attained an intellectual, moral, and material standard of living equal to their own. But practically, such a state would erode their self-understanding. The cleft between the classes was simultaneously a hurdle to ethical goals and a source of safety: "The middle class's sharp outward delimitation made 'raising' the working class difficult but provided a good share of the middle class's internal homogeneity."[38] The text thus presents a subterranean awareness of the forces that had already begun to undermine middle-class ideology at the time of the novella's publication in 1886: the conflict between that ideology's liberal message of universal progress toward the ideal/idyll of middle-class life, on the one hand, and the middle class's continuing use of its economic and social advantage to maintain its position and to distinguish its diverse body of members from the masses below, on the other.[39] The narrator does not set out intentionally to solve the "class question," as Textor does to address enlightened principles and the French Revolution. He does not even intend to absolve himself of guilt. Instead, his is a case of the "involuntary self-incrimination" characteristic of unreliable narrators.[40] Whether or not he is actually unreliable is a question I will return to later.

---

38. Wehler, *Deutsche Gesellschaftsgeschichte* 3, 768.

39. Kocka, "Bürgertum und bürgerliche Gesellschaft," 53–54. Kocka maintains that the period of middle-class decline and defensiveness began in the 1870s. As the general standard of living increased and made some elements of middle-class culture and life available to broader swaths of the population, the middle classes themselves began to feel threatened and attempted to solidify the distinctions between themselves and the lower classes. Wehler discusses the conflict between universal ideology and particular interests, the defensive actions the middle classes took to protect those interests, and the social democratic pressure to realize liberal ideals in *Deutsche Gesellschaftsgeschichte* (3, 769–71). Rudolf Vierhaus summarizes the Socialists' critique, beginning in the 1870s, that the systems and institutions of public education functioned as instruments to preserve the ruling classes' predominance by cementing the educational distinctions between the classes. See "Bürgerliche Hegemonie," 55–56.

40. Zerweck, "Historicizing Unreliable Narration," 156–57. Zerweck paraphrases the concept of unreliability developed in Fludernik, "Defining (In)Sanity."

The Embedded Story: Middle-Class Child Meets Working-Class World

Having sketched how the frame exposes the instability of the narrator's middle-class identity, I devote my close readings to the embedded story's exposure of the narrator's conflicts with the working class. Where others locate the narrator's motivation for his narration in sublimated desire or in a compassionate wish to provide Christine with a comprehensible and mean-ingful history,[41] I attribute it to his disquieting sense of his personal connec-tion to John Hansen's fate. The embedded narrative unquestionably focuses on John, but the narrator appears as an actor and participant at three key nar-rative moments, each of which corresponds to a crucial experience of John's life. Each of these moments shows the narrator's childhood self reinforcing the social distinctions and prejudices that separate him from the Hansens and doom them to destruction.

The first of these episodes provides the transition between the frame and embedded narratives, grounding the narrator's knowledge of the story by describing his youthful acquaintance with John. After learning the identity of Christine's father, he retires to his room and is visited by images of two "bleak places" [öde Orte (531)] from his childhood. The first is an old, abandoned well that he associates with butterfly hunting and with an executioner's hut said to have been there in earlier times. The second is the tiny house at the edge of the village in which Christine spent her early years. As a young boy, the narrator perceives this hut as a "Lilliputian house without parents and without teachers" [Liliputer-Haus ohne Eltern und ohne Lehrer (531–32)] in which it would be delightful to live. As a youth, he knows it as the house in which the wild John Glückstadt beats his wife until the curious gather to listen to the ruckus.

All three of these memories are suggestive of the narrator's relationship to John. The first associates violent death—including John's, which is caused by his fall into the well—with the narrator's childhood play. Moreover, this play involves a potentially aesthetic and cultural dimension, as butterflies were often captured, killed, displayed, and labeled in visually striking collections in the name of scientific and cultural progress and individual self-cultivation. The narrator's childhood butterfly hunting thus bears some resemblance to his adult narration of John's story.[42] The second image of the "Lilliputian house"

---

41. See Bürner-Kotzam, *Vertraute Gäste*, 57, 90–93; Pastor, *Sprache der Erinnerung*, 179, 84–85; Pizer, *Ego–Alter Ego*, 110.

42. I thank Chana Kronfeld for her insight into the cultural significance of butterfly hunt-ing. Pastor asserts that the text's repeated references to hunting evoke a world divided into hunters and hunted, and that the narrator's childhood butterfly hunting places him among

shows the narrator imagining the tiny hovel as a realm free from discipline and learning.[43] I focus on the last image, however, which both includes the narrator's most direct expression of his sense of guilt and ties this feeling to the social gulf that separates him from John. The memory begins with the narrator's presence at the scene of domestic violence.

> Later, when I was already in secondary school, there was something else; there was often a ruckus in these narrow rooms that caused passersby to stop in front of it, and to these I, too, belonged a couple of times. A powerful man's voice cursed and scolded in a torrent of words; thundering blows, the shattering of vessels became audible; between them, scarcely perceptible, the whimpering of a woman's voice, but never a call for help.

> Später, als ich schon Sekundaner war, kam noch ein Anderes hinzu; es gab oft einen Lärm in diesen engen Räumen, der die Vorübergehenden davor Halt machen ließ, und zu diesen gehörte auch ich ein paar Mal. Eine kräftige Männerstimme fluchte und schalt in sich überstürzenden Worten; dröhnende Schläge, das Zerschellen von Gefäßen wurde hörbar; dazwischen, kaum vernehmbar, das Wimmern einer Frauenstimme, doch nie ein Hülferuf. (532)

The narrator's presence is quite natural at the opening, as he locates the memory in the progression of his life. The way he describes that presence, however, suggests his guilty feelings about it. Instead of proceeding directly to his own relationship to the house, as he does when he reports his dreams of living in it, he begins his account of the beatings as an impersonal description: "there was often a ruckus . . . that caused passersby to stop." He numbers himself among this group of listeners only in a second clause that provides multiple linguistic indicators of an uneasy conscience: the slight hesitation at revealing his presence in the group; the "too" that emphasizes this discomfort; and the contrast between the frequency of the beatings and his infrequent spectatorship. Similarly, it is only after he has enumerated the violent noises emerging from the hut that he notes the woman's whimpering and her absent cry for help. The violent clamor attracts the townspeople's attention, perhaps understandably, but the presence of that telling female voice transforms the scene

---

the former. But the narrator is just one of the many examples of "hunters" offered, and Pastor does not discuss the significance of his presence in the list for the story that he tells. See Pastor, *Sprache der Erinnerung,* 187–88.

43. In *Vertraute Gäste,* Bürner-Kotzam interprets the dream of a house without authority figures as a manifestation of the desire that the narrator satisfies vicariously through John (90).

into a more sinister one, one where inactive spectators perhaps assume some responsibility. Years later, the narrator's insistence that Hanna never cried out for help seems an implicit recognition of that unfulfilled responsibility, and the "but" [doch], as the "too" in the earlier sentence, expresses his concentration on this fact. His retroactive unease both indicts him for his youthful presence at the scene and grasps at the ameliorating condition that Hanna never asked for intervention. The absence of sound with which the narrator closes his list testifies to the cry's presence in his mind, however.

The last sentences of the episode, in which the narrator relates how John interacts with his "audience" after one of these incidents, appear to confirm the narrator's vague feeling of guilt:

> He threw back his head with its strong aquiline nose and silently surveyed the crowd; me he struck with a flash of his eyes. To me it was as if I heard him yell: "Go on, go away, you with the fine coat! What's it to you if I knock my wife to pieces!"

> Er warf den Kopf mit der starken Adlernase zurück und musterte schweigend die Umstehenden; mich blitzte er mit ein Paar Augen an, mir war, als hörte ich ihn schreien: "Mach, daß du fortkommst, du mit dem feinen Rock! Was geht's dich an, wenn ich mein Weib zerhaue!" (532)

Among all the onlookers, the narrator feels himself singled out by John's defiant gaze. While John registers everyone present, his eyes "flash" only at the narrator, and the placement of the direct object before the verb emphasizes the narrator's impression of being singled out by John's scorn. The narrator is aware of having injured John's privacy and pride, and instead of defending himself with derision or self-righteous judgment, he imagines himself in John's position and denounces his own action. Interestingly, while John's imagined recrimination charges the narrator with an invasion of his privacy, it also recalls the community's failure to intervene to help Hanna and suggests that most people do not much care whether Hanna is knocked to pieces. Despite John's actions, the narrator is the one scorned, a contemptible, privileged boy in a "fine coat" who intrudes passively on others' suffering. The narrator implicitly judges such behavior again later, when he contrasts the behavior of the passive audience with a neighbor's compassionate aid:

> And boys and young people stopped and stood in the street before their house and took pleasure in the misery that reached their ears from inside. Only one, the old neighbor carpenter, came with goodwill.

Und Buben und junge Leute blieben auf der Gasse vor ihrem Häuschen stehen und ergötzten sich an dem, was von dem Elend drinnen an ihr Ohr hinaus drang. Nur einer, der alte Nachbar Tischler, kam mit gutem Willen. (548–49)

Here—when he is not on the scene—the narrator spells out the voyeuristic enjoyment of others' misery that motivates the onlookers. In the figure of the carpenter, he also presents an image of what those onlookers might have done; the old man arrives either to make peace between Hanna and John, or to remove the innocent Christine from the scene.[44] These passages suggest that the narrator feels a measure of guilty responsibility both for spectating during the Hansens' misery and for failing to intervene in it.

This episode not only betrays the narrator's subconscious sense of guilt about his relationship with John's family but also introduces the means he will subsequently use to deal with it. He never tries to help Hanna; he does not apologize to John. Instead, he begins to construct a story of John's life as he imagines it through John's eyes. Narrative becomes the means by which he tries both to rectify his failings and to downplay them—and, in the end, also to resolve the social conflicts that encourage them. By telling John's story from John's point of view, he acknowledges him as he had not when he was a youth in a "fine coat." Not only does his "half-visionary" story consist largely of events that the narrator has imagined (574), indicating his continuing effort to see John's life from a perspective known only to John and his family, but he also shifts the focalization to John at key moments, such as when John unintentionally kills Hanna (552–53). John becomes an agent worthy of focalization, rather than an object of observation or judgment. This effort to inhabit John's perspective suggests the narrator's attempt to atone for his past failings with a retrospective story. At the same time, the narrator retains control of that story, which diminishes his guilt and its significance, since John's attainment of a simple morality and Christine's emergence from poverty appear to compensate for his tragic fate. Those who criticize the text for sugarcoating its social criticism find fault with it precisely for this aura of redemption, which deflects attention from society's culpability for John's hard life and death. None of these critics notes, however, that it deflects attention

---

44. The mayor, who lends John money, sympathy, and understanding, also demonstrates that it had been possible to support John, rather than persecute him (541–42, 545, 568–69, 574). Niewerth says in "Theodor Storm" (317–18) that he is the only figure who assesses John's situation and character accurately in the embedded story, although the narrator adopts this view in the frame story. He does not remark, however, on this observation's implicit indictment of the narrator.

from the narrator's personal feeling of responsibility. The embedded story departs from the instant when his discomfort about the social rift between himself and John appears most clearly, and, as I will argue, it closes at the moment that rift has been healed. The dual motion of the narrator's story—its implicit acknowledgement of and effort to atone for his guilt, and simultaneous denial of its ultimate significance—suggests that, for the narrator, the story drives not toward social criticism but individual absolution.

Moments of the narrator's personal involvement in John and Hanna's story puncture its tragic progression up until the moment the rift closes. The next occurs at his first mention of Hanna. She first appears in the story as laughter that rings out above the murmur of women's voices on a local chicory field that John has been hired to oversee. The first image of Hanna is focalized by the narrator, however, before it shifts to John:

—Among the women there was one, the same one whose laughter burst forth so brightly from the group, whom I had seen often enough in the entrance to my parents' house, standing as a beggar on the cellar steps; if I happened to step out of my room, she only looked at me mutely with her demanding brown eyes, and if I had a shilling in my pocket, I certainly took it out and laid it in her hand. I still remember well how sweet the touch of this narrow hand was, also that I stood there for a while afterward and looked down as if spellbound at the spot on the steps from which the girl had departed just as silently.

Something similar may have happened to the grim supervisor, under whom she now did honest work; he caught himself devouring the girl, now seventeen, with his eyes, rather than keeping an eye on the lazy women.

—Unter den Dirnen hatte ich eine, dieselbe, deren Lachen aus der Schar so hell hervorschlug, oft genug auf dem Hausflur meiner Eltern als Bettelmädchen an der Kellertreppe stehen sehen; sie schaute mich, wenn ich zufällig aus dem Zimmer trat, nur stumm mit ihren verlangenden braunen Augen an, und hatte ich einen Schilling in der Tasche, so zog ich ihn gewiß heraus und legte ihn in ihre Hand. Ich entsinne mich noch wohl, wie süß mir die Berührung dieser schmalen Hand tat, auch daß ich nachher noch eine Weile stehen blieb und wie gebannt auf die Stelle der Treppe hinabsah, von der das Mädchen sich ebenso schweigend wieder entfernt hatte.

Dem finsteren Aufsichtsmann, unter dem sie jetzt in ehrlicher Arbeit stand, mochte etwas Ähnliches mitspielen; er ertappte sich darauf, daß er mitunter, statt den faulen Weibern auf die Finger zu passen, das jetzt siebzehnjährige Mädchen mit seinen Blicken verschlang. (536)

Pastor and Bürner-Kotzam view this passage as an expression of the narrator's dangerous, norm-defying desire and of his projection of that threatening desire onto the outsider John.[45] Certainly, desire is in play. But in their focus on the desire itself, they overlook the way in which social hierarchy structures that desire. The young boy does not see Hanna and desire the imagined joy and abandon of being with her, as he has earlier dreamed of the imagined freedom in the little house. Instead, he meets her within the constraints of their respective social roles. Hanna appears "as a beggar-girl at the cellar steps" of his parents' home, and when she leaves again, he finds himself "looking down" at the spot where she had stood. He remains above her throughout the encounter. Moreover, he can touch her only through the exchange of money. Reading the passage, one can surmise that the young boy's "certain" decision to put any coin he has into her hand is motivated, at least in part, by his anticipation of the "sweet . . . touch of this narrow hand."

The following paragraph emphasizes that Hanna's relationship to John arises under very different conditions. When she meets him, she is not begging, nor is she receiving money because of his desire; her relationship to him is one of "honest work." The two exchange desirous looks for just a short time before marrying, and when they do, John moves into the little house to live with Hanna and her mother, and to pay half the rent. During the happier phases of their marriage, the two are social equals as well as passionate lovers. In its early days, and even for a time after Christine's birth, both continue to earn honest pay. Despite John's criminal past and his emerging violence toward Hanna, the two maintain a passionate attachment to each other, for Hanna and her mother do not touch the "wound" of his prison time; demonstrating his efforts to inhabit his protagonist's framework of understanding, the narrator concludes that they simply do not perceive John's crime as having made him different from themselves, "for in their own lives, right and wrong often lay next to each other, scarcely distinguishable" [denn in ihrem eigenen Leben lagen Recht und Unrecht oft nur kaum unterscheidbar neben einander (550)]. The argument that leads to Hanna's death begins when this relationship of equality and mutual respect wavers. Plagued by financial worries, John condemns Hanna's earlier begging as shameful and lazy; as he does so, his eyes look at her "as if he wanted to push her down into nothingness" [als wolle er sie ganz ins Nichts hinunterdrücken (552)]. His words and expression demote her to a realm below his own, just as the narrator's earlier "charity" reinforced her lower social position. In fact, these two passages are the only two places where the text refers to her begging; thus, the narrator's presence

---

45. Pastor, *Sprache der Erinnerung*, 184–85; Bürner-Kotzam, *Vertraute Gäste*, 90.

is subtly conjured at the scene of Hanna's death. She responds angrily to her husband's accusations, making her single, fatal mention of John's incarceration—reciprocating his demeaning comments with one of her own. The former romantic and social pact, which had granted even John "his home and castle" [sein Heim und seine Burg (550)], disintegrates.

The narrator not only appears on the periphery of John and Hanna's domestic disputes, connecting himself implicitly with Hanna's death; he also reappears when he imagines John's. Two memories from the days after John's death serve as the transition back to the frame narrative. In the first, a friend of the narrator returns home from a butterfly hunt in the erstwhile chicory field and reports that a ghost has called out his name: "Christian!" The narrator now concludes that the "ghost" had been John, calling for "Christine" and being heard by another human being for the last time (575). In the second, a working-class friend tells the narrator that, mowing grain in the same field, he and his companions had almost caught a foul-smelling falcon that had been feeding on a carcass in the well. The narrator closes his reminiscences with the recollection of his reaction:

> I had not paid this statement much heed, then; now I shuddered as the memory came over me; the damp night wind that wafted over me did me good, above all because it was from now and not then; I knew the well had been filled in a few years before.

> Ich hatte damals dieser Rede nicht geachtet; mich schauderte, da mich die Erinnerung jetzt befiel; der feuchte Nachtwind, der mich anwehte, tat mir wohl, vor allem, weil er von heut und nicht von damals war; ich wußte, der Brunnen war vor ein paar Jahren zugeschüttet. (575)

The first clause of this framing reflection draws attention to the narrator's original lack of thought about John's disappearance. The second is open to at least two interpretations. The narrator could shudder at the realization that the carcass in the well was, in fact, John's corpse. He may also recoil at his casual dismissal of his friend's experience, however; after all, the shudder immediately follows his recollection of that dismissal. His involuntary gesture expresses his horror at the events—and, perhaps, also the mindset—of the past. The winds of "now" are a relief, removed as they are from both the horror and the failure of responsibility it implies. The well has been filled, and nothing more can be done or known about what lies at its bottom.

A load removed from his mind, the narrator orders himself to bed and admonishes John's spirit to accept the peace he has created for it: "You go to bed, too, soul!" [Seele, geh du auch zu Bett! (576)]. He falls asleep and is greeted by a dream image of the child Christine, who "nodded amiably" [nickte freundlich (576)] as she left town for her new middle-class life. This last, closing brush with the world of the past reverses its opening scene. Instead of facing a destitute and angry John who scornfully orders him away, the narrator sees off a newly prosperous Christine who recognizes him affably as she leaves town. In the course of the story, the Hansen family's fate has improved immeasurably, and so has the narrator's relationship to them. Or, at least, so he imagines it. After all, the dream image at the end, like John's words at the beginning, is a product of the narrator's mind.

Historical Voice and the Unequal Distribution of Narrative Power

The narrator's story both depicts social conditions and attitudes as responsible for John's demise and sidesteps a critique of those conditions. It acknowledges the injustices and hardship of the Hansens' past, but it also paints that injustice and hardship as having been overcome—or itself repairs it. John is allowed to focalize the embedded story in parts, but the narrator retains control of that story and its resolution. And it does resolve. I agree with those who claim that the *narrator's* story ameliorates the guilt society bears for John's fate, and that his daughter's elevation into the idyllic middle-class world of the forester's home gives John's story a kind of happy end.[46] To the extent that the narrator can be seen as part of a guilty collective, it also lessens his own culpability. But the narrator's story and horizon are not the same as the implied author's. The narrator is concerned with the social dynamics of his story, but the implied author is also concerned with the story as an element of social dynamics. The narrator emphasizes the importance of language and observes linguistic differences both in the frame, where they threaten middle-class cohesion, and in the embedded story, where they separate the middle from the working class. These observations contribute to his implicit social critique. The structure of the text emphasizes that these linguistic differences translate into differences in what people can do with stories. I want to emphasize this connection between social difference and narrative capability. The text is not only about the transformative power of narrative, taking social critique for granted.[47] Because the characters' capacity for narration is tied to their social identities—because John can only ever be a focalizor, for whom

---

46. Burns, "'Vorbestraft'"; Schuster, "Eine Gegenüberstellung."
47. Cf. Ladenthin, *Gerechtes Erzählen*, 52, 61.

someone else speaks—the novella's statement of narrative as an ethical force is a social critique at the same time.

In the embedded story, the narrator portrays the working-class figures as lacking control over language, and that lack as dooming them.[48] The interactions that lead to John and Hanna's attraction and marriage are visual and physical, rather than verbal. John first meets Hanna when he is overseer of the field where she works: "He caught himself . . . devouring the seventeen-year-old girl with his gaze. In return, she looked silently at him with her hot eyes" [Er ertappte sich darauf, daß er . . . das jetzt siebzehnjährige Mädchen mit seinen Blicken verschlang. Sie mochte ihn dann wohl still mit ihren heißen Augen anschauen (536)]. The marriage proposal takes place after Hanna has run into John and his arms in her flight from a fellow worker, and Hanna begs John to kill her in a striking scene that contains several expressive gazes. Moments of speechlessness alternate with disastrous words throughout their stormy relationship. John beats Hanna for the first time after a snippy verbal exchange. "Back and forth, the words became sharper and less considered" [Red' um Rede ward wechselweise schärfer und unbedachter (546–48)], and after the first blow falls, Hanna both flees and returns to their little house without uttering a word. Her last moment of speechlessness leads her to death; stung by John's accusations about her earlier begging, she is silent and becomes steadily angrier because she cannot respond. When she finally answers by reminding John of his time in jail, he throws her against the stove and kills her. Less fateful scenes also indicate John's inability to use language effectively. When he tries to urge the midwife to Hanna's bed during Christine's birth, for instance, he eventually leaves her to drink her coffee, because "he saw that each of his words only made her more unwilling" [er sah, daß jedes seiner Worte sie nur noch widerwilliger machte (544)].

In contrast, Christine's linguistic accomplishments seem to display her proclivity for middle-class life even as an impoverished child. Instructed by the old woman who cares for her after her mother's death, she learns to read and write, attracting the approving attention of passersby—most of them explicitly or implicitly middle class. "Contemplative people, retired school-teachers, old grandmothers, too" [nachdenkliche Leute, pensionierte Schullehrer, auch wohl alte Großmütter (561)] stop to watch the child move her finger along the page. The little girl is quiet like her mother, but hers is the quiet of obedient learning, rather than the mute suffering of a woman who whimpers without calling for help. Whereas passersby approve her recon-

---

48. On John and Hanna's speechlessness, see also Schunicht, "Theodor Storm: *Ein Doppelgänger*," 177; Neumann, "Text und sein Doppelgänger," 56.

struction of the ordered language on the page, they had previously listened disapprovingly to the wild violence of her father's words. Language out of control and unable to appeal to the world has been replaced by the kind of linguistic behavior the world understands and prescribes.

These linguistic characteristics are not haphazard, and the narrator is clearly aware of them. In his only extended gnomic statement, he highlights the linguistic differences that separate him from John and Hanna:

> Who doesn't know how often those we call "workers" are doomed because their livelihoods depend on their hands alone! When, in the heat of passion, their unpracticed words are not sufficient, the hand reaches in as if by itself, as if it could do something here, too, and what was nothing, a whisper, becomes a grave disaster.

> Wer wüßte nicht, wie oft es denen, die wir "Arbeiter" nennen, zum Verhängnis wird, daß ihre Hand allein ihr Leben machen muß! Wo in der Leidenschaft das ungeübte Wort nicht reichen will, da fährt sie, als ob's auch hier von ihr zu schaffen wäre, wie von selbst dazwischen, und was ein nichts, ein Hauch war, wird ein schweres Unheil. (548)

For such a man as the narrator—who as an attorney makes his living with words; who is at home in poetry and its criticism; who maintains a friendship over many years through letters alone —linguistic deficit must lead to tragedy. People must be able to talk: "no one can endure being silent forever" [ein ewig Schweigen soll kein Mensch ertragen können (562)].

Certainly, the narrator cannot. Reminded of the unfortunate John Glückstadt, and moved to "love or sympathy" [Liebe oder Anteil (577)] for his daughter, the narrator tells a story that acknowledges but tames the ugliness of the past. That story cements the friendship between them, and erases all tension between the former "haves and have-nots." At least, the narrator, the forester, and Christine all believe that the mystery and the pain of the past have been resolved: the well has been filled, the breeze brings in only what is "alive," the honeysuckle is blooming as never before, and a wreath of roses around John's photograph signals that the man and his memory have been rehabilitated (576, 578). As Volker Ladenthin contends, the text grants narrative a unique power to effect a "transformation" of the past.[49]

At the same time the text shows that not everyone can harness that power. Even the narrator recognizes that John and Hanna could not have freed

---

49. Ladenthin, *Gerechtes Erzählen*, 53–54.

themselves from their guilty pasts by telling stories, as he does. As his single gnomic rumination concludes,

> And, having occurred once, [the grave disaster] keeps occurring; for most of these people [workers], not only the worst, live forward in time and have their eyes turned only to today and tomorrow; what was and has passed teaches them nothing.

> Und geschah [das schwere Unheil] einmal, so geschieht's auch ferner; denn die meisten dieser Leute [Arbeiter], just nicht die schlechtesten, sie leben ihre Zeit dahin und haben ihre Augen nur auf heut und morgen; was gewesen und vergangen ist, gibt ihnen keine Lehre. (548)

They do not revisit the past to draw lessons or edification or healing from it, as the narrator does in his tale. Instead, as when Hanna taunts John with his history, their conjuring of the past turns its "whisper" into a "grave disaster." In the narrator's account, John's last act is to cry out his daughter's name. Instead of being heard and saved, however, he is misunderstood and taken for an inhuman spook. In contrast, just two pages later, the forester calls the narrator's story poetry, and within days, that story has restored John to his daughter as a "whole human" [ganzen Menschen (578–79)]. The narrator sees John and his family as cursed by their linguistic incapacity, but he does not see himself spinning the tale that "transforms" the characters' shared past. Only readers see that.

Benevolent Blindness: Narrator Reliability and Reader Judgment

The narrator never admits a sense of guilt about John's fate; perhaps he is not consciously aware of it himself. Nor does he acknowledge that the integrity of his middle-class world depends on the presence and difference of its working-class counterpart. Finally, he shows no awareness that, in using his story to assuage his conscience and confirm his own position, he makes John the object of voyeurism once again and freezes Hanna eternally in her position on the cellar stairs. While these "failings" have been read as a result of his desire to maintain and assert his power as a middle-class male,[50] I think he refrains from confronting these issues directly not because he *will* not, but because he *cannot*. In other words, I do not see him as intentionally obscur-

---

50. Bürner-Kotzam, *Vertraute Gäste.*

ing his motivations for telling John's story. Still, there is a gap between his presentation of the story and the understanding that the implied author supplies.

Within a rhetorical interpretive approach, then, he is unreliable. I do not believe that the implied author judges him for this unreliability, however, nor are readers invited to judge him. The text's language never suggests judgment, and the narrator never appears duplicitous, hypocritical, or malevolent in the narrating present. Indeed, a century of readers viewed him as reliable. I believe that the subtlety of the textual traces of unreliability only partially explains this discrepancy of judgment and that the type of unreliability is also important. In Phelan's terms, the narrator is unreliable neither via misreporting nor via misjudging, but only because he underinterprets the social gulf between himself and John, and misreads his own motives.[51] In the present of the narration, the narrator has the compassion to understand the plight of the poor, and he recognizes that the division of labor affects individuals' abilities. He looks back on his earlier self and is ashamed of the condescension he felt and showed toward John. He still believes, though, in the power and good of a language that can make the world better *for everyone*. The frame story is not a falsifying idyll; it is an ideal.[52] The narrator still believes in the enlightened, utopian vision of a society in which "if something was supposed to be true, good, and beautiful, in principle it was so for everyone"—and so does his ideal audience.[53] In accordance with this belief, his narrative rehabilitates John in terms of middle-class values. His limited frame of reference prevents him from perceiving what the implied author sees.

I suggest that this novella, like many dynamic observer narratives, highlights a kind of unreliability generated solely by faulty interpretation or understanding. Phelan attributes an equal status to unreliability along all three axes: failings of judgment, reporting, or perception and understanding all signal the narrator's distance from the implied author, and any combination of these may cause a bonding or an estranging dynamic.[54] But I think that the axis

---

51. Phelan provides his typology of unreliability in *Living to Tell* (50–53).

52. Cf. Pastor, *Sprache der Erinnerung,* 189. Pastor thinks the narrator does not quite believe the story of salvation the frame story implies. Storm's contemporary Johannes Wedde, on the other hand, saw the frame as an expression of the hope that the class conflict would be overcome. See Grimm, "Theodor Storm," 330–31.

53. Kocka, "Bürgertum und bürgerliche Gesellschaft," 30. On the universal claims and aspirations of middle-class culture, see ibid., 41; Wehler, *Deutsche Gesellschaftsgeschichte* 3, 769. The entirety of Gall's "Selbstverständnis des deutschen Bürgertums" assumes the conflict of an unrealizable utopian ideal with the reality of middle-class life; he specifically uses the term "utopian" on 616.

54. On the third axis of unreliability, see Phelan, *Living to Tell,* 49–50. Booth, too, stipulates that most unreliability is not a function of intentional lying but of "inconscience: the narrator is mistaken, or he believes himself to have qualities which the author denies him." See

Phelan adds to Booth's original scheme—that of perception and understand-ing—has a slightly different status. I agree that this third axis operates the same way insofar as it reveals distance between narrator and implied author and alerts readers that they cannot trust everything the narrator says. But in terms of reader *judgment*, I think this kind of unreliability is distinct. By itself, it does not invite judgment but a lyric bonding, where narrators' failures of perception and understanding help illuminate the interpretive frameworks associated with their particular states of being. Dynamic observer narratives emphasize and help clarify the reasons for this effect. Because their structure highlights the conflicts between interpretive frameworks and their change over time, it is primed to make readers aware of the limitations that these frameworks impose on individuals. While it invites readers to see the nar-rators' failures of understanding, it also promotes an awareness of the omni-present interpretive limitations that individuals face. Moreover, when the narrator's story constitutes a recognition of his past deficiency and an effort to reinterpret the past from an improved vantage point, as it does in this novella, readers may see him as having what Taylor calls an "orientation to the good" and as moving toward it.[55] The bonding effect of the lyricism is heightened, then, when it is accompanied by the narrator's "partial progress toward the norm."[56]

This is not to say that all dynamic observer narrators are sympathetic and undeserving of judgment—far from it. But when they do invite judgment, as they will in the novels examined in the next two chapters, it is because their failures of perception are accompanied by or tied to the two other kinds of unreliability: failures of reporting or failures of evaluation. As Phelan says, these different kinds of unreliability usually co-occur.[57] I suggest that readers experience unreliable narration as estranging, and that they judge the narra-tors who produce it, when these narrators fail to tell the truth (or the whole truth) or when they display distasteful (or inadequate) values. A narrator's failure to see or failure to understand, however—as long as it is not caused by or does not cause the other two faults—encourages readers' understanding of his position. In effect, errors of perception and understanding, which are closely linked to an individual's interpretive framework, serve to illuminate

---

Rhetoric of Fiction, 159. On the three axes and bonding unreliability, see Phelan, "Bonding and Estranging," 225–26.

55. Taylor, *Sources of the Self,* 47–48.

56. Phelan, "Bonding and Estranging," 231.

57. Phelan, *Living to Tell,* 53.

the state of the narrator's "thoughts, beliefs, emotions, specific conditions."[58] They produce a lyric effect.

The narrator makes no break with the liberal belief in the possibility of progress for all; the critical break in this text consists of his realization that he must extend that belief to include even an ex-convict. The implied author does not judge this stance, but he does show that "the realism of the representation penetrates more deeply than the narrator himself can admit"[59]—and perhaps than the author could, either. Many of those who downplay the novella's social criticism do so on the grounds that Storm affirmed the social system of his time.[60] Of course, that the citizen Storm supported the status quo does not prevent his implied author from offering a fundamental critique of it.[61] Here at the end, however, I want to engage in a little speculation. It does not seem improbable that the historical Storm envisioned a reading audience very like his narrator's ideal narrative audience: both ascribe to the universal ideal of the enlightened middle class.[62] Both storytellers' purpose is to affirm the working class's belonging to a universal humanity and to recognize its hardships from a middle-class point of view. This proximity may contribute to the implied author's lack of judgment about the narrator's limited understanding. The historical Storm, a judge who listened to people from all walks of life try to explain themselves, provides observations about the relationship between language and class, but he plants no denunciations of culture, of poetry, of stories. It is the implied author, and the (implied) authorial audience, that can draw connections between social standing, language, narration, and the guilt of the past.

These suppositions are, of course, just that. But the similarity suggested between the historical Storm and his narrator is a similarity that recurs in all of the dynamic observer narratives I examine—and the similarities become ever more striking. The narrators' ideal audiences are often very close to the audiences one might imagine the historical authors wishing for themselves. At the same time, these historical authors repeatedly construct implied authors who reveal the deficiencies of these ideal audiences' perception and judgment. Their (implied) authorial audiences see both these deficiencies and

---

58. Phelan, *Experiencing Fiction*, 23.

59. Neumann, "Text und sein Doppelgänger," 56.

60. See Tschorn, "Verfall der Familie," 50; Goldammer, "Einführung," 92; Böttger, *Storm in seiner Zeit*, 346.

61. Rabinowitz stipulates in "Truth in Fiction" (126) that implied authors can be ethically superior to their creators.

62. Nathalie Klepper also compares author and narrator in their narrative activity. See *Theodor Storms späte Novellen*, 113–14.

the parallels between narrators and historical authors. I do not read these texts sensationally, as the historical authors' veiled self-recriminations and self-defense. They are fiction, and they all reflect on what stories and story-tellers do. They also ask their audiences to consider the historical limitations of figures very like their historical authors, however, and suspend those audiences between judgment and understanding. It seems to me possible that their historical authors invite a bit of both, too.

Conclusion

In terms of a reckoning with the past, Textor and Storm show the emergence of both a narrative model of reckoning with the past and the first inklings of doubt about the process. In Textor the interpretive frameworks and stories of all parties converge: the narrator and implied author are one and the same, and Paul also comes to share their evaluation of Enlightenment ideals and of history. The novel successfully reconciles the diverging accounts of the French Revolution, allowing it to envision a path to peaceful political and social reform.[63] In Storm the ideal narrative audience sees a similar progression. The narrator intuits John's story and weaves it empathetically into an account where middle-class virtues and prosperity triumph, and which John's daughter embraces. In fact, his account allows Christine to integrate her two, disparate sets of childhood memories. Moreover, Christine, the imagined John, and the narrator all share the implied author's fundamental moral framework. The past is laid to rest.

Yet, already in Storm, narrative tension arises. Interpretive distances and instability begin to open between narrator and implied author, between narrator and protagonist, and between these figures' various audiences.[64] I have argued that this distance does not invite readers to judge the narrator, but I think it does begin to cast doubt on the process of a narrative reckoning with the past. Although the implied author does not accuse the narrator of operating with ulterior motives, he does reveal the subterranean motivations that can drive the process of coming to terms with the past. Moreover, by casting the process in the context of class conflict, it introduces power dynamics into that process. It acknowledges the role that social power plays and suggests that the process can itself become an instrument of power. By emphasizing John and Hanna's clumsiness with language, the narrator inadvertently points

---

63. Göttsche, *Zeit im Roman*, 243.

64. This conception of narrative tension derives from Phelan, "Rhetorical Literary Ethics," 634.

out the power that narrative gives him. While they are incapable of telling a meaningful story about their past, he can tell a story that both rehabilitates their memory and defuses the threat that memory holds for the present. The text does not criticize the narrator for telling John's story for him, as will occur in *Stuffcake*. But it does show that it is important to be able to tell a story that others hear and understand.

four

War of the Words

Radical Internarration in Wilhelm Raabe's *Stuffcake*

> The images from my childhood can't be taught and infiltrate everything that I
> see, and as soon as I leave the area, they are all that matters. They don't want
> to be corrected.
>
> —Monika Maron, *Pavel's Letters*

Wilhelm Raabe (1831–1910), like Storm, was a prominent and pro-
lific author of German poetic realism, and his *Stuffcake* (1890), like
Storm's *Doppelgänger,* was one of his last works. Today, it is also one of the
most read. In this novel, the narrator, Eduard, tells of his reunion with his
childhood "friend" Heinrich Schaumann, *aka* Stuffcake [Stopfkuchen] at
the man's farm, the Red Redoubt.[1] In his focus on a childhood acquaintance,
Eduard is very like the narrators of the two novels discussed in chapter 3,
but Raabe's novel departs from the narrative strategies and narrative situation that Storm and Textor employ. Storm's narrator relates the story of John
Glückstadt from a benevolent reverie, speaking for the ex-convict in two
senses: he (1) takes control of the man's story, and (2) rehabilitates his legacy.
Textor's narrator presents Paul Roderich's own words, but his editorializing
provides a clear frame for understanding Roderich's story; in the end, readers are to accept the narrator's account of Paul's life just as surely as Storm's
readers accept his narrator's account of John's. Raabe's novel displays a com-

---

1. I translate the title and title character's name as *Stuffcake* and the name of the farm as
the Red Redoubt, rather than as Red Bank Farm, as Fairley does. The vocabulary of military
defense is important within the logic of the text.

pletely different dynamic. Stories are not primarily benevolent in this novel. Eduard and Schaumann are competing narrators, and neither voice yields to the other. Schaumann tells Eduard his own life story to attack Eduard's self-understanding, and Eduard's retelling of that story tries to parry Schaumann's blow, even as it also implicitly acknowledges his faults as a youth. In short, each narrator struggles to dominate, to be the one to triumphantly "stamp [his] heels on the heads" (304) [den Fuß auf den Kopf setzen (197)] of the hidebound provincial world the other one supposedly represents.

This novel emphasizes what Storm's novel downplays: that the person who tells a story wields power.[2] Its concatenated narratives—Eduard repeats verbatim Schaumann's stories about himself and his wife—emphasize that stories compete with and dominate each other as they impose meaning on history and experience. And it raises the question of whether such domination is right. The narrators of Storm's and Textor's texts never ask, or prompt, this question. Convinced of their own morality and of the validity of their interpretations of their protagonists' lives, they never ask whether those protagonists might better tell their own stories. Raabe does not preach; he is not a moral philosopher or an activist for the oppressed. But he does show his characters' frustration when their stories are usurped, and he shows that some people's stories are more likely to be usurped than others'. He does not advocate a particular formula for narrative justice, but he does show that narrative injustice exists.

Raabe's orchestration of these competing stories affects both the social relationships he depicts and critiques, and the novel's narrative form and commentary on narrative ethics. The novel's social critique adheres in the patterns of narrative dominance and deference that it establishes among its characters, patterns that criticize colonial thought and practice and connect them to "benevolently" oppressive practices in Germany. In the half century of Raabe's literary productivity (1856–1902), mass social movements began to demand the Enlightenment-era rights of freedom and self-determination for new groups of people: workers, women, and slaves. Raabe was never an agitator—he is often read as a resigned humorist—but in a letter to Klara Zetkin, the leader of the socialist women's movement, he characterized himself as a "friend, adviser, and comforter of the burdened of *all* classes, of all those who require courage for living as well as for dying."[3] The only direct statement in his fiction about women's suffrage ridicules the cause, but readers and critics

---

2. Portions of this chapter were originally published in Byram, "German-German Relations."

3. Letter of March 10, 1908, quoted in Hoppe, *Wilhelm Raabe*, 58.

alike noted his many strong female characters and believed him sympathetic to women.[4] Several of his novels suggest a critical stance toward colonialism and the inequalities it both assumes and supports; Raabe's depiction of the Moor figure in the 1873 novella *Master Author* [*Meister Autor*], for instance, contrasts the man's human equality with white Germans to his social inferiority to them.[5] *Stuffcake* suggests parallels between the silenced positions of women and colonial subjects, linking critiques of the domestic and colonial realms and exposing the common power structures that traverse both. The contests of voice in this novel reproduce the tensions between the group that enjoyed self-determination and free speech—white, male Europeans—and those who were beginning to demand them.

Contests of voice also signal the novel's transitional conception of the relationship between narrative and identity. Common wisdom holds that Raabe's late work combines characteristics of German poetic realism with anticipations of modernist concerns and forms. Sandra Krebs reads his depictions of identity and its relationship to narrative as straddling this divide, using key terms of the debate between narrativist and antinarrativist accounts to describe realist and modernist aspects, respectively. Raabe's late novel *The Birdsong Files* (1896) [*Die Akten des Vogelsangs*], she claims, depicts a modernist disintegration of the individual's sense of self and of the intelligible language and coherent stories that would ground it.[6] But *Stuffcake* shows that narrative can also trouble identity in other ways: the open antagonism between the two narrators, Schaumann and Eduard, shows that the story of self can also be undermined from without. Eduard's sense of self does not erode from within; it is besieged when Schaumann denigrates Eduard's material achievements and place in society. The antagonistic stories in the novel portray self-understanding as vulnerable to the stories others tell and show that social identity and social power influence whose story dominates. In other words, the novel highlights the external component of identity. Further, it shows this uncertain identity as tied to a problematic past. The novel, like theories of coming to terms with the past, suggests that a stable present identity requires a successful reckoning with the past, which itself requires a consensus about that past. Where contention persists, both present identity and the past remain unresolved.

---

4. Di Maio, "Wilhelm Raabe's Female Characters."
5. Göttsche, "Der koloniale 'Zusammenhang der Dinge,'" 66–72.
6. Krebs, "Erzählbarkeit des Ich." I discuss the debate between narrativist and antinarrativist views in chapter 1.

Narrative Conflict and the Unresolved Past

The novel's narrative battle originates in old wounds. The text opens as Eduard begins to write his story on board a ship bound for South Africa and his colonial estate. He is returning from a visit to his childhood home in Germany, and the bulk of the text describes this visit. In particular, it details the events of Eduard's last full day there, which he spent with his childhood "friend" Heinrich Schaumann, better known to his schoolmates by the derogatory nickname Stuffcake [Stopfkuchen]. Eduard had been moved to seek out Schaumann at his farm, the Red Redoubt, when he learned that another of his childhood companions, the mailman Störzer, had just died. Upon arriving, Eduard is delighted to find a domestic paradise inhabited by Schaumann and his loving wife, Tine. But his initial pleasure is soon disturbed; as the conversation gets under way and Schaumann begins to tell Eduard how he came to own the Red Redoubt, Tine's family farm, the scene becomes less comfortable. Schaumann's narrative opens with his boyhood, and he quickly accuses Eduard of having belonged to the crowd of boys who made life miserable for the slow, fat Stuffcake. The outcast sought refuge under the hedge of the farmstead, a place forsaken by society because its owner, Tine's father, Andreas Quakatz, was suspected of murdering a man. Eventually, Quakatz and Tine accepted Schaumann as a fellow pariah and ally, and when Schaumann failed in his studies at the university, he moved in at the farm, first as its manager and then as Tine's husband and its proprietor. Under his management, the Red Redoubt yields the couple a prosperous life, and they are living happily ever after.

In the course of this narrative, Schaumann reveals—both to Eduard and to Tine—that he has learned who committed the murder for which Tine's father had been the prime suspect. He refuses to sully the peace of the Red Redoubt by unraveling the mystery on its grounds, however, and accompanies Eduard into town so as to tell him there. On the way, the two pass the neighborhood where the mailman Störzer, Eduard's childhood idol, lies awaiting burial, and Eduard suggests that they stop in to pay their respects. As he stands reverently at the foot of the coffin, Schaumann divulges that the recently deceased man was the murderer. He completes the tale as the two sit in a pub, overheard by a mesmerized barmaid. When Eduard wakes in his lodgings the next morning, he is assaulted by the townspeople's fascinated questions and decides to escape the attention and curiosity by departing for Africa. Störzer's funeral procession, now the sensation of the town, permits him to slip away almost unnoticed. The text closes as Eduard completes his written narrative and the ship sights Capetown's Table Mountain.

The past asserts itself clearly as a disruptive force in this novel, as it does in several of Raabe's late works. All three novels of the so-called Braunschweig trilogy, *Old Nests* (1879) [*Alte Nester*], *Stuffcake,* and *The Birdsong Files,* employ dynamic observer narrators to explore this disruption. Commonly associated with traditional bourgeois society, the narrators of these novels find their comfortable existence disturbed by the reappearance of a friend from the past who rejects or violates that society's values.[7] Nathali Jückstock-Kießling's summary of the narrators' dilemma echoes the guiding question of my book; she writes that the narrators wrestle with social constraints on identity, perspective, and narration, asking, "Who am I and how did I become who I am?"[8] Wolfgang Jehmüller contends that the encounter between narrator and protagonist causes the narrator to undergo an "ironic reversal," what I call a critical break, in which he questions his former beliefs and past actions.[9] The narrator uses narration to tackle this "completely unmastered" conflict; in words that echo narratological descriptions of unreliable narration, Jehmüller characterizes the story he produces as "a kind of confession" or "self-incrimination."[10]

But the contest of voices that pervades *Stuffcake*'s narrative structure complicates the reckoning with the past in this novel and differentiates it from the others. All of the novels highlight the narrator's perspectival limitations.[11] Eduard, however, claims to repeat verbatim a story that Schaumann has told him, so that Schaumann's direct speech consumes much of the text. More importantly, Schaumann challenges Eduard's account of the past and, hence, also his present identity.[12] Jehmüller asserts that the narrating "biographers" of the trilogy create an "epic dualism" because they introduce distinct temporal realms of action in past and present, but he overlooks the narrative dualism generated by the division of narrative labor between Eduard

---

7. See Roebling, *Wilhelm Raabes doppelte Buchführung,* 99–104; Jehmüller, *Gestalt des Biographen,* 49–56; Meyer-Krentler, *Bürger als Freund,* 262. Raabe's late novels *Pfisters Mühle, Meister Autor,* and *Altershausen* share similar narrative configurations but are not usually included in this group. While the parallels are blurred by their divergences from the pattern in the "trilogy," I believe that they share much the same dynamic.

8. Jückstock-Kießling, *Ich-Erzählen,* 318, 192. She explores the implications these issues bear for Raabe's theory and practice of realism.

9. Jehmüller, *Gestalt des Biographen,* 79–91.

10. Ibid., 126–28. This characterization anticipates the descriptions of unreliable narration in Ansgar Nünning, "*Unreliable Narration* zur Einführung," 6; Zerweck, "Historicizing Unreliable Narration," 156; Fludernik, "Defining (In)Sanity," 78.

11. Klopfenstein, *Erzähler und Leser.*

12. Compare to the function of verbatim quotation in *Austerlitz,* which blurs the distinctions between narrator and protagonist. See chapter 7.

and Schaumann.[13] This division of labor affects readers' narrative and ethical assessments of the two figures because, unlike in the other late novels, the two men's competing stories become weapons.[14] The narrators of the other two novels are unsettled by the protagonists and their relationships to them. Yet both construct a stable story in the end, however threatened it may be. In *Old Nests* the narrator accepts his friend Just Everstein's version of the past and reinterprets himself and his history in accordance with it. The narrator of *The Birdsong Files* completes and closes his files about the protagonist, Velten, whose death rules out any challenge to their findings. In contrast, Schaumann is alive and kicking, and the alternative story he tells about the past cannot be a catalyst for narrative realignment and narrative consensus, because neither Schaumann nor Eduard cedes narrative ground. Eduard's ambivalent repetitions of Schaumann narrate his own guilt without ever admitting it, and Schaumann simply refuses to hear Eduard's version of the story.

Schaumann's Narrative Attack

The seed of this narrative dynamic lies in Schaumann's motivation for telling Eduard his story about the past: revenge for wrongs Eduard has committed. From the beginning, his story threatens not only Eduard's story of the past but also his identity; he intends his story "to strike as heavy a blow as possible to the core of Eduard's self."[15] There is no benign proliferation of perspectives here, as in some of Raabe's other novels.[16] Schaumann aims to destabilize Eduard's internal sense of self by assaulting him with the huge discrepancy between his self-understanding and Schaumann's opinion of him.[17] While

---

13. Jehmüller, *Gestalt des Biographen*, 31–32. Indeed, many of Jehmüller's statements about the biographer figure and his relationship to the protagonist indicate that, in order to construct his typology, he sometimes disregards this narrative specificity of *Stuffcake* (as well as specific features of the other novels). He claims, for instance, that because the novels consist of the narrator's subjectively oriented biography of the protagonist, those parts of the protagonists' life stories during which the two are not in contact appear only sketchily (36–37). This is patently not the case in *Stuffcake*, where Schaumann relates the events of these years in detail. In fact, it is Schaumann who narrates the text's crucial events.

14. Compare to the nonviolent confrontation or negotiation of linguistic systems that Wolfgang Preisendanz identifies in Raabe's *Birdsong Files*, and to Jehmüller's characterization of the relationship between the trilogy's biographers and protagonists as friendship. Preisendanz, "Erzählstruktur als Bedeutungskomplex," 217–18; Jehmüller, *Gestalt des Biographen*, 64–65.

15. Sammons, *Alternative Community*, 295.

16. See Hebbel, *Funktion der Erzähler- und Figurenperspektiven*.

17. See also Tucker, "Wilhelm Raabe's *Stopfkuchen*." Tucker argues that the novel's battle between two conflicting modes of historical understanding draws its urgency from their impli-

Eduard views himself as the successful adventurer to Schaumann's sedentary plodder, Schaumann's story casts Eduard as a cruel, irrelevant conformer and himself as a noble and powerful outsider. As he relates the story of his life and unravels the mystery of the long-ago murder, Schaumann blames Eduard for joining in the bullying Schaumann suffered as a child, and implies that Eduard's social conformism implicates him in violence committed in Germany and in Africa. These charges upset Eduard's conception of himself as a respectable, successful, and "harmlessly benevolent" citizen and colonist;[18] of his childhood acquaintances as good, Germanic examples of how "trusting and true people are in the civilized world" [treuherzig es in der Welt und unter den Leuten zugeht (10)];[19] and of the forces of social order as benevolent guarantors of clean streets (175). In contrast, Schaumann casts the histories of Prussian-led Germany and colonial Africa as histories of violence and warns Eduard and Valentine that Eduard is "far more deeply involved in all this than he suspects" (269) [steckt persönlich viel tiefer mit drin, als er es sich jetzt noch vermutet (151)]. Schaumann frames his story as a quest to drive the ghosts of suspicion and persecution from the Red Redoubt, but he tells it in order to make Eduard's ghosts visible to him. Schaumann contends that "in every place you only have to know how to lay the ghosts that have perpetual haunting rites there, and then you'll be all right" (247) [Man muß nur von jedem Ort den von Rechts und Ewigkeits wegen dranhaftenden Spuk auszutreiben verstehen, und man sitzt immer gut (123)], but he intends his story not to facilitate an exorcism but to initiate a haunting.

Schaumann openly declares his story to be a long-anticipated act of revenge: "There, you see, Edward, how the man who is on top of things after waiting quietly for years gets his revenge for the mocks and rebuffs he patiently endured" (226) [Siehst du, Eduard, so zahlt der überlegene Mensch nach Jahren ruhigen Wartens geduldig ertragene Verspottung und Zurücksetzung heim (96)]. Over and over, Schaumann reminds Eduard of the torment he and the other boys visited on their overweight classmate. Early in his visit, for instance, Eduard calls Schaumann by his schoolboy nickname, prompting Schaumann to ruminate about the "worthless, malicious, impudent rascals" (202) [nichtsnutzige, boshaftige, unverschämte Schlingeln (65)] who assigned it to him. Repeatedly throughout his tale, Schaumann places himself "under the hedge" [unter der Hecke] as a designation of the isolation

---

cations for the identities of the present. While Eduard's history emerges from and protects the individual and collective memory that supports stable identities, Schaumann pursues a critical history that destabilizes such accounts (572–77).

18. Jehmüller, *Gestalt des Biographen*, 84.

19. My translation. Cf. Raabe, "Tubby Schaumann," 160.

he endured when abandoned by those same boys. Schaumann's enumerations of his youthful suffering paint Eduard as an active participant in the mob's cruelty. When he first airs his feelings about his "old friends," he includes Eduard among them by using informal, second-person plural pronouns, and when Eduard obliquely suggests that he might be excepted from this blanket condemnation, Schaumann rejects the idea derisively. In fact, Schaumann lumps the other boys into an undifferentiated conglomerate and insists on Eduard's individual presence in the group, twice using pronouns that begin by attributing the damnable behavior to the group but end by singling out Eduard: "Didn't I let you all—or you go . . . Didn't I let you all—or you go without protest?" [Habe ich euch—dich nicht laufen lassen . . . Habe ich euch—habe ich dich etwa nicht ruhig laufen lassen? (66)].[20] In response, Eduard uses pronouns to retreat into the crowd: "And to tell the truth, I—we just left you behind" [Und um der Wahrheit die Ehre zu geben, ich—wir haben dich einfach sitzenlassen (66)].[21] Schaumann acknowledges the collective nature of the group's behavior but emphasizes Eduard's individual responsibility for having played along; Eduard shifts that responsibility to the group as a whole.

In contrast to the picture he provides of Eduard, Schaumann portrays himself as challenging *bourgeois* society and its standards of success. He recognizes at an early age that he is expected to pursue goals counter to his nature: to attend university, acquire a classical education, and surpass his father's professional and social rank. As a youth, he can do little to resist this plan. Though he desires nothing more than to escape the confinement of society's institutions—the "prison" of school is no different for him than the town jail (188)—he dutifully goes away to college.[22] Schaumann's adult situation, however, confirms his tenacity in escaping expectations and following his chosen path to fulfillment. Ensconced at the Red Redoubt, Schaumann lives "the way he must have seen himself a thousand times in the sentimental, idealistic dreams of youth" (192) [wie er sich selber wohl tausendmal in seinen schönsten, elegischsten Jugendträumen als Ideal gesehen hatte (52)]. He has abandoned the cage of middle-class life and its standards of success and entered into "the land of milk and honey" (258) [Schlaraffenland (137)].

He gains entrance to this paradise by aligning himself with society's pariahs, and his narrative emphasizes his affiliation with these victims of social ostracism and prejudice. He describes how he came to belong to the inhabit-

---

20. My translation.

21. My translation.

22. Tine equates these institutions again when she says that her father has been detained under suspicion of Kienbaum's murder just as Schaumann is kept for after-school detention (219).

ants of the Red Redoubt by aiding them in their battles against their persecutors; he first gains entrance to the farm when he gets a bloody nose helping Tine fight off an attack by taunting village youth, and he earns his permanent welcome by translating Latin for her father's endless legal disputes and teaching him about his homestead's historical battles against the town below. Schaumann trades his solitary isolation under the hedge for a communal exile at the Red Redoubt, where, as Tine expresses it, she, Schaumann, and her father are cast adrift from society as if they were "on a desert island" (232) [eine Insel im Meere (104)]. Schaumann even compares himself to Störzer, whose failure to confess to the murder caused Tine and her father years of pain, because Störzer was also a victim of social cruelty. After rehearsing the litany of the abuse he suffered at the hands of Eduard and his ilk, Schaumann finally delivers the punch line of his story: Eduard's childhood idol, Störzer, inadvertently killed a man when his years of similar abuse led Störzer to hurl a stone at his tormenter. Using the alliterative nicknames with which he and Störzer were taunted, Schaumann emphasizes the irony of his position of power over his fellow outsider: "Just imagine Stuffcake and Mutton Chop sitting in the confessional together as priest and penitent, my dear Edward" (297) [Stopfkuchen mit Storzhammel im Beichtstuhl als Beichtvater und -kind, mein guter Eduard! (188)]. Schaumann's whole narrative drives toward illuminating the desperate situation into which ostracized individuals such as Schaumann/Stopfkuchen and Störzer/Storzhammel are forced, but he claims to have escaped this corner by adhering single-mindedly to his own personality and goals. While Schaumann uses his story to portray Eduard as a conforming member and beneficiary of middle-class society, he bills himself as an outcast who has challenged its standards of conduct and success and has established his own framework of orientation.

Schaumann claims affinity with Störzer on the basis of their shared status as outcasts, but the logic of the narrative implies another similarity: both respond to persecution with violence.[23] In both cases, the victim becomes the perpetrator. Clearly, Störzer's unreflected and impulsive manslaughter is different from Schaumann's calculated narrative attack on Eduard's self-confidence. Still, as he casts Eduard as the perpetrator and himself as the victim (and deservedly so), Schaumann's story of the past reverses those roles. That is, in the contest of voices that the novel sets up, Schaumann's voice is not *only* one that urges Eduard to confront his own past crimes; it does

---

23. Julia Hell claims in "Wilhelm Raabes *Stopfkuchen*" that Schaumann brings this additional affinity to Eduard's attention in order to draw a comparison between Störzer and Kienbaum's relationship and his own relationship with Eduard; this comparison is to finish destroying Eduard's illusion that he and Schaumann are friends (171).

not exist only to facilitate a reckoning with the past. In positioning himself as a victim who overcame his trials, he also reverses roles and becomes the aggressor. He criticizes Eduard for his cruelty, but his calculated cruelty as he does so shows that he cannot be trusted entirely, either, by Eduard or by the reader.[24] *Stuffcake* presents a dynamic observer narrator who cites verbatim a story by another narrator whose reliability is also questionable.

Eduard's Narrative Defense

With his story, Schaumann forces Eduard to reassess his past and the criteria by which he had previously measured it. Jehmüller holds that this "ironic reversal" brings Eduard to a Nietzschean "reevaluation of values."[25] But contrary to Jehmüller's reading, which again creates a parallel between *Stuffcake*, *The Birdsong Files,* and *Old Nests,* Schaumann's efforts misfire. Instead of initiating a critical break in Eduard's view of himself and the world, his narrative prompts Eduard to undertake a narrative recuperation. The text indicates repeatedly that Schaumann's narrative affects Eduard deeply, at least for a time. Immediately following their encounter, as soon as he has boarded the ship for Africa, Eduard begins to recount the events of his visit home. His account opens with a description of his walk to the Red Redoubt and Schaumann, and he reports that the stroll called to his memory his last trip there as a youth. His reminiscences of this earlier visit indicate that his encounter with Schaumann has strengthened a long-dormant sense of his comparative inadequacy. As a youth, he watches "like a stupid fool with [his] mouth open" (181) [wie ein dummer Junge mit offenem Munde (38)] while Schaumann hugs and kisses Tine. Displaying all the characteristics of an awkward teenager, he is in turn "taken aback, dazed, uncertain" (187) [verblüfft, betäubt, zweifelnd (45)] and "nervous, bothered, uncomfortable" (189) [verschüchtert, verstört, verlegen (48)] as he witnesses Schaumann's quite adult relationship with his girlfriend. In short, he recognizes the woeful folly of his previous view of Stopfkuchen: "And this was the man we had looked on as not only the fattest, laziest, and greediest among us, not only the most stupid, but as stupidity itself. Oh, what asses we were!" (188) [Und diesen Menschen hatten wir nicht nur für den Dicksten, Faulsten und Gefräßigsten unter uns, auch nicht nur

---

24. Nünning identifies conflicts between a narrator's characterization of others and "his implicit self-characterization or unintentional self-exposure" as a marker of unreliability. See Ansgar Nünning, "*Unreliable Narration* zur Einführung," 28.

25. Jehmüller, *Gestalt des Biographen,* 79–84.

für den Dummsten unter uns, sondern auch überhaupt für einen Dummkopf gehalten, o wir Esel! (47)]. The alliteration and repetitive parallel structure in these passages transmit a sense of the embarrassed youth's internal torment, and of the adult narrator's reliving of it.[26]

As Eduard's adult visit with Schaumann progresses, the fat man's indictment of the world traveler and his implied disdain for Eduard's achievements in Africa continue to erode Eduard's self-conception. Eventually, even Tine's innocuous recollection of her father's relationship with the young Schaumann brings Eduard to self-denigration. After she remarks that her father accepted her young suitor because he was an outsider, too, Eduard launches into a damning self-assessment:

> Naturally Frau Valentina hadn't the slightest notion what a wonderful tribute and testimony she was paying my friend and that she was relegating me to the ranks of the quite ordinary, the quite common individuals found by every roadside, to those who boldly go out into the world, to Africa or somewhere, to have their trivial adventures. (236)

> Frau Tine hatte natürlich nicht im geringsten eine Ahnung davon, welch ein wunderbar Zeugnis und Lob sie jetzt meinem Freunde ausstellte und wie sehr sie mich zu den ganz Gewöhnlichen, den ganz Gemeinen, an jedem Wege Wachsenden warf: zu denen, die nur dreist in die Welt hinaus und nach Afrika laufen mochten, um ihre trivialen Abenteurerhistorien zu erleben. (109)

As Eduard notes, Tine does not judge his character; he extracts his self-interpretation from her matter-of-fact description of her husband. In contrast to the admirable, idiosyncratic Schaumann, Eduard sees himself as nothing but a common (and as the dual meanings of "gemein" indicate, also cruel) man whose life can be reduced to "trivial adventurer stories." Again, the passage's two consecutive alliterative series emphasize this self-incriminating judgment and demonstrate the force with which it impresses itself on Eduard's mind. This understanding of himself and his childhood friend signals that Schaumann's story about the past has completed the shift of perception

---

26. In commenting on Eduard's initial description of the Red Redoubt, Tucker construes Eduard's use of alliteration and rhyme as evidence of the effort it costs him to reconstruct the idyll Schaumann's narrative has disturbed. Tucker, "Wilhelm Raabe's *Stopfkuchen*," 573. Eduard uses such devices frequently in other contexts as well, however, and many, such as the one cited here, can be read as reflecting the intensity of a psychological state rather than as presenting a stylized narrative manipulation of reality.

that had begun during Eduard's last visit to the Red Redoubt as a youth. The weak, untalented, and ostracized Stopfkuchen has become the self-confident, accomplished, and respected Schaumann, and Eduard's belonging to and achievements within society have become liabilities rather than assets in his personal accounting system. Eduard's response to Tine is the pained admission of a man whose vision of self has been shaken to its core.

But the text that Eduard composes onboard his Africa-bound ship shows that his own narrative sets out to repair the damage Schaumann's has done. While it does not succeed entirely in restoring the view of himself and his home that he enjoyed before their encounter, traces of the effort to do so mark his story from beginning to end. His recollections of Störzer, who embodies the link between Eduard's past and present life, exemplify both this effort and its failure. Although Störzer vanishes from the text for fifty pages on three separate occasions, he appears in both the opening and closing segments, occupying Eduard's thoughts as he first sits down to dedicate himself to his writing and again as he completes it. These two passages display remarkable thematic and formal similarities as they raise the questions the text will address and conclude its consideration of those questions. In both segments Eduard offers ambivalent memories of Störzer, testifies to Störzer's influence on his own life path, and expresses mixed feelings about the place to which that path has led him. He attempts, in other words, to reconcile a new view of this central figure of his past with his own identity in the present. He first mentions Störzer as he answers for himself the question that drives his reckoning with the past:

How do people sometimes come to be in places where, when they stop to think, they wonder how they got there?

All I can say at this point is that I honestly think Störzer ought to be held responsible. My old friend Störzer. My dear old friend from the highway of childhood wending its way about my home town—in Arcadia—and so my friend from all the highways and seaways of the wide, wide world. (157)

Wie kommen Menschen dahin, wo sie sich, sich besinnend, zu eigener Verwunderung dann und wann finden?

Ich an dieser Stelle kann nur so viel sagen, daß ich glaube, den Landbriefträger Störzer als dafür verantwortlich halten zu dürfen. Meinen alten Freund Störzer. Meinen alten guten Freund von der Landstraße der Kinderzeit in der nächsten Umgebung meiner Heimatstadt in Arkadien, also—von allen Landstraßen und Seewegen der weitesten Welt. (7)

The equivocal formulation of this answer reveals Eduard's divided sentiments regarding his old friend. He attributes his current position to Störzer's influence, but rather than expressing an unmitigated gratitude for the man's horizon-expanding companionship, he believes that "Störzer ought to be held responsible" for what he has become. This hint of discontent with the man and his own current life inflects the description that follows; even the first-time reader, as yet unaware of Störzer's crime, may sense uncertainty behind the too-insistent characterization of "my old friend Störzer. My dear old friend . . ." Finally, the seemingly positive identification of Störzer with "Arcadia" is actually a double-edged sword. Although Eduard's ensuing memories romanticize his hometown and his imaginative travels with Störzer as a paradise, the previous paragraph has designated his home in Africa as Arcadia also and expressed some dissatisfaction with his life and position there.[27]

The opening passage answers the question of how Eduard landed in Africa simply: Störzer. But the uncertainty that it opens up with regard to Störzer's character and the desirability of Eduard's chosen life remains unresolved in the book's concluding passage.

It was a day and a half before we were able to land, and meanwhile I wandered many a time on the high road at home with Störzer, the country postman, and heard him tell, with curious side-glances at the Red Redoubt, his tales of Le Vaillant and the South African hinterland, all the time with the certain knowledge, full of joyful uneasiness: that I should soon have my wife in my arms again and my young Dutch-German brood clinging to my coattails saying:

"Vader, wat hebt gij uns mitgebracht uit het Vaderland, from the Germany?" (311)[28]

Es dauerte noch anderthalb Tage, ehe wir landen konnte, und während dieser Zeit wanderte ich noch recht oft auf der Landstraße der Heimat mit dem Landbriefträger Störzer und hörte den mit sonderbaren Seiten-

---

27. Eduard may still be undecided about whether Arcadia is a paradise or a fallen realm, but the text is less equivocal. Eduard first invokes the name in his allusion to August von Platen's play *Die Verhängnisvolle Gabel*, and although he intends it to be an innocent reference to his property in Africa, von Platen's text makes reaching the African Arcadia anything but an innocent endeavor. For a discussion of the play and its implications for the text's representation of colonialism, see Dunker, "'Gehe aus dem Kasten,'" 150.

28. The Afrikaans, easily comprehensible to German speakers, translates: "Father, what have you brought us from the Fatherland?" I have altered Fairley's translation here, in the first sentence, to preserve the ambiguity and ambivalence of the original, and in the final question, to include the original code-switched phrase and unidiomatic language.

blicken auf die Rote Schanze vom Le Vaillant und von dem Innern Süd-
afrikas erzählen zu aller froh-unruhigen Gewißheit: nun hängt bald dein
Weib wieder an deinem Halse und dazu deine doppelschlächtige deutsch-
holländische Brut dir an den Rockschößen:
    "Vader, wat hebt gij uns mitgebracht uit het Vaderland, aus dem
Deutschland?" (207)

With the strange phrase "with the certain knowledge, full of joyful uneasiness" [zu aller froh-unruhigen Gewißheit], which must describe Eduard's
state of mind at the time of writing but seems at first to refer to Störzer's long-
ago narratives, the first paragraph conflates past with present and Störzer with
Eduard, demonstrating again the degree to which Eduard's identity is bound
up with Störzer and his adventurous tales. And again, the characterization
of Störzer casts him and Eduard's involvement with him in a doubtful light.
Eduard chooses to spend the remainder of his sea voyage reliving the halcyon
days of his adventures with Störzer, rambling along the same country road
that abuts paradise in the opening. As he does, however, he sees and understands Störzer's intermittent guilty glances toward the Red Redoubt. Finally,
where the first mention of Störzer was occasioned by the question of Eduard's
life path up to this point, his journey from Germany to Africa, the last mention leads to a question about his future, and about the connection between
Germany and Africa. I return to this question in the second section of this
chapter. For now, I note only that it is open-ended. It does not resolve Störzer's
legacy—or the value of Eduard's life in past or present.

Störzer links Eduard's past and present because he stands both for the
values and foibles of the petty bourgeois society to which Eduard belonged
as a child, and for the colonial life he lives as an adult. In Eduard's childhood world, Störzer was an icon of dutiful middle-class virtue, whom his
father held up as a model. At the same time, Störzer introduced Eduard to
the romance and adventure of Africa through the travelogues of François Le
Vaillant. Eduard's ambivalence about him thus signals his uncertainty about
his own course through life. This ambivalence is visible in Eduard's continuing
references to the accidental murderer in terms that correspond to the view he
held of Störzer before he learned of his deed: "harmless old friend" (161) or
"my dear friend, the faithful and weary wanderer" (276) [meinen harmlosen
Jugendbekannten (19), der liebe Freund, der getreue, müde Wandersmann
(167)]. Such terms point toward his desire to preserve the Störzer he knew
as a child, and his present, positive self-conception.[29] His indecision about

---

29. Cf. Detroy, *Humor als Gestaltungsprinzip,* 17–25, who construes Eduard's opening

whether he "owes" Störzer for setting him on the path to earning a fortune in Africa or whether his friend should be "held responsible" for it, however, shows that he cannot sustain this vision entirely (168, 157). Eduard's story of the past and its connection to the present remains open, as "an on-going process of interpreting and clarifying himself."[30] His account hovers between the narrative of self and society he harbored before his visit and Schaumann's alternative, aggressive version. Eduard's narrative response indicates that he is both struck by the assault and resistant to it. He does not succumb to it fully, nor does he overcome it entirely. The narrative process of coming to terms with the past remains suspended—unresolved, yet inescapable.

Narrative Conflict, Colonialism, and German Identities

As Schaumann's story accuses Eduard of social violence, it also reveals his childhood idol to be guilty of physical violence. Eduard's idyllic childhood roaming the countryside and reading colonial travelogues with the guilty Störzer becomes the precursor to his own romanticized colonialism. His connection to Störzer thus taints Eduard's current existence, as do Schaumann's pointed comments about colonial events. In effect, Schaumann charges Eduard with living a violent life cloaked in romantic rhetoric, in adulthood as well as childhood. The association of sea travel and murder in the novel's subtitle, *A Tale of Murder and the High Seas* [*Eine See- und Mordgeschichte*], suggests that Schaumann's antagonistic story about the violent past is, at the same time, a story about a violent colonial present—and, in its juxtaposition with the silly nickname Stuffcake, also a ridiculing of romanticized, sensationalist rhetoric. Indeed, as has been shown, the novel exposes both colonialism's violence and its romanticized, escapist discourse.[31] Reading this critique in connection with the narrative conflict that structures the novel suggests another dimension to its colonial commentary. The patterns of narration and the power relationships to which they correspond show that colonial influences structure relations between Germans in Germany, as well.

---

descriptions of Störzer and their idyllic hometown as consistently ironic. I do not claim that there is no irony in Eduard's descriptions of Störzer, but as Eric Downing also observes, the fact that Eduard does not relinquish these designations indicates that he cannot abandon this version of reality completely. Downing, *Double Exposures*, 232–35.

30. Jehmüller, *Gestalt des Biographen*, 121.

31. On the novel's critique of colonialism, see especially Brewster, "Onkel Ketschwayo in Neuteutoberg"; Dunker, "'Gehe aus dem Kasten'"; Krobb, *Erkundungen im Überseeischen*, 161–87.

Schaumann and Eduard

The novel's opening lines raise immediately the question of verbal facility and power within a colonial context, as Eduard expresses an urgent concern about his ability to speak: "Before I proceed with the setting down of this narrative, I would like it understood that I still consider myself an educated man" (157) [Es liegt mir daran, gleich in den ersten Zeilen dieser Niederschrift zu beweisen oder darzutun, daß ich noch zu den Gebildeten mich zählen darf (7)]. Proof of his educated status is to substantiate his right to speak and be heard "in the Fatherland" (158) [im alten Vaterlande (8)]. Being able to produce the right kind of language is to secure the emigrant colonist's position as a speaker among other speakers in his homeland. Having begun with Eduard's worry about whether he is qualified to speak in Germany, the book ends with a question that indirectly denies his children's capability to do so. Imagining his return home, Eduard envisions his children asking: "Father, what have you brought us from the Fatherland, from the Germany?" (311) [Vader, wat hebt gij uns mitgebracht uit het Vaderland, aus dem Deutschland? (207)]. This simple question shifts from colonial Afrikaans to (unidiomatic) German in mid-sentence, showing that the children cannot open their mouths without proving that they cannot "count themselves among the educated." Indeed, policies in both the Dutch and the German colonies made cultural competence, such as fluency in the European language, a key prerequisite to attaining full European status,[32] or the right "to speak in the old fatherland." Although such policies often applied to "mixed-race" applicants for European status, Eduard's description of his children as "feral young German-Dutch half-breeds" (161) [verwilderte[n], halbschlächtig deutsch-höllandische[n] Schlingel (12)] emphasizes their mixed heritage and suggests that they have been "contaminated" by "wild" (i.e., native African) influences.[33] In Eduard's own description, their language and wildness demonstrate that they belong to the ranks of the "Boers and Kaffirs and Hottentots" (161) [Buren, Kaffern und Hottentotten (12)] who are entirely unsuited for European society. Boers who have become "wild" are no better than the natives. Being a colonist threatens the ability to assert oneself at home.

Both Schaumann and Eduard seem to justify their right to be heard with their respective positions in Germany and Africa. Early in his visit, Eduard expresses frustration that Schaumann shows no curiosity for his exploits in Africa; instead, Schaumann regales him with the Red Redoubt's history,

---

32. Stoler, *Carnal Knowledge*, 17; Wildenthal, *German Women for Empire*, 126–27.
33. "Feral" preserves the sense of wildness; Fairley uses "rowdy."

which Eduard holds to be an "utterly insignificant piece of history, thunder of cannon, trembling citizens, shrieking women and children, fire, and bloodshed" (207) [grenzenlos unbedeutendes Stück Welthistorie, Kanonenlärm, Bürgerangst, Weiber- und Kindergekreisch, Brand und Blutvergießungen (72)]. When Eduard rebels at Schaumann's meandering narrative, Schaumann replies that his story is the revenge of a wise man who has stayed at home: "This is the satisfaction I have been waiting for in the cool shade while you and your Le Vaillant were out hunting elephants, rhinoceroses, and giraffes in burning Africa or sweating yourselves to death in some other useless way" (226) [Darauf, auf diese Genugtuung, habe ich hier in der Kühle gewartet, während du mit deinem Le Vaillant im heißen Afrika auf die Elefanten-, Nashorn- und Giraffenjagd gingest oder dich auf andere unnötige Weise ab- und ausschwitztest (96)]. He admonishes Eduard to be quiet and listen and suggests that "you may judge for yourself afterward whether you regard [the murder victim's], your, or my story as the more important" (226) [nachher magst du ja selber beurteilen, ob du deine, seine [the murder victim's], oder meine Geschichte für die wichtigere hältst (96)]. Eduard is to see his lack of power in his relationship with Schaumann as associated with his status as a mere adventuring colonist returning to Germany. He eventually accedes to Schaumann's dominance, and by the time the two part, he can say nothing more than good-bye in answer to Schaumann's final words (303). Before his visit, he had thought himself superior to those who remained at home, but Schaumann's story teaches him the hard lesson that becoming an economic "baron" in Africa does not guarantee him a respected voice in Germany. On the contrary, "mankind might be calm, tranquil, fat perhaps, but it could muster the power to hold its own with the brawniest, leanest, most reckless of adventurers. Heinrich Schaumann, alias Stopfkuchen, had taught me this lesson very thoroughly" (309) [die Menschheit hatte immer noch die Macht, sich aus dem Fett, der Ruhe, der Stille heraus dem sehnigsten, hageren, fahrigen Konquistadorentum gegenüber zur Geltung zu bringen. Heinrich Schaumann, genannt Stopfkuchen, hatte dieses mir gegenüber gründlich besorgt (204)]. Eduard's passive use of Schaumann's childhood nickname only emphasizes that the tables have been turned. The fat boy "under the hedge" has bested the bully turned conquistador.

As a result, Eduard finds himself compelled first to listen to Schaumann's story, and then to reproduce it verbatim in his own written account of his visit. The novel calls repeated attention to this reproduction, and to Eduard's inability to do anything else. Even before Schaumann completes his story, Eduard can signal his potential criticism only by repeating Schaumann's words. Horrified by the imperturbability Schaumann displays when he discovers who had committed the murder for which his father-in-law had long been blamed, Eduard voices his astonishment:

> SCHAUMANN: "Then [Tine] was called out into the kitchen and so I filled my pipe and thought things over."
> EDUARD: "You thought things over!" (287)

> SCHAUMANN: "Als [Tine] dann in die Küche hinausgerufen wurde, stopfte ich mir natürlich eine Pfeife und überlegte."
> EDUARD: "Du überlegtest!" (176)

Moments later, his exclamatory surprise has devolved into a weak echo of passive acceptance:

> SCHAUMANN: "Fortunately my pipe went out and I had to light it again."
> EDUARD: "You had to light it again." (288)

> SCHAUMANN: "Mir ging glücklicherweise die Pfeife dabei aus, und ich hatte sie wieder anzuzünden."
> EDUARD: "Du hattest sie wieder anzuzünden." (176)

In the end, Eduard seems to regard himself as Schaumann's passive mouthpiece. He imagines being occupied by his friend's massive presence and speaking his words (304), and before he leaves town, he realizes that Schaumann intends for him to repeat his story and to disseminate its lessons (305–6). The manuscript that he produces on board the ship suggests that Schaumann has persuaded him of its import, and its relatively greater importance than Eduard's tales of adventure. The sentimentalized colonial story Eduard wishes to tell about his present life, his "sea tale" [*Seegeschichte*], is yoked to Schaumann's "murder tale" [*Mordgeschichte*] from the past.

Schaumann and Valentine

When Eduard frames Schaumann's story within an account of his trip home and of the visit with Schaumann and his wife, he also affects the story that Schaumann tells about himself. The juxtaposition of Schaumann's narrative with Eduard's narrative frame allows readers to establish a critical distance from both men's views. In particular, Eduard's commentary on Schaumann's relationship to his wife, along with the colonial discourse and logic that saturate Schaumann's stories about her and the Red Redoubt, reveal that Schaumann replicates much of what he criticizes in colonialism in his relationship with Tine. Following a move in postcolonial studies to examine "colonized and colonial within the same analytical field,"[34] I consider how the novel shows the relationships and discourses of colonialism as implicated in and affecting the culture, politics, and social relations within Germany. Axel Dunker began this work on *Stuffcake,* holding that the novel reveals how colonialism's violence and the silences that obscure it pervade the supposedly civilized homeland. But where he emphasizes the silences that mask colonialism's violence, I examine the contest of voices in what *is* said to illuminate how the discourse of colonialism exposes hierarchical, "colonial" power relations at home.[35] At the same time, this contest of voices comments obliquely on the "woman question" and the quest of the women's movement for equal rights.

Schaumann uses the language of colonialism unabashedly to describe his infiltration and eventual "complete conquest" [völlige Eroberung (94)] of Tine's family property.[36] He repeatedly describes his tenure there in terms that compare both his mastery of it and Eduard's control over his lands in Africa to the absolute power of a feudal lord; he is "head and master" of the Red Redoubt or "Quakatz's castle" just as Eduard is "baron" of his "feudal estate" in Africa (252, 224, 247, 304) [Herr und Meister (129); Quakatzenburg (94); Baron (123); Rittergut (198)].[37] In talking about his wife, Schaumann employs the rhetoric of culture and domestication that accompanied much colonial activity, in words that betray the element of forcible control such domestication implies:

> "Haven't I fed her well, the wildcat of Quakatz's castle, and made her pretty and chubby and nice and forced her down comfortably in the comfortable sofa-corner with the customary and ever-so-cosy knitting in her hand?" (234)[38]

---

34. Cooper and Stoler, "Between Metropole and Colony," 15.

35. In a related article, I focus on the place the colonist assumes in this hierarchy by highlighting the similarities between Eduard and Valentine. See Byram, "German-German Relations." For a similar argument about the reproduction of colonial patterns at home, again using Valentine as the primary example, see Jürgen Meyer, "'Of Our Time Distinc(t)ly.'"

36. My translation. Dunker and Claudia Liebrand both note the colonial flavor of Schaumann's relationship to the Red Redoubt and his wife, but neither pursues the implications of this characterization for the novel's commentary on colonialism. Dunker, "'Gehe aus dem Kasten,'" 154; Liebrand, "Wohltätige Gewalttaten?" 97.

37. Fairley translates "afrikanisches Rittergut" as "my place in Africa," which does not retain the feudal connotations.

38. I have amended Fairley's translation to retain the element of force.

"Habe ich die hagere Wildkatze von Quakatzenburg nicht recht hübsch und rund und nett und fett herausgefüttert und sie behaglich mit dem gewöhnlichen und deshalb um so komfortabelern Weiberstrickzeug in die behagliche Sofaecke niedergedrückt?" (106)

Tine, the former wild creature, may be prosperous and "comfortable" in her sofa's corner—the sentence insists three times that she is—but she has been pressed and oppressed there, nevertheless.

In a move that reasserts his role as civilizing benefactor, Schaumann also claims to have given Tine language, or at least the "cultured" language of the bourgeoisie. In a telling scene in which Schaumann temporarily relinquishes the narrative to his wife, he interrupts her three times to tell Eduard that she has acquired her words from him. The words he emphasizes, *traktieren* [nego-tiate; treat badly], *Geschmack* [taste], and *Genügsamkeit* [moderation], evoke the virtues (and vices) of the middle class. Via the related *Traktat* [treatise], *traktieren* calls to mind the middle-class adulation of *Bildung* and classical learning, while the verb itself suggests the aggressive potential of such facility. *Geschmack* signals the middle classes' high valuation of "culture" and those who are discerning of it, and *Genügsamkeit* its denunciation of luxury and dissipation. After the third interruption, Tine displays one of few moments of discontent with her married life:

"Of course. I got everything from you," cried Frau Valentina, now really becoming a bit jittery and excited and irritable. "Well, it's a comfort that you let me claim my good conscience as something of my own. And if you say that I got my inner self-content from you, I at least had some of it in me to begin with, and all you did was to—" (239)

"Natürlich! Alles habe ich von dir!" rief Frau Tine jetzt wirklich etwas zitterig, aufgeregt, ärgerlich. "Nun, da ist es ja noch ein Trost, daß du mir wenigstens das gute Gewissen als mein eigenstes Eigentum läßt! Und wenn ich denn einmal die Genügsamkeit auch von dir haben soll, so hat doch gewiß wenigstens etwas davon auch schon in mir gelegen, und du hast mir nur—" (112)

Here, her husband cuts her off again and finishes her sentence for her. For a moment, Tine rebels against Schaumann's paternalistic attitude and his self-congratulatory approval of her. His repeated claims to have made her every-thing she is drive her to declare herself an independent, equal human being with a conscience of her own and an intrinsic potential for good, or at least for the good life. As scholars from Edward Said to Susanne Zantop and Ann Stoler have shown, colonial relations were often expressed in such gendered tropes.[39] Zantop asserts that the dynamic of the conquering man marrying and bringing culture and well-being to the "wild" woman was a particular fantasy of German colonialists.[40] Of course, this idea was a fantasy; in the decade following the publication of Raabe's novel, prominent colonial personalities, such as Heinrich Leist and Carl Peters, were convicted of crimes ranging from forcing women into prostitution to executing native "concubines."[41] At home in Germany, Tine's frustration reveals a seed of discontent underneath the conjugal bliss both Schaumann and she profess, a resentment of the colonialist troping of their relationship and the subjugation that this characterization supports. Raabe may not have supported female suffrage, but his representation of Tine shows an awareness of and empathy with many women's plight. In the presence of Tine's repressed resentment, Schaumann's claim of unmitigated success in domesticating the loving and grateful "natives" in Germany is somewhat absurd.[42] Schaumann's colonial rhetoric undermines the notion that his civilizing project in Germany differs fundamentally from the overseas activities he criticizes.

Like colonialism's power, Schaumann's mastery depends on more than physical domination. When Schaumann interrupts Tine, he appropriates her story and history. In fact, Eduard's most overt criticisms of his "friend" arise from this narrative appropriation. When Schaumann reveals that he knows the truth of the old crime that has haunted Tine's family but has withheld that truth from her, Eduard calls him an "ogre" and comments editorially on the "cold-bloodedness" with which Schaumann has treated her (224–25) [Ungeheuer (94); Kaltblütigkeit (95)]. Later, he demands that Schaumann end her suspense and tell her the identity of the true murderer: "Monster, I've had enough of it. You simply must stop and not go on torturing your wife a moment longer" (268) [Unmensch, ich bin satt! Jetzt hörst du endlich hiermit

---

39. The idea of a passive, feminized Orient opposite an authoritative, masculine West runs throughout Edward Said's *Orientalism*. For an examination of a specifically German use of gender tropes, see Zantop, *Colonial Fantasies*, ch. 2–3. For an investigation focusing on discourse and practice in the Dutch colonies, see Stoler, *Carnal Knowledge*, 44.

40. Zantop, *Colonial Fantasies*, 2–15.

41. Wildenthal, *German Women for Empire*, 69–75.

42. In general, the scenes that detail the couple's interaction contribute substantially to the novel's humor. Schaumann's ridiculously self-satisfied and superior reign over Tine in her caricatured deference offer standard comedic entertainment. This combination of complete asymmetry and complete contentedness corresponds to Peter Detroy's concept in *Humor als Gestaltungsprinzip* of the novel's humor, which he sees as arising from the reconciliation of seemingly incommensurate objects or attitudes.

auf und quälst mir deine Frau in diesem Augenblick nicht länger! (150)].[43] In the end, Eduard finds that, "strangely," he is more concerned with Tine than with Störzer, the murder victim, or Schaumann: "the dear, the poor dear woman" (304) [Die Gute! Die Arme und Gute! (197)], he concludes, imagining the plight of this virtuous and oppressed creature.

Valentine suffers no physical hardship; instead, Eduard's sympathy is a response to her husband's inconsiderate domination of her story. Claiming to know what is best for her, Schaumann tells it "for" her, meanwhile enlisting her support for his tale; not only does she supply a portion of the narrative at his request, but she literally fuels the story with the parade of food that sustains him and his guest. Schaumann also appropriates Tine's story by making it a record of his own plans, desires, and achievements. In casting himself as her story's hero, he reenacts the drama of the text that had inspired Eduard to emigrate to Africa, François Le Vaillant's 1790 African travelogue. Mary Louise Pratt describes Le Vaillant's text as "an explicitly experiential, narcissistic narrative structured around human dramas of which he is the protagonist," and Schaumann's accounts of his interactions with the residents of the Red Redoubt run in the same vein.[44] In one episode, for instance, Le Vaillant describes a hunt for a tiger that had been raiding a colonist's livestock; when all of the colonists run in fear, he holds his ground and kills the beast, earning their admiration and the settler's gratitude.[45] Similarly, Schaumann fends off the predators who threaten Tine, standing with her against the taunting village children and appearing in the middle of a snowstorm to subdue her surly servants. Florian Krobb argues that Le Vaillant's text signals Raabe's critique not of colonial practice per se but of the rhetoric that invested the unknown overseas with heroism and adventure.[46] As he narrates his conquest of the Red Redoubt, Schaumann constructs himself within exactly such heroic tropes. As Sara Friedrichsmeyer, Sara Lennox, and Zantop argue in *The Imperialist Imagination,* the logic, experience, and discourse of colonialism have saturated and helped shape the relations and self-understanding of those in Germany.[47] Dunker maintains that by preventing Eduard from speaking about his experiences in Africa, the novel reproduces the silences

---

43. The passage's linguistic construction suggests that Eduard identifies with Tine's suffering; the indirect object "mir" presents him as being affected by Schaumann's narrative tormenting his wife. For further discussion of the parallel between Eduard and Tine, see Byram, "German-German Relations," 61–73.

44. Pratt, *Imperial Eyes,* 89. Schaumann's name also corresponds to Pratt's "seeing man," whose eyes and voice support colonial power (7).

45. Le Vaillant, *Anecdotes in Travels,* 28.

46. Krobb, *Erkundungen im Überseeischen,* 171–75.

47. Friedrichsmeyer, Lennox, and Zantop, *Imperialist Imagination.*

that elide colonialism's violence.[48] But Schaumann's rhetoric shows how colonial discourse converts forcefully asserted power into heroism with its narrative of civilization. Although he adopts the sentimentalizing, heroic mode of narration that Le Vaillant uses to efface the violence of his actions, he does not deny that violence.[49] He justifies it by making it the condition of civilization and its "comforts." Raabe's novel thus highlights what Stoler and Frederick Cooper term the "polyvalent discourse of civility" that supported the consolidation of (male) bourgeois power both at home and abroad in the nineteenth century.[50] Telling Tine's story as his own, Schaumann exemplifies how relating the story of another's life can help justify relationships that might otherwise be unacceptable. Raabe's novel suggests that wives should no more have to suffer having their lives' stories and meanings determined by others than their husbands should.

Radical Internarration and the Ambiguity of an Unresolved Past

Up to this point, my reading of the figures of Eduard and Stopfkuchen has engaged very little with their critical reception. My assessments of both of these characters as two-sided—Schaumann as an ambivalent figure who is both victim and aggressor, and Eduard as a figure who both registers Schaumann's narrative attack and tries to shield himself from the reckoning with the past that it might initiate—correspond to many recent interpretations of the work.[51] But the history of the critical reception of both of these figures has been very uneven. While some have read Schaumann as an exceptional and superior individual,[52] many view him as morally compromised because of the motivations for and effects of his vengeful storytelling.[53] Some assessments of Eduard accept Schaumann's characterization of him as a social conformist, a spineless philistine bound by and servile to social norms;[54]

---

48. Dunker, "'Gehe aus dem Kasten,'" 155–58.

49. Pratt in *Imperial Eyes* classes Le Vaillant among those who produce sentimentalized colonial accounts. By emphasizing personal experience and interactions, these accounts conceal the lopsided political and economic relations of colonialism (88–90, 69–85).

50. Cooper and Stoler, "Between Metropole and Colony," 10.

51. On Eduard as both comprehending and defensive, see Göttsche, *Zeitreflexion und Zeitkritik*, 152; Hell, "Wilhelm Raabes *Stopfkuchen*," 172–74; Mein, "Raabes *Stopfkuchen*," 129–31; Bird, "Scham, Beschämung und Gesellschaftskritik," 61.

52. See Herman Meyer, "Raum und Zeit," 111; Ohl, "Eduards Heimkehr," 25–50.

53. See Bird, "Scham, Beschämung und Gesellschaftskritik," 59–60; Liebrand, "Wohltätige Gewalttaten?" 93–96; Sammons, *Alternative Community*, 295–98; Eisele, *Dichter und sein Detektiv*, 14; Downing, *Double Exposures*, 247, 52–55.

54. See Herman Meyer, "Raum und Zeit," 111; Kokora, "Ferne in der Nähe," 67; Downing, *Double Exposures*, 231.

others contend that Schaumann's depiction of Eduard makes him more contemptible than he actually is.[55] Some believe that Eduard fully comprehends and accepts Schaumann's story and its lessons. His repetition of Schaumann's story shows that he has undergone the fundamental change in perspective that Schaumann's narrative requires.[56] Others portray Eduard as impervious to his friend's challenge and say that his narrative framing allows him to deny any effects from Schaumann's tale.[57]

In effect, these readings all rest on judgments of both Eduard's and Schaumann's reliability as narrators, since narrator reliability, whether from a cognitivist or a rhetorical viewpoint, depends largely on the adequacy of the narrator's moral and interpretive frameworks. The great discrepancies between these readings can be explained within the cognitivist account of unreliability, since both historical and literary historical factors have influenced whether readers perceive Schaumann and Eduard's behavior (narrative and otherwise) and beliefs as "normal."[58] Over time, readers have grown much more skeptical about both figures' reliability, and one could argue, as Vera Nünning does for the *Vicar of Wakefield*, that this change has occurred as readers' cognitive frames of reference have grown ever more distant from those typified by Schaumann and Eduard.[59] For instance, Schaumann's domineering relationship with Tine is often cited as a count against him in recent criticism, but the asymmetry of the husband-wife relationship was unlikely to disturb many of Raabe's contemporaries, who perceived Schaumann as "good" and reliable. Literary conventions and their associated epistemological assumptions have likely also played a role. Early readers, relying on Raabe's claim that Schaumann was a largely autobiographical figure, read Schaumann as representing the author's (reliable) views.[60] Eduard, in this understanding,

---

55. Göttsche, *Zeitreflexion und Zeitkritik,* 150–51.

56. For interpretations that read Eduard as adopting Schaumann's superior worldview in its entirety, see Klopfenstein, *Erzähler und Leser,* 219–20; Detroy, *Humor als Gestaltungsprinzip,* 48–49, 108, 22–25. Christa Hebbel's *Die Funktion der Erzähler- und Figurenperspektiven* maintains that each figure keeps his initial position, but that Eduard adopts Schaumann's humorous narrative style; Margret Walter-Schneider's "Erzählen" (106) focuses solely on Eduard's adoption of the narrative style, downplaying the differences in their content. Brewster's "Onkel Ketschwayo in Neuteutoberg" sees Eduard as having learned empathy for social outsiders, perhaps including African natives.

57. Jeffrey Sammons writes that Eduard's insistence on sentimentalizing Schaumann and Tine and on describing Schaumann as "comfortable" betray his determination to avoid registering Schaumann's criticism. Sammons, *Alternative Community,* 285–88, 95. Likewise, in *Bürger als Freund,* Meyer-Krentler maintains that Eduard uses his narrative to bury and deny the implications of Schaumann's tale (257).

58. See Ansgar Nünning, *"Unreliable Narration* zur Einführung," 22–23; Vera Nünning, "Historical Variability," 236–37.

59. Vera Nünning, "Historical Variability."

60. See both Raabe's statements and editorial commentary in Hoppe, "Stopfkuchen," 424–27.

was a model reader, accepting Schaumann/Raabe's lessons.[61] Moreover, unreliable narrators were unusual in late nineteenth-century German literature. Raabe's contemporaries did not anticipate the unreliability that Raabe's transitional realist/modernist texts contained,[62] but as readers became increasingly conditioned to look for narrator unreliability, they began to read Eduard, and then Schaumann himself, as unreliable. Today, dual unreliability has become the dominant reading.[63]

Certainly, reader expectations and frameworks influence interpretation. But recent interpretations do not simply impose unreliability on narrators who could just as well be read as reliable. Unreliability is present in the text. As I have shown, it emanates from both the antagonistic narrative structure and the dynamics of the social relationships depicted. Per Krogh Hansen calls the unreliability that results from conflict between different narrators' accounts internarration; a radical internarration is the structuring principle in this novel, where the discrepancies between Eduard's and Schaumann's accounts render *both* narrators suspect.[64] Eduard undermines himself by repeating Schaumann's story, in which Schaumann offers withering criticism of Eduard and his interpretive framework. In a combined act of penitence and admission of inferiority, Eduard tells a story in which he gives Schaumann the floor. To say that Schaumann speaks for himself is not to say that his perspective goes unchallenged, however. Eduard transmits Schaumann's language intact, but his commentary as he reproduces it colors Schaumann's tale. His experience of Schaumann and his domineering relationships with others frames that story, showing that even telling one's own story can be an act of violence or oppression. Two distinct voices and vantage points appear, and neither can dispel the force of the other's words entirely. Rather than the optimistic comparison that causes bonding unreliability, a kind of mutually pessimistic comparison erodes the audience's trust in both figures. The moral valence of both characters is ambivalent, and the narrative structure prevents textual features from resolving that ambivalence. The contest of voices prevents any final authority.[65]

---

61. See Detroy, *Humor als Gestaltungsprinzip*, 104–8; Walter-Schneider, "Erzählen," 106–7.

62. Zerweck contends that unreliable narration is a defining feature of the transition to modernism. Zerweck, "Historicizing Unreliable Narration," 161.

63. See Jürgen Meyer, ""Of Our Time Distinc(t)ly,'" 199–200; Downing, *Double Exposures;* Eisele, *Dichter und sein Detektiv;* Sammons, *Alternative Community;* Graf and Kwisinski, "Heinrich Schaumann, ein Lügenbaron?"

64. Internarration is one of four textual modes that Hansen identifies as signaling narrator unreliability. Hansen, "Reconsidering the Unreliable Narrator," 241–42.

65. Tucker and Krobb see a similar undecidability in the text, but do not consider how the text's narrative structure contributes to it. Krobb, *Erkundungen im Überseeischen,* 186; Tucker,

This suspension of final authority or the judgment it would allow helps illuminate how dynamic observer narratives both relate and reflect on the relationship between the narrative and lyric modes. Readers see Eduard using narrative to try to reconcile different interpretive frameworks and the ways of being that they shape: his own colonialist worldview and experience and Schaumann's idiosyncratic disdain for society and his isolated life at the Red Redoubt. Such conflicts between interpretive frameworks appear prominently in Phelan's discussions of lyric narrative hybrids, too, suggesting that combinations of the narrative and lyric modes may often be used to explore the clashes between states. Phelan presents these conflicting frameworks as producing a resistance to narrative and interpretive resolution, what he calls "the stubborn," and he views the resulting interpretive openness as an achievement of the lyric narrative form.[66] But there is an important distinction between the ways the stubborn operates in the two examples he cites. In one, Frost's "Home Burial," the resistance derives largely from the incompatibility of the frameworks themselves. In the other, the staged character narration of "Doc's Story" contributes to the interpretive instability. In one case, the stubborn exists between lyric states; in the other, a narrative is depicted as precipitating or prolonging a stubborn conflict. *Stuffcake,* too, highlights the role that narrative plays in generating and sustaining interpretive instability; the novel's multiple narratives suggest that as long as competing stories proliferate or persist, narrative(s) cannot resolve the conflicts between frameworks.

Not incidentally, I think, "Doc's Story" is also a dynamic observer narrative. I suggest, then, that dynamic observer narratives call attention to a particular kind of "stubbornness": the irresolvable interpretive instability that lies dormant in the space between cultural and interpretive frameworks and that is drawn out by the narratives that bring them into contact. This realm of instability—of indeterminacy engendered by conflicts *between* interpretive frameworks, rather than of circumstances that mitigate judgment *within* a given framework—is a product of the contrasts between narrator and protagonist perspectives and between past and present interpretive frameworks that characterize the form. As a class, then, dynamic observer narratives highlight a very modern variety of indeterminacy: that provoked by narratives

---

"Wilhelm Raabe's *Stopfkuchen*," 580. The abiding contradictions of these two perspectives also generate humor, as Wolfgang Preisendanz understands it in *Humor als dichterische Einbildungskraft:* they help make visible the disjuncture between narrative representation and "reality" in each character's account (11–13).

66. Phelan, *Living to Tell,* 192–96; Phelan, "Rhetorical Literary Ethics"; Phelan, *Experiencing Fiction,* 205–14.

attempting to reconcile the shifting and conflicting moral and interpretive frameworks of the modern age. *Stuffcake* makes this interpretive conflict concrete by presenting it as an open conflict between two characters' stories, but the same instability plagues nearly all of the texts I discuss.

This interpretive instability affects the identities of the present, and also the possibility of coming to terms with the past. The concatenation of Eduard's and Schaumann's histories does not combine or reconcile the two original tales but creates a tug-of-war between two accounts that have remained fundamentally intact. If successful reckoning with the past entails reaching a "societal consensus" about a shared story of the past,[67] then the unresolved conflict between Schaumann and Eduard precludes a successful resolution. Eduard and Schaumann cannot agree about the past because neither one is willing to relinquish his own story. Eduard never admits any guilt about his treatment of Schaumann. Instead, he attempts to deflect attention from his role in the cruel taunting. Perhaps in response, Schaumann refuses to let Eduard speak; he leaves no room for disputing his account of the past, and his insistence that he has become his own ideal indicates his determination to maintain his current identity and self-understanding.[68] The end of the novel shows both figures withdrawing from any future dialogue or negotiation; Schaumann retreats to the Red Redoubt with no intention of entertaining Eduard again, and Eduard leaves town to avoid having to disseminate Schaumann's tale about Störzer. Neither is willing to undertake the "process of understanding" that is required for a reckoning with the past, and that changes the current "identities of those involved" as it reinterprets the story of the past.[69]

The logic of the novel suggests that Eduard and Schaumann resist such a process of understanding because the stakes of retreating from their respective stories of the past are too high. In the generation before Eduard and Schaumann, bullying became a matter of life and death when the victim finally attacked his persecutor. Schaumann threatens no physical violence, but the parallels between Schaumann and Störzer suggest that his threat is similarly potent when he attacks Eduard's sense of self. No consensus is possible.

---

67. Wertgen, *Vergangenheitsbewältigung*, 362.

68. Tucker writes in "Wilhelm Raabe's *Stopfkuchen*" that, although Schaumann claims to pursue a critical history, he practices monolithic history when he attempts to drown out and dominate Eduard's affirmative version (579–80). In *Erkundungen im Überseeischen*, Krobb sees Schaumann's museum as a symbol of his drive to control history in order to support the "claims to dominance" in the present (185). Hell asserts that Schaumann's claim to have achieved his ideal self, with the status of a public figure, is false, since he is trapped in the limited world of private action. "Wilhelm Raabes *Stopfkuchen*," 177–83.

69. Wertgen, *Vergangenheitsbewältigung*, 110.

Nor does either make overtures to a "bridging discourse" that might allow both to retain their core frameworks while constructing a shared account of events that both could agree on.[70] Perhaps the persistent logic of the system hinders such attempts. The history of relations in the town, from its historical wars to the two generations portrayed in the novel, is a history of violence and a struggle for power.[71] The players in this generation have reversed roles; Eduard now plays the victim, and Schaumann the aggressor. But the dynamics of the system remain the same.[72] Werner Wertgen asserts that "wherever the same schemata that caused harm are still in effect, a reckoning with the past cannot be said to have taken place," because these conditions encourage the repetition of wrongs, even if the original aggressor rues his earlier deeds.[73] In the end, all the old interpretive frameworks remain in place in this novel, if ever so tenuously. Schaumann asserts his idiosyncratic vision of a domestic paradise won from ignominy and exclusion. Eduard clings to his story of a romantic, adventurous colonial life founded on comfortable, respectable middle-class tradition. Both see their stories of self as being in violent competition with one another. Retreat—or benevolence—is not an option.

---

70. Barkan and Karn, "Group Apology," 14.

71. The Red Redoubt was a fortification built by Prince Xavier of Saxony during his successful siege of Wolfenbüttel in 1761, during the Seven Years' War. From this vantage point, he, like Schaumann, attacked the town below.

72. Similarly, Krobb argues in *Erkundungen im Überseeischen* that the "horizontal," geographical expansion represented by Eduard and the "vertical," historical investigations undertaken by Schaumann have comparable methods and results and share a common hubris (183–86).

73. Wertgen, *Vergangenheitsbewältigung,* 354.

PART III

Evolving Responses to National Socialism

five

Günter Grass's Litanies of the Past

Performative Language and *Vergangenheitsbewältigung*

> It's easy for storytellers to think stories are wonderful, but some stories burden
> and curse you; some stories you're better without.
> —Rebecca Solnit, *A Faraway Nearby*

he conviction that narratives *do* something underpins both narrativist theories of coming to terms with the past and rhetorical narrative
theory.[1] So, too, does it underlie Günter Grass's life and artistic production,
both of which display a deep belief in the need for a break with the past and
in the power of narrative to effect that break. In the 1961 novella *Cat and
Mouse,* the narrator, Pilenz, receives advice that Grass might well have given
himself: "You've got a style of your own: take up the fiddle or write yourself
free—the good Lord knew what He was doing when He gave you talent" (529)
[Sie verfügen doch . . . über eine eigenwillige Feder: greifen Sie zur Geige
oder schreiben Sie sich frei—der Herrgott versah Sie nicht ohne Bedacht mit
Talenten (4:106)].[2] Yet neither Pilenz nor Grass succeeds in writing himself
free. In this chapter, I use the theories of linguistic performatives and speech
acts developed by J. L. Austin and John Searle both to characterize Grass's fictional and nonfictional writing as reliant on a faith in the power of a narrative

---

1. For a theoretical exploration of the relationship between narrative and performance,
see Breger, *Narrative Performance,* 7–40.

2. Manheim's translation altered. In this chapter, elisions in quotations are marked by an
ellipsis in brackets, to distinguish them from the numerous ellipses in the original texts.

reckoning with the past, and to analyze why it so often fails.[3] I examine how Grass's narrators try to "do things with words" and how they fail to meet the conditions of satisfaction that successful performatives require.[4]

Some would say that Grass's own efforts to "do things with words" have been just as wanting. For more than five decades, Grass was a highly visible advocate for a German reckoning with the past. His political speeches and journalistic writing called for fellow Germans to confront and confess their past crimes and shared responsibility. From his debut novel *The Tin Drum* (1959) [*Die Blechtrommel*] to *Cat and Mouse* to the novella *Crabwalk* (2002) [*Im Krebsgang*], his literary work critiqued Germany's mode of dealing with its National Socialist past and exhorted Germans to reflect on the degree to which their present identity has remained tied to, and constrained by, this past. In awarding him the Nobel Prize for Literature in 1999, the Swedish Academy cited his literary efforts to "portray the forgotten face of history."[5] Then, shortly before the publication of his autobiography in August 2006 (*Peeling the Onion*), Grass stunned the world with a confession. In the last year of World War II, he had belonged to the notorious Waffen-SS. His revelation prompted a barrage of astonished commentary and criticism. For the most part, this criticism was not aimed at the fact itself; few faulted the seventeen-year-old Grass for his brief service, and Grass had long declared that, as a teenager, he had been an enthusiastic Nazi and a stubborn believer in Germany's eventual victory. The outrage was directed instead at his delay in confessing the fact. Some called for him to renounce his Nobel Prize;[6] others, defending the continuing value and merit of his literary work, nevertheless declared the "end of a moral authority" or expressed disappointment that he had remained silent about this episode for so long.[7] The contradiction

---

3. For another, complementary explanation of the lack of resolution, see Minden, "Figures of Shame," 23–27. In Minden's reading, shame (as opposed to guilt) cannot be resolved because it attaches to a person, rather than to an act. Moreover, it occurs on the edges of identity, where the human meets society and is "implicated in . . . the collective existence of a given society," and where values and codes are thrown into question. It thus shares many points of contact with the shift of identity associated with a reckoning with the past.

4. Austin, *How to Do Things*.

5. "The Nobel Prize in Literature 1999."

6. The Associated Press reported in "Günter Grass gilt den meisten" that, in an interview with the *Bild-Zeitung*, Lech Walesa had included the Nobel Prize in the list of honors Grass should relinquish. According to a poll by n-tv, the majority of Germans felt differently, however. Of those surveyed, only 8 percent thought he should have to sacrifice the prize, while 87 percent believed he should keep it.

7. Grass's biographer Michael Jürgs was widely quoted as proclaiming that Grass's confession meant "the end of a moral authority." See "Ende einer moralischen Instanz"; Keil, "Kritik und Verständnis." Numbering himself among Grass's supporters, Erich Loest stated, "He is late, but he has still brought the truth to light. . . . But again: I don't understand this long silence." See Reents, "Er hätte sagen sollen."

between his moralizing calls for confession and his own failure to confess brought disillusionment, and then discussion about whether his personal revelation must discredit his literary achievements.

I do not intend to intervene in this dispute or to judge Grass, perhaps Germany's most prominent postwar literary figure, in political terms. Rather, sharing Paul Dawson's conviction that both fictional and nonfictional writings operate as statements by the author in the public sphere, I examine how both develop Grass's notion of the relationship between narrative and the past.[8] Even as his work departs from a confidence in narrative's performative power to break with the past, it shows a preoccupation with two narrative behaviors that undermine a confessional break: a litany-like language that encourages repetition rather than revision and the habit of deflecting attention from one's own actions by focusing on others and their stories. In other words, Grass's writing epitomizes the tension of the dynamic observer narrative in its simultaneous need for and self-reflexive questioning of narrative. My focus in this chapter will be on how Grass generates this tension stylistically and narratively, and on what these characteristics suggest about the general enterprise of a narrative reckoning with the past.

Performative Language and *Vergangenheitsbewältigung* in the Federal Republic of Germany

Grass's loud public calls for active engagement with the National Socialist past belonged to the current of postwar German thought and political culture in which the idea of *Vergangenheitsbewältigung,* or coming to terms with the past, arose. Proponents of such a reckoning called for self-reflection, confession, and the development of a new, untainted language and political culture that would allow Germans to break with past moral and interpretive frameworks and to lay the foundation for a democratic, moral future. Such ideas, which also inform current notions of transitional justice, rest on an implicit belief in the performative power of language; language not only describes one's relationship to the past but can also define and change it.[9] Austin first developed this idea of language's power to "do" as well as to "state."[10] Although he initially distinguishes between "performative" and "constative" utterances (or statements), this demarcation quickly erodes. A confession, for instance, can be explicit: "I confess that I belonged to the National Socialist party," but

---

8. Dawson, "Real Authors," 104–11.

9. See Teitel, "Transitional Justice."

10. Austin, *How to Do Things,* 5.

the seemingly simple statement of fact, "I belonged to the National Socialist party," may also count as a confession under certain circumstances.[11] These dual functions emerge because a single utterance often contains three acts: a locutionary act, in which a verbal utterance bears some meaning; an illocutionary act, in which convention accords the utterance a certain force; and a perlocutionary act, in which the utterance generates an effect, whether intentional or not.[12] The locutionary utterance "I belonged to the National Socialist Party" can, in certain circumstances, bear the illocutionary force of a confession. This confession, in turn, may provoke various perlocutionary responses; although the intended effect may be forgiveness, a confession may just as easily incite denigration, judgment, or identification.[13]

To analyze how the confessional break with the past goes awry in Grass's narrative *Vergangenheitsbewältigung,* I use the conditions of satisfaction that John Searle isolates as necessary for the successful execution of an illocutionary act. Four major conditions would need to be met for this confessional break to be "nondefective."[14] (1) The essential feature (or illocutionary point) of confession is the speaker's admission of wrongdoing. (2) The propositional content of a confession, then, must be a statement of the speaker's past actions. Grass, for instance, might say, "I believed in Hitler and joined the Waffen-SS." (3) Preparatory conditions must also make the confession appropriate. Grass must have actually believed in Hitler and joined the SS; he must consider these acts to be wrong; and the facts must be unknown (or denied) prior to the confession. (4) The speaker must be sincere, having the psychological state appropriate to the illocutionary act. Grass must be convinced that he did believe in Hitler and join the SS, acknowledge that to do so was wrong, and feel remorse or guilt about it. In the case of a confessional break with the past, the preparatory and sincerity conditions are brought about by a critical break: a new moral framework causes the speaker to acknowledge previously accepted acts as wrong.

In the postwar Federal Republic of Germany, many saw individual and political self-examination and confession as illocutionary acts that could produce highly desirable perlocutionary effects: they were to transform Germany and its citizens, ushering in a positive future for the nation despite its

---

11. Ibid., 67–82.

12. Ibid., 94–147.

13. Austin terms intended perlocutionary effects "objects" and unintended ones "sequels" (118–19).

14. For Searle's explanations of the conditions of satisfaction, see Searle, *Speech Acts,* 57–71; Searle and Vanderveken, "Illocutionary Logic," 119–29. For Austin's initial outline of the requirements for a "felicitous" performative, see *How to Do Things,* 14–15.

ugly past. Jaspers, for instance, began his 1947 lectures on *The Question of German Guilt* by rejecting the tendency he saw among Germans as a nation to evade responsibility for their situation by blaming others, particularly the occupation powers, for postwar conditions. Jaspers asserted that Germany's national and political regeneration could occur only if the members of its populace reckoned with their guilt on an individual level, by undergoing a process he termed purification. This purification, although it encompasses outward acts of restitution and atonement, rests on "inner renewal and metamorphosis"; it "is an inner process which is never ended but in which we continually become ourselves."[15] This characterization of the process suggests that, while it also satisfies the desire to do justice to the past, its primary aim is to provide hope for the future: "clarification of guilt," Jaspers insists, "is at the same time clarification of our new life and its possibilities."[16] Among the possibilities such a new life offers is the promise of freedom, both individual and political. Indeed, this freedom seems to be the goal of Jaspers's lectures: "For only consciousness of guilt leads to the consciousness of solidarity and co-responsibility without which there can be no liberty. . . . In short: without purification of the soul there is no political liberty."[17]

Adorno and the Mitscherlichs also traced the ills of postwar German society and politics to a lack of individual reckoning with the past. As the Mitscherlichs' title and presentation of psychological case studies reveals, they believed that the "principles of collective behavior" reside in individual neuroses and behaviors rooted in a denial of past guilt and trauma; Adorno's advocacy for psychoanalysis or comparable self-reflection shared a similar impulse.[18] Like Jaspers, Adorno saw a self-critical engagement with the past as the key to understanding and strengthening the self; fundamentally, such engagement consists of a "turn toward the subject: reinforcement of a person's self-consciousness and, with that, of a sense of self."[19] This increase in self-awareness or self-confidence permits the individual subject, now seen as a citizen, to view himself as a subject rather than an object of social and political processes. In other words, fortification of the self facilitates both independent action and a sense of responsibility for the action of the whole. Adorno maintained that such identification with the democratic system was lacking in the German population. Because the people failed to see themselves as active subjects of the political system, the population as a whole

15. Jaspers, *Question of German Guilt,* 97–98, 114.
16. Ibid., 113.
17. Ibid., 114–15.
18. Mitscherlich and Mitscherlich, *Inability to Mourn;* Adorno, "Coming to Terms."
19. Adorno, "Coming to Terms," 128.

failed to recognize that system "as the expression of their own maturity" or the "union of the individual and the collective interest."[20] The result was social and political apathy and disengagement. This disengagement, which persisted into the full blossoming of the *Wirtschaftswunder* [economic miracle] of the 1950s and early 1960s, prompted the Mitscherlichs' work as well. The individual failure to confront the past led to a "blockage of social imagination [and] tangible lack of social creativity," "sterile patterns of reaction," and "psychic immobilism in the face of the acute problems confronting German society."[21] Like Adorno's Germans, the Mitscherlichs' Germans had failed to identify with their country's postwar democracy, instead associating themselves solely with its economic system.[22] All three of these writers on *Vergangenheitsbewältigung* (and contemporaries of Grass) thus conceived of individual self-reflection about the past as the condition for a future that held out the hope of personal and political freedom.[23]

As a public and political figure, Grass displayed a similar point of view. In his famous letter to Kurt Georg Kiesinger published in the *Frankfurter Allgemeine Zeitung* on December 1, 1966, for instance, Grass exhorted Kiesinger to remove himself from consideration for the post of chancellor. Although he maintained that Kiesinger's membership in the National Socialist party and service as director of radio broadcasts in Ribbentrop's foreign ministry were understandable on a human level, he asserted that this past compromised Kiesinger's ability to lead Germany into a respected and democratic future. Grass ends his letter with a series of questions that ask Kiesinger to consider how his history will affect Germany's future if he becomes chancellor.[24] In a 1967 campaign speech, Grass called on voters to undertake a similar self-questioning and to recognize that adherence to old values endangered the country's fragile democracy. Individuals had to learn to view their pasts in a new and painful light. His example is of particular relevance for the novella *Cat and Mouse,* the key event of which is the protagonist's theft of a war hero's

---

20. Ibid., 118.

21. Mitscherlich and Mitscherlich, *Inability to Mourn,* 13.

22. Ibid., 26–27.

23. Although Jaspers, Adorno, and the Mitscherlichs all stress the democratic freedom that self-reflective engagement with the past can bring, none contends that it is possible to leave the past behind. Jaspers holds that the moral and metaphysical guilt borne by Germans who lived through the war "are by their very nature not atoned for. They do not cease. Whoever bears them enters upon a process lasting all his life." Jaspers, *Question of German Guilt,* 111. Adorno writes that to attempt to escape this past is unjust, for it is still "intensely alive" in German society. "Coming to Terms," 115. For a comparable statement by the Mitscherlichs, see ch. 1, n. 11.

24. Grass, *Werke,* 11:195–96.

Knight's Cross. In the speech Grass calls on those who had been decorated with the Knight's Cross to acknowledge the senselessness of their courage and sacrifice and the systemic criminality and murder that the cover of war made possible. Refusing to wear his decoration, a self-reflective soldier would eschew the "wrongful upholding of tradition" [falsche Traditionspflege] and continued celebration of military heroism, instead recognizing that the democratic postwar nation requires a different kind of bravery: "Our country demands civil, not military, courage" [Unser Land verlangt nach ziviler und nicht nach militärischer Tapferkeit].[25]

This same impulse toward reevaluation and the renewal it promises permeated much of the era's discussion about poetics and literary production. In the decades following the war, writers and cultural critics, particularly those who had been in exile and those of the emerging postwar generation, declared the necessity of breaking with the linguistic and literary traditions that had been polluted by their support of the National Socialist regime. Poetic practice had to reclaim the German language to affirm the new reality, values, and hopes of the German people. The sense of urgency about this mission came not only from a generalized need to abandon the language of the past but also from the specific character of National Socialist language. Postwar critics saw this language as having a performative effect diametrically opposed to self-examination and confession: in its reliance on and elevation of ritualized language, it encouraged an unexamined affirmation of old beliefs and an abdication of personal responsibility. The nature of the language itself worked against a critical break and a reckoning with the past.

Ritualized language is not deficient or despicable in itself; "uttering certain words" is an essential component of performatives of many kinds.[26] But seen from a postwar German perspective, ritualized National Socialist language became the foundation of a litany that necessarily undermined efforts for *Vergangenheitsbewältigung*. The utterance of litany is a speech act in which a community affirms its articles of belief by repeating conventionalized language. Under National Socialism, secular litany was a powerful mode of bringing Germans everywhere to affirm and circulate the party's propaganda and articles of belief in everyday interactions and activities. To continue to use that language in the postwar context was to continue to affirm those views. Second, while litany relies on communal recitation of ritual language, the speech act of confession demands an individual utterance that details the specific act the individual has committed: such a confession cannot be captured in ritual

---

25. Ibid., 11:243. Grass never suggests that the decorated soldiers themselves might be guilty of murder or crimes.

26. Austin, *How to Do Things*, 14.

language. By providing communal, formulaic expressions for portraying the past, such language absolves the individual of responsibility for addressing his own history. Under the rule of National Socialism, litany encouraged a culture of belief and obedience, a squelching of individual initiative within a quest for a homogenous, unified national community. Such systemic suppression of individual responsibility was exactly what postwar advocates of *Vergangenheitsbewältigung* wanted to dismantle.

In 1947 Victor Klemperer provided the first analysis of the role language played in supporting National Socialist culture and policy, publishing revised excerpts from his wartime journals under the title *LTI: A Philologist's Notebook* [*LTI (Lingua Tertii Imperii): Notizbuch eines Philologen*]. For the most part, Klemperer's study analyzes the lexical features of National Socialist language. But as he describes the way these lexical features were deployed, he paints that language as deriving its incredible power less from the rhetorical genius of the speeches of Hitler or Goebbels than from its formulaic reproduction. According to Klemperer, National Socialism gained control through "the individual words, the expressions, and the sentences that it imposed on the masses in millions of repetitions and that the masses adopted mechanically and unconsciously."[27] In their unconscious, mechanized speech acts, the masses affirmed National Socialist ideology and institutions.

For Klemperer, this mechanical repetition leveled all difference within the German people by creating a homogenous national language. In sketching the fundamental poverty of that language, he casts Goebbels as National Socialism's linguistic dictator. By the later years of the war, Goebbels's Friday radio broadcasts determined what would be printed and opined for the following week; he and a select few others established "the only valid linguistic model. . . . Indeed, at the end it was perhaps Goebbels alone who determined what language was permitted" (32). In this system of "clichés predetermined for everyone," the voices of individual Germans merged together (32). Klemperer abhors this eradication of the individual that linguistic dictation enacts. In Klemperer's view, such linguistic practice transforms the people into an animalistic or inanimate mass driven by forces over which they have no control: "The *LTI* is aimed toward robbing the individual of his separate existence, numbing him as a personality, making him into an unthinking and undesiring member of a herd that is driven and hunted in a particular direction, into an atom in a rolling block of stone" (33).

In fact, Klemperer compares National Socialist language to religious dogma, denouncing the perverted "language of belief" that National Socialism

---

27. Klemperer in an annotated edition by Watt, *Notizbuch eines Philologen*, 21. All translations from Klemperer are my own.

derived from Christianity in general and Catholicism in particular (143). Nor is Klemperer the only one to understand National Socialist language in this way. In his 1990 lecture *Writing after Auschwitz* [hereafter *Writing; Schreiben nach Auschwitz*] Grass described himself and his contemporaries at the end of the war as having been stunted by secular National Socialist dogma, or "articles of faith" [Glaubenssätze (12:239)]. Many postwar writers wanted, above all, to break with these National Socialist "articles of faith," and attempts at a new language and literature surfaced almost immediately after the war's end, in the movements that came to be known as *Trümmerliteratur* [rubble literature] and poetic *Kahlschlag* [clear-cutting]. In his introduction to a 1947 anthology of poems written in prisoner-of-war camps, Hans Werner Richter justified its publication by referring to the new "tone" that suffused this writing. This tone was, above all, one of realism in content and style, and Richter saw in this realism the hope for regeneration.[28] Early hopes for a new literature and a new language were largely dashed in both East and West in the 1950s, however.[29] Thus, in 1962 the poet Hans Magnus Enzensberger was still insisting on the need for revolutionary poetry properly understood: for a poetry that strove to effect revolutionary change in society through its innovative use of language, rather than in overt support of a political program.[30]

Decades later, Grass outlined the "commandments" of literary production for his generation in the first postwar decades. Their writing was to jettison "belief" and embrace "doubt" (*Writing* 12:246). For Grass as for Enzensberger, this doubt was to manifest itself in language itself, by eschewing bombastic color and "ideological black-and-white" [ideologische[s] Weiß oder Schwarz] and revealing the potential of a more subtle exploration of the world:

> In addition, this commandment demanded richness of another kind: the sorry beauty of all recognizable shades of gray was to be celebrated with the means of a damaged language. That meant lowering the flag and spreading ashes on geraniums.

> Obendrein verlangte dieses Gebot Reichtum neuer Art: mit den Mitteln beschädigter Sprache sollte die erbärmliche Schönheit aller erkennbaren Graustufungen gefeiert werden. Das hieß, jene Fahne zu streichen und Asche auf Geranien zu streuen. (*Writing* 12:246)

---

28. Hans Werner Richter, *Deine Söhne, Europa.*

29. See Ralf Schnell's *Geschichte der deutschsprachigen Literatur seit 1945* (61–225) for a balanced and thorough assessment of developments in both the FRG and the GDR.

30. Enzensberger, "Poesie und Politik," 352.

Like Enzensberger, Grass sought a language whose very existence would critique the status quo and point toward the future. As the percussive and glass-shattering modes of expression of his most famous character, Oskar Matzerath, demonstrate, he sought a language that disrupted rather than smoothed, rankled rather than soothed—one diametrically opposed to the lulling rhythms of ritualized language.

Litany in *Cat and Mouse*

A Future in the Past

If *The Tin Drum* shatters a ritualized language of avoidance, *Cat and Mouse* shows that language in action. In combination with the narrator's ruinous lack of self-examination, this language undermines the reckoning with the past that the narrator—and the Germany he represents—desperately need. The novella consists of the narrator Pilenz's retrospective account of his boyhood with the protagonist, Joachim Mahlke, in Danzig during the Third Reich. Pilenz's brief and scattered metanarrative statements show that he intends his story to be a freeing confession. In the quotation cited in this chapter's opening, a clerical friend, Pater Alban, encourages Pilenz to "write [himself] free" of what Pilenz calls the story of "cat and mouse and *mea culpa*" (529, 517) [Katz und Maus und mea culpa (4:106, 86)]. Pilenz tries to follow this advice, admitting, "I am writing, because I must be rid of it" [ich schreibe, denn das muß weg (4:89)].[31] The novella begins with an anecdote illustrating Mahlke's status as a bullied outcast, and its various episodes recount the ridicule he suffers for his physical appearance and his passionate religious devotion. Over time, however, Pilenz and his classmates are moved to grudging admiration as Mahlke develops amazing diving skills and makes himself a hideaway in a sunken ship; steals a Knight's Cross from a war hero who visits the boys' school and is expelled as a result; and himself wins a Knight's Cross for his bravery and feats as a tank gunner. Mahlke's story ends when, refused the honor of appearing as a war hero at his former school, he deserts from the army and asks Pilenz to ferry him to his aquatic hideaway. Pilenz's help is as ambivalent as his feelings, and his last glimpse of Mahlke is the naked feet that kick down into the water as the boy dives. The book ends with Pilenz's vain attempts to find Mahlke after the war.

Despite Pilenz's stated intention to write about his own guilt, the novella

---

31. My translation.

displays anything but the straightforward report of misdeeds and the sin-cere remorse that the confessional act demands: Pilenz constantly equivo-cates about his actions and attitudes toward Mahlke. The opening anecdote establishes this pattern. In this scene, which yields the novella's title and central symbolic image, a young cat attacks the "mouse" of Mahlke's enor-mous Adam's apple as he lies dozing on an athletic field amidst a group of his classmates. Although later discussions of the incident reveal Pilenz as the likely instigator of the attack, his initial description of it obscures the agent, suggesting uncertainty as to whether the cat acted independently or whether he or one of the other boys brought it to pounce. Subsequent reports of the event name various perpetrators, and Pilenz either interrupts them when they threaten to isolate him as the prankster or refrains from commenting on the accuracy of reports that name others (483, 489, 525, 528, 538). The final episode of Mahlke's desertion, too, is riddled with uncertainties gener-ated by Pilenz's narrative contradictions and obfuscations. He reports that Mahlke's mother is not home when he goes to get him provisions for his dive into the ship, but when Mahlke asks about her, Pilenz implies that she has been taken away because of Mahlke's desertion from the army. His account of the last minutes before Mahlke descends into the ship obscures whether he reminds Mahlke to take the can opener crucial to his survival or con-ceals it from him so that he will leave it behind (although he clearly pitches it into the ocean after Mahlke has dived). Finally, it is unclear whether he ever intended to go back to help his friend (although, again, it is clear that he never does). In his "confessional" narration, Pilenz blurs his account of his potential "crimes."

Another crucial instance of narrative obfuscation occurs when Pilenz converts the ambivalently perceived Joachim Mahlke of his childhood into the "Great Mahlke" he attempts to construct in his adult recollections. Pilenz reports that after the Knight's Cross is stolen, the other boys quickly con-clude that Mahlke must be responsible. After a moment of hesitation, Pilenz credits himself with coining the nickname that attributes legendary status to Mahlke, the former outcast: "But Schilling, no, it was I, dreamed up a new title. [. . .] 'The great Mahlke. The Great Mahlke did it, only the Great Mahlke can do such things'" (515) [Nur Schilling, nein ich führte einen neuen Begriff ein, sagte [. . .] "Der große Mahlke. Das hat, das kann nur, das tat der Große Mahlke" (4:83)]. In the next paragraph, Pilenz reiterates and secures his role in this conversion of the temporarily admired "great Mahlke" into "the Great Mahlke," insisting that "my spontaneous cry" (515) [erst mein spontaner Ruf (4:83)] spawned a fitting nickname for the boys' peculiar peer. Pilenz's moments of narrative equivocation show that, rather than enacting a confession, his narrative undertakes a strained act of narrative commemoration of Mahlke.

Pilenz's insistence that he is telling Mahlke's story, rather than his own, makes visible the impulse that informs almost all of the dynamic observer narratives, and one that necessarily undermines the act of confession: the narrators' avoidance of self-examination via a determined focus on their protagonists. The novella's first sentence locates the opening anecdote within Mahlke's development and life (it takes place "after Mahlke had learned to swim" [469]), and the remainder of the narrative focuses on Mahlke's exploits as a schoolboy and a young war hero. In the past-tense narrative, Pilenz functions primarily as a witness to these deeds, and his appearances as historian and writer in the frame narrative are brief, offering little information about his adult life. While Mahlke's full name appears on the first page, Pilenz tells more than half of his story before naming himself, and even then insists that his first name is irrelevant (517). Metanarrative commentary reveals his conscious effort to focus on his friend. After a brief report of where he lived as a boy, Pilenz interrupts himself: "But this isn't supposed to be about me, my story is about Mahlke, or Mahlke and me, but always with the emphasis on Mahlke" (479) [doch soll nicht von mir die Rede sein, sondern von Mahlke oder von Mahlke und mir, aber immer im Hinblick auf Mahlke (4:22)].[32] Pilenz's repeated apostrophe to the absent Mahlke also aids him in deflecting attention from himself and his guilt. With each "you," he directs readers' attention to the other boy. Even as the apostrophe presupposes Mahlke's absence, as it does in the conventions of traditional lyric poetry, Pilenz's continual attempts at conversation with his "friend" show him trying desperately to conjure Mahlke in the present, a feat that would obviate his need for confession.[33] As it encourages readers to focus on a larger-than-life Mahlke in past and present, the apostrophe displaces Pilenz's intended admission of guilt with a memorialization.

Memorialization is another avenue to a reckoning with the past, of course, and, as a form of restitution, can be a responsible reaction to guilt.[34] Yet Pilenz does not succeed in memorialization, either. His depictions of Mahlke are ambivalent, and the narrative as a whole provides a remarkably

---

32. Manheim's translation altered. Similar statements appear on 495, 529, and 535.

33. On apostrophe as an attempt at invocation, see Johnson, "Apostrophe"; Kacandes, *Talk Fiction*, ch. 4; Waters, *Poetry's Touch*, 49. On apostrophe in *Cat and Mouse*, see Kacandes, *Talk Fiction*, 162–70.

34. Adorno writes in "Coming to Terms" that when the crimes of the Holocaust are forgotten or denied, "the murdered are . . . cheated even out of the one thing that our powerlessness can grant them: remembrance" (117).

flat picture of the boy.[35] Instead, in an unintended perlocutionary effect, the narrative ambiguities in his account of Mahlke suggest the contours of the shadowy and marginal Pilenz, much as Jonathan Culler argues that lyric apostrophe emphasizes the speaker's act of poetic self-constitution.[36] This inadvertent illumination of Pilenz's present position is predictable from a narratological standpoint; each statement he makes about Mahlke in the past gives contour to his own present identity by revealing his attitudes toward and thoughts about his "friend." It is also congruent with Werner Wertgen's understanding of the "performative symbolic acts" that constitute many efforts at *Vergangenheitsbewältigung*. Such acts cannot change the past, but are aimed at transforming their agents' present identities.[37] Pilenz's narrative strategies are determined not only by the demands of representing his object but, more importantly, by the image of himself he wishes to project.[38] In Searle's terms, the perlocutionary effects he seeks are aimed primarily at himself;[39] his ostentatious and ambivalent hero-worship notwithstanding, he hopes to influence his audience's "feelings, attitudes, and subsequent behavior" toward himself, rather than toward Mahlke. The aim of confession is, after all, forgiveness or absolution.

Or, for Pilenz, freedom. But the audience of Pilenz's text is unauthorized to forgive and seems unlikely to absolve,[40] and the glimpses the text gives of Pilenz's postwar life show that he remains bound to his past. Trapped by his "gloomy conscience" (535) [mürrische[s] Gewissen (4:116)], he resentfully earns a modest living as a social worker in a residential facility he rarely leaves. His only real human contact appears to be with Pater Alban, and, night after night, their interactions circle around Mahlke or pass in endless, issueless conversations about faith. Despite his occupation, he thus displays

---

35. In fact, it can provide no real picture at all. Neither Pilenz nor his friends can remember what Mahlke looked like, and Pilenz recognizes that his lack of intimacy with Mahlke bars him from depicting his inner life (489, 485). With the exception of occasional speculation about Mahlke's thoughts and feelings, Pilenz reports only Mahlke's observable actions. This style may be read as noncommittal or as simultaneously truthful and superficial, as in Hollington, *Günter Grass*.

36. Culler, *Pursuit of Signs*, 143.

37. Wertgen, *Vergangenheitsbewältigung*, 329–30. Like Austin and Searle, Wertgen specifies that such acts can fail if those performing them do so in bad faith, for instance, if they employ them for deceptive purposes (330).

38. See also Bruce, "Equivocating Narrator," 144–49; Pickar, "Intentional Ambiguity," 236–37. On the effects of Pilenz's narrative equivocation, see Fickert, "Use of Ambiguity"; Spaethling, "Günter Grass."

39. On perlocutionary acts, see Austin, *How to Do Things*, 117–20; Searle and Vanderveken, "Illocutionary Logic," 118–19.

40. Searle specifies that perlocutionary effects are never guaranteed. Searle and Vanderveken, "Illocutionary Logic," 119.

the kind of detachment from and apathy about society that Adorno and the Mitscherlichs bemoan. In fact, with the exception of his almost compulsive music consumption (itself a seeming attempt to top his youthful experiences with Mahlke), he mentions contact with the outside world only in connection with his ongoing search for his lost classmate. The book ends with brief accounts of three failed attempts to locate his friend. He watches films of diving expeditions in hopes of seeing Mahlke's face emerge from a diving helmet, attends circuses to ask the clowns about a colleague named Mahlke, and travels to a meeting of Knight's Cross recipients to have Sergeant Mahlke paged to the door. But Mahlke never appears, and Pilenz is left to ask, "Who will supply me with a good ending?" (556) [wer schreibt mir einen guten Schluß? (4:150)]. The self-examination and confession that were the touchstones of calls for postwar *Vergangenheitsbewältigung*—including Grass's own public statements—fail miserably in his novella. Pilenz's confession fails to fulfill the essential condition of satisfaction for confession, and its propositional content is all wrong: rather than detailing his own past misdeeds or omissions, Pilenz deflects attention from himself with an (also inadequate) memorialization and invocation of Mahlke.[41]

Litanies of a National Socialist Childhood

Grass's novella also exposes the forces that hinder Pilenz's confession: the persistence of the old moral framework and language that Pilenz claims to have left behind. This framework prevents him from fully inhabiting the psychological state appropriate to the act of confession. Like Klemperer's and Grass's nonfiction writing, *Cat and Mouse* compares National Socialism's language to the ritualized language of belief found in traditional religion, demonstrating how National Socialism transformed secular language into a litany that encouraged communal affirmation of its ideology; the novella also depicts these habits of rote, communal recital carrying over to Pilenz's peer group's discussions of Mahlke. An abundance of secondary literature considers the novella's depictions of religious iconography, practice, and belief, but none links the ritualized language within the past-tense story to the language of Pilenz's narrative reckoning with his past.[42] I contend that the novella

---

41. For a similar reading, see Gerhard Kaiser, *Günter Grass*, 40.

42. Mahlke's obsessive and sexually tinged adoration of the Virgin Mary has often been interpreted as analogous to a fanatical devotion to Hitler. Thomas, "Religious Themes," 231–34; Leonard, *Günter Grass*, 36. Others note the text's depiction of the church's collusion with the National Socialists and the machinery of war. See Frank-Raymund Richter, *Vergangenheitsbewältigung*, 44; Reddick, *"Danzig Trilogy"* 166; Neuhaus, *Günter Grass*, 74. Pilenz has been

presents Pilenz's acculturation to these litanies as a key factor in the failure of his postwar confession. By revealing the similarity between ritualized wartime languages and Pilenz's postwar story, the novella posits a continuity underlying the supposed critical break of the war's end. The postwar confession is thwarted because the narrator is still under the thrall of (or hiding behind) the affirmative language of his boyhood.

The most striking illustration of the convergence of religious and secular language occurs in a scene that Pilenz dismisses as peripheral to his story of Mahlke.[43] There, Pilenz describes the deplorable behavior of his fellow altar boys, who carry on a conversation about military statistics during mass. A punctuated sequence from the opening of the mass demonstrates the result, as snatches of liturgical Latin and military statistics follow one upon the other. The lines cited from the mass associate the approach to God with youth and strength—virtues of a military culture—and affirm the eternity of the military-religious complex:

"I will go the altar of God—Say, when was the cruiser *Eritrea* launched?—Thirty-six. Special features?—To God who gives joy to my youth—Only Italian cruiser in East African waters. Displacement?—God, my strength [...] And I will go to the altar of God [...] As it was in the beginning [...] is now and ever shall be [...] and in ages of ages, Amen." (495)[44]

"Introibo ad altare Dei—In welchem Jahre lief der Kreuzer *Eritrea* vom Stapel?—Sechsunddreißig. Besonderheiten?—Ad Deum, qui laetificat juventutem meam.—Einziger italienischer für Ostafrika. Wasserverdrängung?—Deus fortitudo mea—[...] Et introibo ad altare Dei—[...] Sicut erat in principio—[...] et nunc et semper—[...] et in saecula saeculorum, Amen." (4:49)

By inserting military language into the rehearsed repetition of the liturgical service, this passage depicts a ritualized litany of war. The question-and-

---

read as desperately seeking the comfort of established belief. See Johanna E. Behrendt, "Auf der Suche," 318; Frank Richter, *Die zerschlagene Wirklichkeit,* 17. Finally, Mahlke and Pilenz appear in the critical literature as figurations of Christ and Judas, respectively. See Ziolskowski, *Fictional Transfigurations of Jesus;* Ruhleder, "Pattern of Messianic Thought"; Croft, "*Katz und Maus,*" 255–57; Gerhard Kaiser, *Günter Grass,* 15; Reddick, "Trilogie des Leidens," 112; Neuhaus, *Günter Grass,* 77.

43. Roman Catholic liturgical texts appear at several crucial junctures in the action, as well, illuminating the relationship between Mahlke and Pilenz (535, 545–46).

44. Manheim's translation retains the Latin to preserve the effect of the original; I provide a translation here to make Grass's commentary accessible.

answer format of the boys' conversation echoes the call and response of liturgical litany, and their unerring recitation demonstrates their complete command of the militaristic, militarized affirmation of faith. Elsewhere, Pilenz uses the verb "vorbeten" (4:29) [to lead a prayer; to hold forth] to describe the boys' knowledge of the Polish fleet.[45]

In fact, a ritualized secular language permeates all spheres of the boys' lives. Military institutions, school officials, journalistic public discourse, and athletic organizations all produce variants of the same repetitive, litany-like language, a ubiquity that corresponds to claims that National Socialist language penetrated all spheres of life.[46] Two formal features, fused phrases and ellipses, set this formulaic language off from "normal" discourse. Graphically most striking are the phrases that eliminate the spacing between words, transforming statements into units of indivisible meaning that resemble what Bakhtin terms authoritative discourse. The headmaster Klohse emits a torrent of such phrases as he concludes the presentation by the first military hero to visit Mahlke and Pilenz's school. Strung together with dashes, the phrases resemble the beads of a rosary as they extol the virtues of military readiness and self-sacrifice and link them to the German literary tradition:

"Thosewhocomeafterus—Andinthishour—whenthetravelerreturns—but-
thistimethehomeland—andletusnever—quicktoughhard—pureofheart—
asIsaidbefore—pureofheart—andifanyonedisagreeslet—andinthishour—
keepclean—ToconcludewiththewordsofSchiller—ifyourlifeyoudonot-
stake—thelaurelneverwillyoutake—Andnowbacktowork!" (499)[47]

"Jenedienachunskommen—Undindieserstunde—Wandererkommstdu—
Dochdiesmalwirddieheimat—Undwollenwirnie—flinkzähhart—sauber—sagteschon—sauber—Undwernichtdersoll—Undindieserstunde—sauberbleiben—Mitschillerwortschließen—Setzetnichtlebenein
niewirdeuchgewonnensein—Undnunandiearbeit!" (4:55)

The phrase "Wandererkommstdu" further truncates a Greek line praising Spartan military bravery that Heinrich Böll had used as a title for his 1950 story, "Wanderer, kommst du nach Spa . . ." Like *Cat and Mouse,* this story

---

45. Grass also uses the verb "to pray" to describe his boyhood knowledge of maritime statistics in *Beim Häuten der Zwiebel* (Werke, 10:220). Cf. the translation in Grass, *Peeling the Onion,* 13.

46. Klemperer in Watt, *Notizbuch eines Philologen,* 321–43; Seidel and Seidel-Slotty, *Sprachwandel im Dritten Reich,* vii.

47. Manheim's translation slightly altered.

reflects critically on National Socialism's appropriation of the humanistic tradition and on the educational system's role in converting a generation of idealistic schoolboys into soldiers. The two phrases "ifyourlifeyoudonot-stake—thelaurelneverwillyoutake" [Setzetnichtlebenein niewirdeuchgewon-nensein] are sung twice in succession in a song that celebrates the soldier's life just before the curtain falls in the eleventh scene of Schiller's *Wallenstein's Camp* [*Wallensteins Lager*]. Klohse's recitation omits three syllables from each line, changing Schiller's varied meter into a sing-song meter reminiscent of nursery rhyme.[48] If a glorious military tradition had ever existed, National Socialism's twisted repetitions of it—in speech acts as well as military ones—undermine its successful replication.

The fused phrases concretize the monolithic nature of the speech's author-itative discourse, which "enters our verbal consciousness as a compact and indivisible mass."[49] Pilenz presents them as calcified chunks of ideology and nonsense (or nonsense ideology), discredited expressions of the rejected authority of National Socialism that appear as "an object, a *relic*, a *thing*."[50] Bakhtin asserts that "authoritative discourse cannot be represented—it is only transmitted"; as a result, he holds that it plays little role in the dialogic dis-course of the novel, where it can appear only as "a dead quotation."[51] In Grass's novella, however, these "dead quotations" play a central role. While the novel depicts them as inert, anachronistic holdovers from a dead (and, coinciden-tally, authoritarian) language and moral framework, it also illustrates their power as speech acts of affirmation.

Ellipses used to conclude phrases often serve a similar function. Klohse begins his speech introducing the second war hero with quotations that appear as clichéd, cemented phrases. As he moves to welcome the speaker to the podium, however, he offers a seemingly inconclusive statement: "One of us, from our midst, a product of our school and its spirit, and in this spirit let us . . ." (507) [Einer von uns, aus unserer Mitte, aus dem Geist unseres Gymnasiums hervorgegangen, und in diesem Sinne wollen wir . . . (4:69)]. The incomplete statements and ellipses seem at first to suggest what Bakhtin calls internally persuasive discourse. Unlike authoritative discourse, such dis-course is open and can be adapted to new contexts and meanings: it "awakens new and independent words, . . . and does not remain in an isolated and static

---

48. The original lines read "Und setzet ihr nicht das Leben ein, / Nie wird euch das Leben gewonnen sein." Schiller, *Werke und Briefe*, 4:53.

49. Bakhtin, *Dialogic Imagination*, 343.

50. Ibid., 344.

51. Ibid.

condition."[52] But Klohse's statements in fact evoke the same kind of inviolable units of fixed meaning (or of no meaning at all) as the fused phrases present. The ellipses signal a conclusion that need not be written because it follows so self-evidently from the introduction. In describing the first military hero's speech, W. G. Cunliffe says that Grass marks the falsity of this speech "by running together incomplete commonplace phrases with the air of one who is too weary to trouble finishing them."[53] In the case of the ellipses, too, repetition has made language and its meaning predictable and durable. Many of the ellipses contained in the second military hero's speech, as well as those that conclude Klohse's announcement of Mahlke's expulsion from school, produce a comparable effect (508, 521). The two reports of Mahlke's military achievements at the end of chapter 11, although in a slightly different form, amount to the same thing. Closing with the words "and furthermore, etcetera etcetera" (538) [und so weiter und so weiter (4:121)] followed by a period, both the parade ground announcement and the newspaper article explicitly signal the continuation of the familiar rhetoric. The nearly identical language of the two reports indicates the degree to which the discourses of military parade ground and "civilian" newspaper have merged, again reflecting the "truly totalitarian" language of the National Socialist state.[54] Finally, because many of the novella's Roman Catholic texts appear in the same form, the book underscores the similar form and function of the ritualized languages of National Socialism and of traditional religion.[55]

If the novella's fused phrases and concluding ellipses evoke the repetitions and established meanings of litany, several of the text's direct discourse exchanges mimic its call-and-response format, highlighting the way litany organizes individuals into a communal body that shares and affirms knowledge and beliefs. The novella's most extended passages of direct discourse record the two military heroes' speeches and the exchanges between Mahlke and Pilenz in the final scenes, but much of the remaining dialogue occurs in brief conversations whose speakers remain unidentified. The three longest of these depict schoolboy chatter about Mahlke and his athletic and military feats (483, 538, 548–49). In these segments, each speaker contributes only a short statement or question, each of which is set off by a paragraph break. Many of these utterances express incomplete thoughts or leave their referents

---

52. Ibid., 345–46.

53. Cunliffe, "Günter Grass," 181.

54. Klemperer in Watt, *Notizbuch eines Philologen,* 323.

55. Examples include a snippet from a Lenten service, Mahlke's beloved *Stabat dolorosa,* and Father Gusewski's final celebration of communion (477, 535, 545–46).

unidentified and can be understood only in the context of the conversation or of a previously existing common body of knowledge:

> "What's the matter with him?"
> "I say he's got a tic."
> "Maybe it's got something to do with his father's death."
> "And what about all that hardware on his neck?"
> "And he's always running off to pray."
> "And he don't believe in nothing if you ask me."
> "For that he's too realistic."
> "And what about that thing on his neck?"
> "You ask him, you're the one who [verb missing] the cat [preposition missing] him . . ." (483)[56]

> "Was hat er nur?"
> "Der hat nen Tick, sag ich."
> "Vielleicht hängt das mit dem Tod von seinem Vater zusammen."
> "Und die Klamotten am Hals?"
> "Und ewig rennt er beten."
> "Dabei glaubt er an nischt, sag ich."
> "Da ist er viel zu sachlich für."
> "Und das Dinglamdei und nun auch noch das?"
> "Frag du ihn, du hast ihm doch damals die Katze . . ." (4:28)

This format, visually arresting in a text whose sparse dialogue is otherwise incorporated into longer paragraphs, demonstrates the communal nature of the meaning being constructed. The line breaks emphasize that distinct individuals utter each statement, but the statements' anonymity indicates the irrelevance of those individuals' identities; their voices are registered only insofar as they belong to the group. As this group speaks, it constructs a single unit of meaning, a shared assessment of Mahlke's personality. Beginning with a call and response of question and answers, the conversation proceeds with each speaker adding an observation or explanation. The statements' seemingly final periods are belied by their initial words; in a string of five statements, four begin with coordinating conjunctions. The exchange demonstrates the way individual language and identity are subsumed by the shared opinions and

---

56. Manheim completes the phrase "sicked the cat on him," but the original obscures the crucial information by leaving out the verb and preposition.

meanings generated in the litany-like language of Pilenz's childhood.[57] The perlocutionary effect of the litany is, as Klemperer notes, a dissolution of individual identity. The exchange also ends with the telltale ellipsis . . .

Litanies of a Postwar Narrative

. . . just as Pilenz's postwar narrative starts with one. Taking the narrative device of beginning *in medias res* to the extreme, the novella begins with an ellipsis: ". . . and once, after Mahlke had learned to swim, we were lying in the grass, in the Schlagball field" (469) [. . . und einmal, als Mahlke schon schwimmen konnte, lagen wir neben dem Schlagballfeld im Gras (4:5)]. This same introductory ellipsis and phrase (and once/und einmal) also initiates four more episodes, all of which detail the achievements for which Mahlke is famous among his peers: his submarine trophy-hunting, his frighteningly long dives into the shipwreck, his discovery of its dry radio cabin, and his (asserted) liaison with Tulla Pokriefke (474, 476, 501, 545). These ellipses seem to function very differently from those in the conversations of the past-tense narrative. There, ellipses at the ends of phrases mark monolithic discourse that the audience, whether composed of schoolboys, newspaper readers, or worshippers, can complete by rote. Here, in the narrative discourse of Pilenz's present, they begin sentences and the stories they tell. I maintain, however, that their symmetrical usage exposes Pilenz's postwar narrative as belonging to the same cycle of repetition that plagued National Socialist society. They are a typographical sign that the language of the past persists, inhibiting Pilenz's critical break with a supposedly discarded moral framework and language.

This continuity contrasts with Pilenz's conscious treatment of the language of the past. The highly stylized fused phrases of Klohse's speeches suggest that Pilenz himself marks this language as foreign rhetoric.[58] He explicitly says that he is writing his story, so the narrative audience within the fictional world sees the typographically highlighted fused phrases, just as the authorial

---

57. The ubiquitous presence of ritualized language in the past-tense story supports interpretations that read *Katz* as a critique of National Socialism's perversion of religious, humanistic, and literary traditions. See Gerhard Kaiser, *Günter Grass,* 33; Reddick, "*Danzig Trilogy,*" 167–68; Neuhaus, *Günter Grass,* 71–73; Roberts, "Cult of the Hero"; Plagwitz, "Crux des Heldentums."

58. Cf. Hasselbach, *Katz und Maus,* 106–7, who attributes the marking to a higher-order narrator. This attribution seems to stem solely from her general disregard for Pilenz's intelligence and insight, since she offers no textual grounds for it.

audience does. Pilenz uses this blatant stylization to distance himself from the rhetoric of his youth; the illocutionary force is one of parody, and the ideal narrative audience is to recognize that. His conscious treatment of language thus parallels postwar authors' rejection of a linguistic and literary tradition polluted by National Socialism,[59] suggesting that he has undergone the "change of perspective" or critical break essential to the reinterpretation of history that takes place in *Vergangenheitsbewältigung*.[60] In contrast, his use of ellipses in the time of narration allows the implied author to show that, despite his conscious effort to break with the past, Pilenz unconsciously replicates its language and forms. Again, the narrative audience sees these ellipses. But Pilenz's introductory ellipses seem to designate something different than do those associated with ritualized rhetoric in his story about the past—his own mental processes, perhaps. There are no suggestions that he perceives the symmetry of the two types. Nor would his ideal narrative audience, the postwar Germans who themselves lean comfortably on a conditioned rejection of National Socialism without recognizing the similar, rote quality of wartime and postwar rhetoric. Ann Mason mentions in passing that Pilenz's "formulaic repetition of his 'litanies' but serves to recall him again and again to the unresolved sources of his guilt," and argues that they illustrate art's inability to serve a redemptive function.[61] The ritualized language in Pilenz's present-day narrative discourse does more than depict him as ensnared in old fascinations and antipathies, however, and does less than declare the impossibility of using writing and narration to come to terms with the past (although it does highlight the difficulty of the undertaking). It demonstrates the degree to which his current existence, cognition, and language continue to be structured by the same patterns that guided his youth. Furthermore, it allows him to avoid the self-examination that might bring him to acknowledge its continuing influence over his narrative—and the guilt that narrative at once obscures and emphasizes. Pilenz, the proclaimed postlitany writer, proves to be in thrall to the rhythms and mechanisms of the language from which he has declared his independence.

The introductory ellipses do not elicit a rehearsed conclusion. Nor, as John Reddick contends, do they "point back as it were into empty space."[62] Instead, they indicate that what precedes a statement may be as predictable as what

---

59. For readings that view Grass's employment of the form of the novella similarly, as a subversive critique of its tradition and ideology, see Durzak, "Entzauberung des Helden," 28; Frank Richter, *Die zerschlagene Wirklichkeit*.

60. Wertgen, *Vergangenheitsbewältigung*, 108–10.

61. Ann Mason, *Skeptical Muse*, 64.

62. Reddick, *"Danzig Trilogy,"* 89.

follows it. In Pilenz's case, stories about Mahlke follow other stories about Mahlke as if on an endless, looping reel. In one of few passages alluding to his postwar life, Pilenz reveals that he sits with Pater Alban night after night, debating theology and relating stories of Mahlke's life. The list that describes his recollections suggests that these anecdotes proliferate uncontrollably, as Pilenz talks about

> Mahlke and Mahlke's Virgin, Mahlke's neck and Mahlke's aunt, Mahlke's sugar water, the part in the middle of his hair, his phonograph, snowy owl, screwdriver, woolen pompoms, luminous buttons, about cat and mouse and *mea culpa*. I tell him how the Great Mahlke sat on the barge and I, taking my time, swam out to him alternating between breast stroke and back stroke. (517)

> Mahlke und Mahlkes Jungfrau, von Mahlkes Gurgel und Mahlkes Tante, von Mahlkes Mittelscheitel, Zuckerwasser, Grammophon, Schnee-Eule, Schraubenzieher, Wollpuscheln, Leuchtköpfe, von Katz und Maus und mea culpa, auch wie der Große Mahlke auf dem Kahn saß und ich, ohne mich zu beeilen, in Brustlage, Rückenlage zu ihm schwamm. (4:86)

Pilenz wants to "write himself free" of Mahlke, but his effort is in vain. In some of the most often cited lines of the text, Pilenz laments the impossibility of ever writing a conclusive story: "Are there stories that can [end]?" (534) [Gibt es Geschichten, die aufhören können? (4:113)]. By the end of his tale, he knows that he, at least, is incapable of finishing them. "Who will supply me with a good conclusion?" (556) [Wer schreibt mir einen guten Schluß? (4:150)], he asks, as if to seek aid from the reader or the hauntingly empty air.

Pilenz is trapped in an unending recitation of the story of Mahlke's life. The ritualized introductory phrase ". . . and one time" [. . . und einmal] exposes the degree to which he condemns himself to this repetition by unwittingly adhering to the language and perspective of his youth; the phrase marks Pilenz's adult narration as a continuation of the litany of Mahlke's exploits that Pilenz and his friends had established during Mahlke's lifetime. Two scenes demonstrate the role this litany plays in defining the boys' relationship to the simultaneously admired and ridiculed outsider. In the first, Pilenz and another boy launch into a recitation of Mahlke's summertime achievements in a clumsy attempt to impress Pilenz's visiting girl cousins. Pilenz's representation of this recitation, much like his account of Klohse's auditorium speech, omits connective words and strings together key terms that evoke the whole:

"Metal plates, absolutely, and a fire extinguisher, and tin cans, he opened them right up and guess what was in them—human flesh! And when he brought up the phonograph something came crawling out of it, and one time he . . ." (492)

"Schildchen hat er, na und den Feuerlöscher, Konserven, sag ich Euch, gleich mit nem Büchsenöffner, war Menschenfleisch drinnen, und aus dem Grammophon, als er's oben hatte, kroch was, und einmal hat er . . ." (4:44)

The final "and one time, he . . ." [und einmal hat er . . .], which echoes Pilenz's adult use of the phrase, gestures toward the next rehearsed adventure story just as Klohse's incomplete statements point to the next propagandistic phrase or the priest Father Gusewski's to the next line of the mass. Similarly, when Pilenz and his classmates brag at their first military barracks about their acquaintance with Mahlke, they recite a catalogue of his deeds that includes three items that conclude with ellipses (538). The last of these initiates the story of the day at the athletic field and the drama of cat and mouse, closing the circuit that begins with the novella's opening ellipsis.

The ellipses thus mark the story of Mahlke's life as an endlessly repeated litany. By appearing in Pilenz's accounts of Mahlke on both narrative levels—in Pilenz's narrating present *and* in the story he tells about the past—these ellipses expose the similarities in Pilenz's assessment of and relationship to "the Great Mahlke" across the great divide of the war's end. Neither Pilenz's fundamental relationship to Mahlke nor the language he uses to describe it has changed. The old language and moral framework act as "an unconscious corset on the capacity for conscious interpretation."[63] Old language can, of course, be put to new use,[64] as Pilenz's parodic use of the fused phrases shows. In this novella, however, Grass creates a narrator who fails to confess his old guilt in part because he speaks a "new" language that resembles the "old" one. His ostentatious apostrophe to Mahlke betrays this continuity, too. Mahlke's beloved apostrophic prayer, the *Stabat dolorosa,* indicates his search for salvation in an external instance—with the prayer, in the Virgin Mary, but as a heroic military recruit, from far less admirable sources. As it echoes this prayerful apostrophe, Pilenz's postwar address to Mahlke suggests the same kind of reliance on external salvation. Rather than assuming responsibility for his wartime sins and his postwar condition, he continues to seek

---

63. Wertgen, *Vergangenheitsbewältigung,* 101, 55.

64. On language's openness to resignification, see Butler, *Excitable Speech;* Bakhtin, *Dialogic Imagination,* 280–82.

absolution from without.[65] Pilenz's ritualistic language inhibits the development of the new interpretive framework (or, to use Searle's terminology, psychological state) that would allow him to confess successfully. Although Pilenz's perlocutionary *object* as he parodies litany is to establish his distance from the past, the perlocutionary *effect* is the reader's conviction that he remains entrapped in it. Language here is not a resource for future development but an anachronistic burden.

Litany in Grass's Fictional(ized) Danzig Writings

The novella shows confession and a reckoning with the past foundering on old language and an avoidance of self-examination. To be more specific, the implied author reveals the narrator's failure by exposing the continuities between his past and present language and obsession with Mahlke. In the last section of the chapter, I argue that Grass portrays ritualized language and other-focused narration similarly in three other major fictional and non-fictional works dealing with the past and with Danzig, the city of his childhood: *Crabwalk, Writing,* and *Peeling the Onion.*[66] Although I do not conflate Grass with his implied authors, I argue that this persistent concern with the speech acts of ritualized language and other-focused narration has signaled his self-reflexive literary processing of his own guilt and shame over decades. My intent here is not so much to make an argument about the biographical Grass as it is to examine his ongoing (biographically relevant) reflections on and literary stylization of narrative as a means of reckoning with the past. In this goal, my project resembles recent efforts to reconstruct Grass's development of and reflections on his authorial persona in both literary and nonliterary spheres.[67]

The narrator of *Crabwalk,* Paul Pokriefke, tells the intertwined stories of his mother, Tulla, and his son, Konrad. Grandmother and grandson share an obsession with the ship named after the German nationalist Wilhelm Gustloff and with its sinking at the end of World War II, as it carried refugees (and troops) westward from Danzig. This obsession culminates in Konrad's

---

65. Kacandes reads Pilenz's efforts at an apostrophic resurrection of Mahlke as an effort to obtain salvation from him. *Talk Fiction,* 166–70.

66. English quotations from *Crabwalk* refer to the translation by Krishna Winston, unless otherwise noted. German citations refer to *Im Krebsgang* in Grass, *Werke,* 10:5–205. As many have noted, the autobiography is often highly fictionalized. See Ahlberg, "Grass as Literary Intellectual," 217; Rebecca Braun, "Ethics of Autobiography"; Fuchs, "Autobiographical Confession."

67. See Rebecca Braun, *Constructing Authorship;* Pietsch, "*Wer hört noch zu?*"

murder of another youth. The book's interwoven narratives emphasize the conflicts between the three family members' interpretations of the *Gustloff* story, producing what Anne Fuchs terms a "memory contest": "memory contests edit and advance competing narratives of identity with reference to an historical event perceived as a massive disturbance of a group's self-image."[68] The core of the dynamic observer narrative appears clearly in this definition, and, not coincidentally, all three of Fuchs's literary examples are also dynamic observer narratives (the other two are Monika Maron's *Pavel's Letters* [*Pawels Briefe*] and Uwe Timm's *In My Brother's Shadow* [*Am Beispiel meines Bruders*].[69] While Fuchs identifies features of post-1989 German memory contests that are not common to all dynamic observer narratives, then, the memory contest phenomenon should be viewed within the tradition of the dynamic observer narrative.

Paul writes on behalf of a figure he calls "the old man" [der Alte], who has charged him with defusing the incendiary potential of the story of the *Wilhelm Gustloff* and its legacy. The old man has recognized, too late, the consequences of leaving the topic of German wartime suffering to the political right:

> Never, he said, should his generation have kept silent about such misery, merely because its own sense of guilt was so overwhelming, merely because for years the need to accept responsibility and show remorse took precedence, with the result that they abandoned the topic to the right wing. This failure, he says, was staggering . . . (103)

> Niemals, sagt er, hätte man über so viel Leid, nur weil die eigene Schuld übermächtig und bekennende Reue in all den Jahren vordringlich gewesen sei, schweigen, das gemiedene Thema den Rechtsgestrickten überlassen dürfen. Diese Versäumnis sei bodenlos . . . (10:93)

In constructing his account, Paul uses the same sources Konrad had used for his propagandistic version, but he refuses the rhetoric of conspiracy and victimization that suffuses his son's tale, instead representing the event from multiple perspectives and resisting a focus on the suffering it caused.[70] His

---

68. Fuchs, "Generational Memory Contests," 179. See also Twark, "Landscape, Seascape, Cyberscape," 147–49; Schmitz, *On Their Own Terms*, 270–73.

69. Note that Fuchs's examples of memory contests include both fictional and nonfictional texts, as I see dynamic observer narratives as appearing in both realms.

70. See also Dye, "Günter Grass's *Im Krebsgang*," 481; Hall, "Danzig Quintet," 173, 78–79; Schmitz, *On Their Own Terms*, 269.

narrative rebels against the litanies of German victimhood that are epito-
mized by his mother's eternal reminiscences of her experiences aboard the
ship; she and her parents had been among the refugees trying to escape when
the ship sank, and Paul's birth was brought on by the trauma of the experience. Throughout the text, her recitations of the details of the disaster almost
inevitably end with the ellipsis of familiar rhetoric (28, 58, 95, 140, 223).

The novella suggests, however, that the complaints of those who mili-
tantly proclaim the unending guilt of the German people are no better.
Konrad murders a boy whose online persona is a Jewish youth named
David after the two argue in an Internet chatroom. In a striking passage,
Paul reproduces snatches of David's direct discourse alongside direct
speech from Hitler and Tulla. David baits Konrad with an elliptical phrase:
"You Germans will forever be branded with Auschwitz as a sign of your
guilt . . ."[71] [Euch Deutschen wird Auschwitz als Zeichen der Schuld ewig-
lich eingebrannt sein . . . (10:111)]. Konrad informs David that Hitler's last
speech was broadcast on the *Gustloff,* and, confirming this statement, Paul
cites the speech: "Twelve years ago, on 30 January 1933, [. . .] Providence
placed the destiny of the German Volk in my hands . . ." (126) [Heute vor
zwölf Jahren [. . .] hat mir die Vorsehung das Schicksal des deutschen Vol-
kes in die Hand gelegt . . . (10:112)]. Finally, Paul records his mother's recollection of the broadcast: "It sure gave me the creeps when the Führer went
on that way about destiny and stuff like that . . ." (126) [Richtich jegrault
hab ech miä, als der Fiehrer vom Schicksal ond ähnliche Sachen jeredet
hat . . . (10:112)]. The radical right and those who shirk responsibility for the
events of World War II do not have a monopoly on ritualized language; the
"anti-fascist prayer wheel" (142) [antifaschistische Gebetsmühle (10:127)] of
the other side is just as predictable.[72]

Ritualistic language is dangerous here, as is an avoidance of personal guilt
and self-reflection. Paul harbors a feeling of responsibility for his son's corruption and crime. Visiting Konrad in jail and seeing the model *Gustloff* he
has just finished assembling, Paul asks himself whether he could have prevented Konrad's obsession by buying, building, and discussing the model ship
with him earlier. Yet, even as he recounts the ship's history, Paul resists associating himself with the distasteful story, just as he has sought to distance
himself from the calamity throughout his entire life (29, 40, 71–72, 122, 148).
Indeed, although he provides much more information about himself than

---

71. My translation.

72. Others have pointed out that Grass indicts German memory practices of all political
stripes as inadequate. Thesz, "Against a New Era," 298–301; Ó Dochartaigh, "Memory Contest
without Jews."; Schmitz, *On Their Own Terms,* 280.

Pilenz does, Paul's story of Tulla and Konrad's obsession with the *Wilhelm Gustloff* still presents the family history as hinging on others' stories, rather than his own. In particular, while his reflections on the signs of Konrad's obsession and his own failings as a father betray that he, like Pilenz, feels guilt about past events (75, 91–92, 161, 197–98, 208), he insists again and again that his mother is responsible for Konrad's crime: "It's her fault and hers alone that things went so wrong with the boy" (69) [Sie, nur sie ist schuld, daß es mit dem Jungen danebenging (10:64)]. Although Paul acknowledges and reflects on his guilt much more openly than Pilenz does, he, too, deflects attention from it by pointing to someone else.

Paul tells his family's story to break their cycle of rhetoric, but the novella's last lines explicitly assert the impossibility of reaching a qualitatively different future as long as formulaic language reigns. His son in jail, Paul finds an Internet site dedicated to the prisoner. "'We believe in you,' the site proclaims, 'we will wait for you, we will follow you . . .' andsoon [*sic*] andsoforth" (234) ["Wir glauben an Dich . . . wir warten auf Dich, wir folgen Dir . . ." Undsoweiter undsoweiter (10:205)]. In response to this fanatical devotion, expressed in the now familiar combination of ellipsis-completed and fused phrases, the narrator expresses his fatalistic assessment of the situation: "It doesn't end. Never will it end" (234) [Das hört nicht auf. Nie hört das auf (10:205)]. So ends the book.

Similar conventions pervade Grass's critical and autobiographical prose, often with similar intent.[73] In *Writing* Grass uses ellipses to present the "articles of faith" [Glaubenssätze] that penetrated all of German society during National Socialism: "We Germans are . . . being German means . . . and finally: A German would never . . ." [Wir Deutschen sind . . . Deutschsein heißt . . . und schließlich: Niemals würde ein Deutscher . . . (12:239)]. For Grass, this last item, the denial of the possibility of the Holocaust, survived the war and the collapse of Hitler's regime (*Writing* 12:240). Likewise, in *Peeling the Onion*, ellipses mark the incorrigible litanies of the unreformed Nazis who were Grass's coworkers in the postwar period; they stubbornly hum "Raise the flag . . ." [Die Fahne hoch . . .], the first line of the National Socialist Party's official hymn, and warn, "If the Führer were alive today, he would [verb missing] the lot of you . . ." (226) [wenn der Führer noch leben würd, würd er euch alle . . . (10:433)].[74] Here, too, Grass highlights the durability of

---

73. Ellipses do not always denote litany-like recitations. They can, for instance, mark a drifting off in the face of uncertainty (*Crabwalk* 75), regret (*Crabwalk* 80, 103), or old memories (*Peeling* 3–4). Stuart Taberner contends in "'Political' Private Biography" that in *Die Box* (2010), ellipses signal true gaps that leave the "authentic," private self unspoken (507).

74. The title of the song is the "Horst-Wessel-Lied." Heim supplies the verb that the ellipses in the original elide.

ritualized language and its ability to shore up moral frameworks across social and political breaks that would seem to require their abandonment.

Like *Crabwalk,* the autobiography also acknowledges that all worldviews have their ritualized language. There are litanies of postwar regrets and pro-testations of innocence (18, 29), litanies of parents' hopes for and admonish-ments of their children (68, 243), litanies from Grass's Danzig relatives about the plight of German refugees (236), litanies of Marxist ideology from East German tour guides and of false promises from West German publishers (322, 412),[75] and litanies of freedom in the occupying Americans' imported music: "Don't fence me in . . ." (270). In addition to the many elliptical phrases, Grass employs a fused phrase to represent the single act of true resistance he wit-nessed during the war. Day after day, a young man in his military training camp refused to so much as touch a gun, always uttering the same phrase: "Four words fusing into one: Wedontdothat" (86) [Vier Wörter schnurrte zusammen, wurden zu einem: Wirtunsowasnicht (10:294)]. This formulaic phrase thus becomes a mode of unflagging counter-litany and a (speech) act of resistance, and Grass reports that "his unvarying reply became a catchword that has never left me" (86) [seine nie variierte Antwort geriet zur Redensart und ist mir fur alle Zeit zitierbar geblieben (10:293)]. In two passages, the fig-ure of the young Grass even utters recurrent litanies himself. He echoes the Latin of the Catholic mass from *Cat and Mouse,* "Introibo ad altare Dei . . . ," and Grass the narrator remarks that he still knows the prayers after decades of nonbelief (60). Grass also tells of how his mother listened to "the litany of my boasts, that would open with 'When I'm rich and famous, I'll [verb miss-ing] with you . . .'" (48) [die litaneihaft so begannen, "Wenn ich mal reich und berühmt bin, werde ich mit dir . . ." (10:254)].[76] Grass figures himself and his contemporaries in the nonfictional world as entrapped, enamored, and empowered by ritualized language and the speech acts and stories it supports, much as his fictional figures are.

His play with the author function in *Cat and Mouse* and *Crabwalk* also shows extradiegetic figures very like himself as susceptible to the "the tempta-tion to camouflage oneself in the third person" (*Peeling the Onion* 1) [Versu-chung, sich in dritter Person zu verkappen (10:209)].[77] That is, he emphasizes storytellers' propensity to tell someone else's story to avoid their own. The figure whom Paul refers to as "the old man" or "my employer" [mein Arbeit-

---

75. The English translation omits the ellipses in the promises.

76. Heim's translation supplies the missing verb.

77. For discussions of the relationship between narrator, extradiegetic figure, and Grass, see Rebecca Braun, *Constructing Authorship,* 167–75; Pezold, "Weiterführung oder Zurücknahme?" 192; Midgley, "Memory, Medium, and Message," 63; Hall, "Danzig Quintet," 161–62.

geber] is a much more concrete character than the invisible instance to which Pilenz occasionally alludes, but in both cases shadowy figures push the narrators to write, who then insist they are writing about others. Pilenz alludes to this figure only briefly, saying that he "must write" because "over and over again the fellow who invented us because it's his business to invent people obliges me to take your Adam's apple in my hand" (469) [der uns erfand, von berufswegen, zwingt mich, wieder und wieder Deinen Adamsapfel in die Hand zu nehmen (4:6)]. He is male, perhaps an author, and Pilenz seems to have difficulty separating himself entirely from him: "If only I knew who made up the story, he or I, or who is writing this in the first place!" (528) [wenn ich nur wüßte, wer die Mär erfunden hat, er oder ich oder wer schreibt hier? (4:105)]. *Crabwalk* provides a fuller picture of "the old man" who guides Paul's writing process, practically obliging the reader to equate him with Grass. Paul is to write in his place, to compensate for the old man's failure to tell the story (103–4). Paul's "employer" explains that he ought to have told this story himself because "properly speaking, any strand of the plot having to do directly or loosely with the city of Danzig and its environs should be his concern" (79) [eigentlich müsse jeder Handlungsstrang, der mit der Stadt Danzig und deren Umgebung verknüpft oder locker verbunden sei, seine Sache sein (10:73)]. The older man should have taken up the further story of Tulla and her family immediately: "Soon after the publication of that mighty tome, *Dog Years,* this material had been dumped at his feet. He—who else?— should have been the one to dig through it" (79) [Gleich nach Erscheinen des Wälzers *Hundejahre* sei ihm diese Stoffmasse auferlegt worden. Er—wer sonst—hätte sie abtragen müssen (10:73)]. But the author of *Dog Years* (Grass) failed to do so, for he admits "that around the mid-sixties, he'd had it with the past [. . .] . . . Now it was too late for him" (80) [daß er gegen Mitte der sechziger Jahre die Vergangenheit sattgehabt habe [. . .] . . . Nun sei es zu spät für ihn (10:73)].

Paul's suggestion that Tulla forces "the old man" to force Paul to write might be seen as reducing the Grassian character to a mere figure in a playful interpenetration of factual and fictional worlds (104). But Grass portrays himself as a real counterpart to his fictional narrators in less ambiguous contexts, as well. In *Writing* he explains his temporary retreat from prose writing after the completion of *Dog Years* in terms that associate him not only with the extradiegetic figure from *Crabwalk,* but also with his narrators: "Not that I was exhausted, but I believed too hastily that I had written myself free of something that now lay behind me, not erased, of course, but at least brought to an end" [Nicht daß ich erschöpft war, doch glaubte ich voreilig, mich von etwas freigeschrieben zu haben, das nun hinter mir zu liegen hatte, zwar nicht abgetan, aber doch zu Ende gebracht (12:254)]. Like Pilenz, he has told others' stories in an attempt to "write himself free." For Grass as for his fictional characters, however, it is a delusion to believe that he could attain freedom from the past by narrating another's story. "It is certainly the case that I believed I had done enough with what I had written" [Es ist sicher so, daß ich glaubte, mit dem, was ich schreibend tat, genug getan zu haben], Grass explained in his August 2006 *Frankfurter Allgemeine Zeitung* interview.[78] But over time, this belief that telling others' fictional stories was "enough" faded. These stories could not compensate for his failure to tell his own; a successful confession demands speaking of one's own past actions: "That oppressed me. My silence through all the years is one of the reasons I wrote the book. It had to come out, finally" [Das hat mich bedrückt. Mein Schweigen über all die Jahre zählt zu den Gründen, warum ich dieses Buch geschrieben habe. Das mußte raus, endlich].[79]

Perhaps Grass's literary career has been a long, spiraling recitation of a litany of the other, a litany that for decades allowed him to ignore and bury the story of his own past. Perhaps his flesh-and-blood readers, accepting and affirming this litany, served as real-world counterparts to the ideal narrative audiences of his fictional narrators. His fiction permitted him to externalize his own guilt, or, in the Mitscherlichs' words, served "the alienation [*Verfremdung*] of one's own past."[80] Commenting on Grass's long silence about his history with the Waffen-SS, Arno Widmann, too, notes his dissociation from his own past: "Like most, [. . .] he was able to make the leap into the new world of democracy only by separating himself from himself. He jumped out of his skin in the hope of escaping himself."[81] With his confession, Grass appears not exceptional but representative, "like most." Indeed, Stuart Taberner argues that Grass uses his autobiography to present himself as exemplary, in both senses of the word: both in his representative German experience, and in his emulation-worthy means of addressing it.[82] Nor is Taberner alone in thinking that because the (fictionalized) autobiography continues to render the abiding difficulty of dealing with Germany's National Socialist history, its "baroque litany of guilt and shameful feelings" may still qualify as "great German literature."[83]

---

78. Schirrmacher and Spiegel, "Eine deutsche Jugend."

79. Ibid. In "Autobiographical Confession," Fuchs also writes of Grass's autobiographical confession as a speech act that he felt compelled to complete.

80. Mitscherlich and Mitscherlich, *Inability to Mourn*, 20.

81. Widmann, "Unser Wegweiser," 3.

82. Taberner, "Private Failings."

83. Vogel, "Literaturskandale," 35. Rebecca Braun reads the autobiography as "perhaps Grass's greatest ethical achievement yet" because it undermines the idea that one can provide a

However, my purpose in the end is not to weigh in on Grass's worthiness as a person, or as a political or public figure, or even as a politically engaged author—an undertaking that has been complicated yet again by his controversial "poem" condemning Israel's nuclear policy.[84] Rather, I contend that the continuities in his fictional and nonfictional writing over time indicate an ongoing engagement with the poetics of the relationship between guilt and narrative. Through decades, his fiction has captured the modern dilemma of desiring and believing in the performative power of language and the narratives that use it, while simultaneously mistrusting them and being aware of their many modes of failure. It depicts the shadowy grip of habitual language, the teller's eternal temptation to deflect attention from his faults and weaknesses by focusing attention on someone else, and the impossibility of telling a story that ends. And yet Grass's writings continue to evince a great faith in— or, at the least, hope for—the power of stories to achieve great perlocutionary effects: to transform their tellers, affect their audiences, and change the world. Whatever else his controversial poem may do, it expresses this faith; as did his publication of *Peeling the Onion;* as did his Nobel Prize lecture, which held out hope for literature as the realm that might undermine the "new dogmatism" of capitalism. "Our common novel must be continued" [Schließlich muss unser aller Roman fortgesetzt werden], he writes. As the speech's title insists, one thing is always predictable in human language and stories: they are "To Be Continued . . ." [Fortsetzung folgt . . .].[85]

---

single, truthful account of one's self. "Ethics of Autobiography," 1065–66. She thus reads Grass as rejecting a strongly narrativist paradigm.

84. Grass, "Was gesagt werden muss," or, in English translation, "What Must Be Said." The poem sparked a controversy in the media and the public sphere, and has been heavily criticized by academic audiences, as well, as in a panel titled "What Has to Be Said about Günter Grass" at the German Studies Association annual conference in Milwaukee, Wisconsin, in October 2012.

85. Grass, "Fortsetzung folgt." Translation at Grass, "To Be Continued."

My Mother, My Self

Language and (Dis)Identification in Postwar Mother Books

> A change in meaning is, essentially, always a reevaluation: the transposition
> of some particular word from one evaluative context to another.
> —V. N. Voloshinov, *Marxism and the Philosophy of Language*

or many people, parents are the first and most important interlocutors in the "web of interlocutions" that, as Taylor argues, initiate individuals into the "language[s] of moral and spiritual discernment" grounding their identity.[1] It should come as no surprise, then, that the attempt to define one's own moral language and identity often entails reckoning with the moral languages of one's parents. David Parker suggests that Taylor's concept of identity is particularly useful for understanding the dynamics of intergenerational auto/biography, in which narrators seek to understand themselves by telling the story of a parent or other influential family figure. In this chapter, I explore texts along the continuum between fictional dynamic observer narrative and intergenerational auto/biography to explore the operation and boundaries of each, and to highlight again the rhetorical function of the ideal narrative audience. Traditional autobiography often thematizes personal development, and narration *about* a younger, more naïve self is a common feature of the genre. Narration *by* a staged younger self with a different interpretive framework represents a step away from such traditional life-writing. Essentially, such narration takes a step along the continuum of fictionaliza-

---

1. Taylor, *Sources of the Self,* 36, 35.

tion. Whereas authorial, narrative, and ideal narrative audiences coincide in traditional autobiography, an author who stages narration by a younger incarnation of herself communicates indirectly with readers about that former self: she employs an unreliable character narrator. This narrator and her ideal narrative audience know less (or think differently) than the implied author does. To at least some degree, the aim of the book thus fictionalized is to reflect on, question, or expose the interpretive framework that the fictionalized narrator and her ideal narrative audience share. The fictionalized texts discussed in this chapter operate in this way.

Parker maintains that classic modern examples of intergenerational auto/biographies, such as Edmund Gosse's *Father and Son* (1907), often document the narrator's attempt to establish autonomy from the parent, but that since about 1980, this drive has often been complicated by a desire for relationality. Rather than simply declaring themselves free of their parents, the narrators of such works "discover significant sources of self in parents and grandparents" and attempt to unearth and preserve the (often overlooked) values these figures represent.[2] This wave of auto/biographies tends to illuminate forebears who would otherwise remain obscure; Parker takes as his illustrative example Carolyn Steedman's *Landscape for a Good Woman* (1986), which reckons with her mother's experience as a working-class woman and with its legacy for Steedman's own self-understanding. For such writers, the moral frameworks of the past are no longer simply encumbrances to be jettisoned. Tension arises as they seek to salvage some building blocks for the moral framework of the present.

Within autobiography studies, the move to broaden the definition of autobiography to include what Paul John Eakin calls "relational autobiography" also takes women's life-writing and feminist autobiography studies, which emphasize the relationality of women's life-writing, as its point of departure.[3] In fact, this feminist intervention in autobiography studies took place during the same era that Parker pinpoints as the turning point in intergenerational autobiography.[4] Given this wave of concern, it would hardly seem surprising for contemporaneous German-language life-writing about mothers to show a similar pattern. In the postwar German context, however, such an approach *is* surprising, since it has been generally assumed that there can be no desire to recognize a "source of the self" in National Socialism. Reading relational German-language "mother books" that broadly span this era thus suggests

---

2. Parker, "Narratives of Autonomy," 141–42.

3. Eakin, *Lives Become Stories.* See also Miller, "Representing Others."

4. See, for instance, Mary G. Mason, "Other Voice"; Stanton, "Autogynography"; Susan Stanford Friedman, "Women's Autobiographical Selves."

the need for a new understanding of the landscape of postwar German cultural memory and literary history. In addition, reading these books within the context of the tradition of dynamic observer narrative calls for a reevaluation of second-wave feminism's quest for relationality and the recovery of lost and oppressed female voices. As they excavated and liberated these voices, feminists took the crucial step of making this work explicit and of bringing the operation of moral languages to consciousness. Still, the dynamic observer narrative tradition shows that the effort to do justice to others by making their voices heard was not entirely new. The women in the relational autobiographies of the 1980s are the descendants of John and Hanna Glückstadt and Valentine Schaumann. New narrative strategies, such as extensive metanarration and prominent discourse markers, bring this effort to the forefront of attention and make it explicit. But those "lost" voices had long been sought in dynamic observer narratives.

Life-Writing in Postwar Germany

While I have already discussed the dynamic observer narrative at length, my argument about the significance of mother books in postwar German-language life-writing requires some contextualization. In the 1970s and early 1980s, intergenerational writing in German-speaking Europe was associated with the "New Subjectivity," a movement in which writers emphasized interiority and self-reflection in often autobiographical explorations. This movement is usually understood as a resigned retreat from the political and social protest movements that rocked Germany in the late 1960s and early 1970s, and from the politically engaged literature that accompanied them. In these protest movements, young adults of the first postwar generation had begun to confront their parents' generation for its complicity with National Socialism. The confrontations occurred both in the public sphere, with challenges to those who retained positions of public influence despite their past National Socialist associations, and in the private sphere, with parents as the primary targets. Indeed, the protesters insisted that these two spheres were linked—that the social and authority structures that produced National Socialism in the political realm were the same as those that warped families and individuals in the home. The "New Subjectivity," too, while it has the reputation of apolitical resignation, conducts its self-examinations with the understanding that personal identity and experience cannot be divorced from political and social issues. Two currents of writing within New Subjectivity reckoned with parents' influence on their children's character, self-understanding, and moral language. Feminist self-exploration and redefinition required a confrontation with mothers' conceptions of female identity, as in Gabriele Wohmann's *An Outing with My Mother* (1976) [*Ausflug mit der Mutter*] and Katja Behrens's *The Thirteenth Fairy* (1983) [*Die dreizehnte Fee*]. Continuing the central concern of the 68er movement, the genre known as *Väterliteratur* [father literature] investigated fathers' culpability for both the crimes of National Socialism and the painful deformation of the postwar German family.

These mother accounts and father books share many points of contact. Both present themselves as largely autobiographical and deal with parents of the war generation, including their experiences during National Socialism. Both attempt to deal with the moral and linguistic legacies that the authors have inherited from their parents. Both feature children who narrate about their parents' lives to try to cement what Taylor calls an "epistemic gain," or what I term a critical break: "a move to a new way of looking at things, a new understanding of the good."[5] The feminist daughters, like the children of former Nazis, declare their opposition to their parents' moral languages and struggle to loosen the hold those languages still exert on them. And yet, these two strands of personal and social introspection remained quite separate—or, at least, literary criticism has considered them separately and has read them through very different theoretical frameworks: feminist theory on the one hand, and discourses of *Vergangenheitsbewältigung* on the other. In this regard, the texts (or the scholarship) reproduce the dynamics of the activist movements of the 1960s, where feminist activism remained mostly distinct from antifascist, antiauthoritarian activism,[6] or, at least, where feminists received very little support from the "politically oriented" movement.[7] Similarly, feminist accounts of women's narratives have been read as treating a special phenomenon, while the generalized story of generational writing in this era has been told as a story of sons and daughters who write about their fathers and their fathers' ties to National Socialism to separate themselves absolutely from their parents.[8] Compared to English-language generational

---

5. Parker, "Narratives of Autonomy," 148; Taylor, *Sources of the Self*, 73–75.

6. Susanne Maurer argues in "Gespaltenes Gedächtnis?" that historiography about the period reproduces this division, too. The famous incident in which a tomato was thrown at the male student leaders unwilling to discuss discrimination against women, for instance, is frequently invoked as a founding moment of the feminist movement, but almost never as an important indicator of student movement politics.

7. Altbach, "New German Women's Movement," 455. On the Swiss context, see Kunz, "Rebellion zur Emanzipation," 283.

8. Two influential accounts have been Michael Schneider's "Fathers and Sons, Retrospectively," and, in the United States, Ernestine Schlant's *Language of Silence*, 80–98. Mathias Brandstädter's recent, more differentiated (but as yet little recognized) *Folgeschäden* uses a corpus approach to establish the "simultaneity of different *Väterliteraturen*."

auto/biography, which saw a shift toward an affirmation of relativity in the 1980s, the German-language generational writing appears to follow a postwar *Sonderweg* [special path].[9] Or so the story has gone.

This chapter challenges this characterization. The seeming disparity between the English-language and German-language writing results from slippage between discussions of "fathers" and discussions of "parents." It arises because the story of the fathers has eclipsed the story of the mothers to become the story of the parents' generation as a whole.[10] Even Matthias Brandstädter's important, corpus-based effort to reconstruct the differences within father literature elides the gender differences that affect the texts' view of history, the ethical value of narrative identity that they assume, and the way others read these accounts of history and identity.[11] By reading mother narratives against the backdrop of *Vergangenheitsbewältigung*, I provide an alternative picture of postwar generational writing and its efforts to articulate a new moral language and orientation. For all their similarities with "canonical" *Väterliteratur*, these mother books cannot simply be subsumed into existing paradigms under a new, gender-neutral rubric. The mothers are not like the cold and culpable fathers of paradigmatic *Väterliteratur*, and they also differ from each other. Moreover, the narrators' efforts at self-positioning are complicated by a range of emotional, psychological, and ethical factors that make a simple distancing not only impossible but also undesirable.[12] Their narratives are openly relational.

In this chapter I track the movement of language between mother and child in three mother books to complicate and enrich the story of generational self-positioning that has been constructed on the basis of *Väterliteratur*. Rather than reading the narrators' critique of their parents' language as a complete rejection lacking in self-reflexivity, as the father books have often been read,[13] I argue that the mother books show the narrators' struggle to

---

9. The historiographical theory of the German *Sonderweg* posits National Socialism as the product of Germany's insufficient development of liberal values in the nineteenth and early twentieth centuries.

10. Such generalizations elide other differences, as well. The story of the "war generation" told here is actually the story of National Socialist sympathizers, or at least of passive witnesses. For a critique of such generation-based generalizations, see Weigel, "Generation."

11. While he refers nearly exclusively to fathers and often mentions "father-son conflicts," his corpus includes a number of books about mothers, a fact that he never mentions. For a list of the corpus, see Brandstädter, *Folgeschäden*, 104–14.

12. For a similar reading of postwar books *by* women, see Schaumann, *Memory Matters*, 145–54.

13. Schlant, *Language of Silence*, 92–94. Hinrich Seeba distinguishes between the father texts' degree of linguistic self-awareness but finds that the majority show little. Seeba, "Erfundene Vergangenheit," 181.

reckon with the persistent language of the past that they find in themselves. As in Grass's texts, narrative strategies highlight language as an often ambivalent cultural, social, and historical force that can undermine the critical break with the past. Here, too, narrative clearly possesses—or is hoped to possess— a performative force. Unlike in Grass, however, the question of if and how another person's story ought to be told moves to the center in these texts. Grass's narrative strategies draw attention to the consequences that telling someone else's story has for *self*-identity. These books openly question what that story does for or to the other person. Mahlke remains a blank slate. These mothers do not.

Isolated studies have taken a political approach to representations of war-generation mothers. Erin McGlothlin examines the mothers who appear in *Väterliteratur,* and others have discussed Peter Handke's treatment of the National Socialist era in *Sorrow.*[14] Caroline Schaumann's book on women's accounts of the Nazi era considers some texts about mothers, but these were all composed after the reunification of Germany in 1990. No study has investigated the body of texts that constitute a *Mütterliteratur* [mother literature] counterpart to the *Väterliteratur* of the 1970s and 1980s. Nor do I have the space to examine them all here, or to account for all the gender dynamics that influence their representations. In this study, I focus on the impact the parent's gender has on the representations, largely bracketing the writing child's. My text selection relies on three criteria. First, the books I consider must all be dynamic observer narratives, where the story of the mother takes center stage. Second, National Socialism must figure as an important episode in the story of the mother's life and moral language. Finally, I focus on texts where a negotiation with the mother's historical language, or voice, features prominently.[15] While Anne Fuchs celebrates the autobiographical writing of this era for its effort to "restore the notion of individual historical agency and responsibility" rather than to foreground "the analysis of the social and linguistic structures that precede individual agency,"[16] I argue that the authors' efforts to excavate the linguistic detritus of the past is part of the project of taking responsibility for it. Three examples of *Mütterliteratur* from the 1970s to the early 1990s ground this claim and show a continuity of concerns from the

14. McGlothlin, *Second-Generation Holocaust Literature;* Barry, "Nazi Signs"; Schindler, "Nationalsozialismus als Bruch"; Parry, "Vorzügen einer Fiktionalisierung."

15. Other texts that belong to the larger body of mother literature include Helga Novak's *Die Eisheiligen,* Barbara Bronnen's *Die Tochter,* Behrens's *Die dreizehnte Fee,* Christa Wolf's *Kindheitsmuster* [*A Model Childhood*], Karin Struck's *Die Mutter,* Wohmann's *Ausflug mit der Mutter,* and Hans Frick's *Die blaue Stunde.* Wolf's is the only one of these to have appeared in translation.

16. Fuchs, "Generation and Masculinity," 63.

early aftermath of the student movement to the first years after the fall of the Berlin Wall: Handke's *A Sorrow beyond Dreams* (1972), Stefan's *It Was a Rich Life: Report on My Mother's Dying* (1993), and Ortheil's *Hedge* (1983).

Whose Words Are They? Handke and Stefan

I begin with *Rich Life* and *Sorrow,* which represent the nonfictional to "less fictional" end of the spectrum, respectively. Together, they also illuminate the boundaries of the dynamic observer narrator form. Although the maternal biographies they relate are strikingly similar, their different relationships to the dynamic observer form are immediately evident. In *Rich Life* the first five paragraphs present the instability of the mother's looming death; in *Sorrow* the first instability introduced is that of the son's conflicted attitudes toward writing about his mother and her death. These contrasting narrative launches accurately signal the difference in form: *Rich Life* is not a dynamic observer narration, but *Sorrow* is. In *Rich Life* both the conflict between mother and daughter and the daughter's attempt at narrative reckoning lie in the past. The story of that narrative reckoning and of the relationship it yields appears only in the epilogue, the events of which precede the composition of the book the reader has just completed. Stefan's book is actually a memoir *of* a dynamic observer narration, in which authorial, narrative, and ideal narrative audiences coincide. In this coincidence, it is conventionally nonfictional. Handke's dynamic observer narrative troubles the waters of both the internal textual and the authorial-readerly relations. Although his narrator has negotiated the linguistic boundaries between himself and his mother, their relationship remains unstable in the present-tense narrative track, and the past-tense narrative constitutes the narrator's effort to resolve it. The authorial-readerly relationships are variable. In some places, as in the passage relating the mother's life during National Socialism, author and narrator, and authorial, narrative, and ideal narrative audiences, appear to merge. In many of the self-reflexive or highly stylized passages, on the other hand, the artistic detachment suggests an implied author with a more sovereign view of the situation than the narrator seems to have. At such moments, as in the book's conclusion, the implied author offers a distanced, somewhat critical view of the narrator and those like him, the ideal narrative audience for whom he writes.

Although my introduction to these texts highlights their differences, most of the remaining discussion focuses on their similarities. First, they relate parallel biographies. Young women, oppressed by provincial life and its traditional gender roles (in Austria and Switzerland, respectively), reach adulthood during National Socialism and briefly break out. They marry and move to Germany and the city. After the war, both return to their home-towns, wither under the deadening physical and emotional demands of a traditional domestic routine, and suffer long, painful declines and deaths. As their children tell these stories from Germany, where they have established independent lives, their concern with language leaps from the page. Typo-graphical conventions—all uppercase words in Handke and italics in Ste-fan—highlight words and phrases throughout the books, generally marking bits of the mothers' free indirect speech. I argue that these marked phrases register the tension between the desire for both autonomy and relationality *vis-à-vis* the mother that drives the two accounts. Such phrases appear in many generational accounts of this era, including the *Väterliteratur,* and they tend to mark language that expresses deeply ingrained patterns of thought and belief, whether individual or social.[17] Often, in fact, it is difficult to tell whether the speech emanates from the main "relational" figure, or that fig-ure's spouse, or some unnamed person in the social environment. Such usage reflects the contemporaneous, burgeoning focus on language now often referred to as the linguistic turn. In Handke and Stefan, the language that appears in this form is to be understood as formulaic and, often, clichéd.[18] The phrases have been repeated so many times by so many people that they have become fossilized and representative of those who voice it, rather than communicative; Stefan calls them "preserves" [Konserve (60, 62)]. As in *Cat and Mouse,* such formulaic language resembles Bakhtin's authoritative dis-course, which "enters our verbal consciousness as a compact and indivisible mass. . . . Authoritative discourse cannot be represented—it is only transmit-ted . . . [as] a dead quotation."[19]

In both mother and father books, the society that the children wish to reject is crystallized in these "compact and indivisible" expressions, and the fossilized phrases help the narrators put distance between themselves and their parents, as the fused phrases help *Cat and Mouse's* Pilenz parody National Socialist rhetoric.[20] Christoph Meckel, for instance, highlights his

---

17. For instance, Peter Henisch, *Die kleine Figur meines Vaters;* Christoph Meckel, *Suchbild: über meinen Vater;* Wohmann, *Ausflug mit der Mutter;* Elisabeth Plessen, *Mitteilung an den Adel;* Helga Novak, *Die Eisheiligen.*

18. Many Handke commentators characterize it in this way. See Norberg, "Economy of the Phrase"; Nancy A. Kaiser, "Identity and Relationship," 49; Stoffel, "Antithesen," 43–44; Rey, "Provokation durch den Tod," 299; Zorach, "Freedom and Remembrance"; Varsava, "Auto-Bio-Graphy," 131.

19. Bakhtin, *Dialogic Imagination,* 343–44.

20. See also Norberg, "Economy of the Phrase"; Rey, "Provokation durch den Tod," 299.

·

dissociation from his father's National Socialist ideology when he notes that his father's house was built in the "ARYAN BUILDING STYLE mandated d uring the Third Reich" [im Dritten Reich vorgeschriebenen ARISCHEN BAU- WEISE] and describes his father's attitude toward the German occupation of Eastern Europe: "we were NOT MONSTERS and showed understanding" [man war KEIN UNMENSCH und brachte Verständnis auf].[21] Handke seethes against the way his mother accepts and makes light of her poverty and homebound drudgery, as in her cozy designations of the outdated household tools that make her a slave as she makes do: "the GOOD OLD washboard, the COZY hearth, the often-mended FUNNY cooking pots, the DANGER- OUS poker, the STURDY wheelbarrow" (41–42) [die BEHÄBIGE Waschrum- pel, der GEMÜTLICHE Feuerherd, die an allen Ecken geflickten LUSTIGEN Kochtöpfe, der GEFÄHRLICHE Schürhaken, der KECKE Leiterwagen (64)].[22] Stefan rejects her mother's self-blame for her husband's lack of interest in her and her conclusion that she must simply *"wait for it more patiently and hum- bly"* [*geduldiger und demütiger darauf warten* (51)]. The content of Meckel's phrases is "political," Handke's and Stefan's "domestic," but all three narrators mark their parents' language to separate themselves from the ideology and values that it expresses. Nor are these values unrelated. As Claudia Koonz has shown, the domestic whitewashing of millions of women provided National Socialism's venom and violence with a veneer of domestic stabili- ty.[23] Analyses that read Handke's text without the backdrop of *Väterliteratur* do not capture the full scope of the social function these phrases perform.

Ernestine Schlant and Hinrich Seeba charge that the narrators of the *Väterliteratur* fail to recognize their continuing entanglement in their par- ents' language.[24] In Handke and Stefan, however, the fossilized phrases fulfill a dual role: they signal not only the narrators' efforts to distance themselves from this language but also their awareness that they cannot escape it. The narrators do not present these phrases in direct quotations. Rather, they weave them into the text as free indirect speech, using typographical con- ventions to designate it as a foreign object within the narrative stream that surrounds it. In so doing, they present it as embedded within their own nar- ration and stories. The typographical conventions allow them to characterize themselves as individuals who find themselves reliant on this language that they would like to see pass away. Marked phrases that emanate from the nar- rators highlight this entanglement. Stefan, for instance, uses the italics of the

---

21. Meckel, *Suchbild: Über meinen Vater*, 28, 68.

22. Manheim's translation amended slightly.

23. Koonz, *Mothers in the Fatherland*.

24. Schlant, *Language of Silence*, 92–94; Seeba, "Erfundene Vergangenheit," 181.

fossilized phrase to acknowledge that the language she shares with her generation is just as ritualized as her mother's. Describing her youthful rebellion against her parents' norms, she recalls the idolized screen stars and fashions of her teen years and concludes, "Otherwise, everything important is *high* and *hip, flower* and also already *power.* Anything that counts can be said only in English, and only in the loudest-colored pens" [ansonsten ist alles, was wichtig ist, *high* und *hip, flower* und auch schon *power.* Was zählt, läßt sich nur auf englisch sagen und nur in den grellsten Filzstiftfarben (56)]. The "loud" colors of her imagery "highlight" the terms just as the italics do in the text. By occasionally using fossilized phrases to represent their own speech and viewpoint, the narrators show themselves to be self-critical and aware of their own attachment to the traditions and conventions propagated through language.

It is likely that these phrases fulfill such a dual function in some of the more self-reflexive father books, as well. But they have a second, fundamentally different function in these two mother texts, because the mothers possess a fundamentally different relationship to language. The narrators of *Väterliteratur* can take the domineering fathers' voices for granted; breaking free of them demands a vociferous rejection and declaration of autonomy. The mothers in Handke and Stefan, on the other hand, do not speak for themselves. They aren't heard in tape-recorded monologues, as in Peter Henisch's *Negatives of My Father* [*Die kleine Figur meines Vaters*]. They don't speak through journal entries, as in Meckel's father account. Instead, they are nearly speechless—except when their voices echo in these dead phrases.[25] The narrators of these fictionalized autobiographies approach their mothers' voices like much feminist life-writing of the 1970s and 1980s did, trying to reclaim the silenced voices of the oppressed.[26] Yet, they have access to their mothers' voices only through fossilized clichés, a circumstance that heightens their awareness of the social and cultural conditions inflecting her voice. Moreover, their need to reconstruct the mothers' silenced voices encourages them to reflect on the relationship between those lost voices and their own. They reflect on the writer's difficulty in resurrecting such a voice, and the child's difficulty with the mother's alternating speechlessness and clichéd utterances. As Katharina Aulls writes, "A trend becomes visible to respect the

---

25. In their speechlessness, they seem to resemble the storyless mothers in Hartwig, "Geschichtslosigkeit der Mütter." Yet the narrators' efforts to find a voice and a story belie an understanding of mothers that equates a life in the domestic sphere with an unstoried one, as she does.

26. See Smith and Watson, *Reading Autobiography,* 84–85.

'mother's' voice and to trace the maternal discourse in the texts."[27] These narrators cannot be glib about representing their mothers' voices. Perhaps it is the mothers' very silence that encourages the "linguistic sensibility" that the fathers' thundering seems to repel.[28]

Both texts emphasize this silence, returning to it again and again. As an adult woman and mother, the mother in Handke's text is isolated by her lack of speech. She lacks a language that would allow her to talk with her husband, so their communication is limited to "gestures, involuntary mimicry, and embarrassed sexual intercourse" (27) [unwillkürliche Mimik, Gestik und verlegenen Geschlechtsverkehr (43)] and, later, mute physical abuse (37). Her society—provincial, respectably poor, and patriarchal—does not allow her to speak about herself, except in confession; women can be silent, or, if they go a little crazy, they can scream (33–34). In the end, in her profound depression, she can no longer speak at all (54). Accordingly, instances of her direct speech are few. A rare example allows readers to "hear" her report on her inability to talk to others: "I talk to myself, because I can't say anything to other people anymore" (59) [Ich rede mit mir selber, weil ich sonst keinem Menschen mehr etwas sagen kann (88)]. Stefan's mother struggles to speak,[29] and when she does, no one wants to hear what she has to say; her husband, for instance, doesn't want to listen to her feelings of uselessness, of unfulfilled exhaustion, of frustrated longing (50). To be able to speak of her life, she writes voluminous journals, and, as she grows older, she is dogged by the urgent need to bring "order" to her scribblings, jottings, and sketches. But this attempt fails, so that her journals become a symbol of the inadequacy and futility of her life as a whole: "Order plagues her, a derisive grimace. *You've failed, you've made nothing of your life, too weak, too weak, only cooked and forever scribbled your notebooks full of boring nonsense*" [Ordnung plagt sie, eine höhnische Fratze. *Du hast es nicht geschafft, du hast nichts aus deinem Leben gemacht, zu schwach, zu schwach, nur gekocht und ewig deine Hefte vollgekritzelt mit langweiligem Zeug* (31)]. Consumed by the labor of maintaining a house, a family, bodies that need food and clothes, she has been unable to construct a coherent, sustained narrative of her life. The value she attributes to this elusive narrative, its potential to grant her life meaning, resonates with narrativist approaches that see narrative as the ground of individual identity and ethical status.[30]

Stefan's narrator explicitly links her mother's struggles with language and

---

27. Aulls, *Verbunden und gebunden*, 238.

28. Seeba reads such linguistic sensibility as a marker of quality in the father books. "Erfundene Vergangenheit," 181.

29. For examples, see 46, 145–46.

30. See the discussion in chapter 1.

narrative to contemporary feminist theory. Remembering her first feminist gatherings, she recalls that transformation began "because each woman could hear her own voice. . . . Each had the experience that her voice counted, that her words were worth something, that others were listening" [weil jede ihre eigene Stimme hören konnte. . . . Jede konnte erfahren, daß ihre Stimme zählte, daß ihr Wort etwas galt, daß andere zuhörten (60)]. She represents the effort to forge an adult relationship with her mother as an effort to find a common language. Unable to talk about babies and diapers, the childless daughter and her mother enter uncharted and uncertain, but open, interpersonal and linguistic territory: "The undiscussed space between them remains discussable. What has gone unarticulated is entirely unprocessed; it can be shaped. It can succeed or fail" [Der unbesprochene Raum zwischen ihnen bleibt besprechbar. Das Ungesagte ist vollkommen roh; es ist formbar. Es kann gelingen mißlingen (60, 62)]. Later, mother and daughter linger over the daughter's emerging translation of Adrienne Rich's *The Dream of a Common Language*. Even at the end of her mother's life, when their relationship has become deep and tender, Stefan's narrator anticipates her mother's death as the moment when "broken women's language" [gebrochene Frauensprache (74)] will become unnecessary. These characterizations echo second-wave feminist theory, in which Hélène Cixous, Luce Irigaray, and Julia Kristeva advocated the search for a subversive female language that would oppose the patriarchal hierarchies encoded in existing language and open up a realm of feminine expression and meaning-making.[31] Against the intellectual backdrop of feminism, the mother's sense of failure about her writing itself takes on meaning. Her disjointed, fragmented writing does not satisfy the normative demand for a coherent, linear life-narrative that developed in the context of the male-dominated genre of post-Enlightenment autobiography.[32] She lacks the framework for accepting, let alone celebrating, the "messy," kaleidoscopic *écriture féminine* that her self-narrative might be seen to represent. Handke's account is less explicit in making these links, and the son learns something of his mother through discussions of literature (by males), rather than through a hard-won, shared language. But he clearly presents his mother's speechlessness as a product of her identity as a poor woman in provincial Austrian society.[33]

---

31. Three of the founding texts of this line of thinking were published in the mid-1970s: Cixous's *The Laugh of the Medusa* (1975), Irigaray's *Speculum of the Other Woman* (1974), and Kristeva's *Revolution in Poetic Language* (1974).

32. For an overview of feminist critiques of autobiography as a genre, and of the opposition that has often been posited between life-writing by men and life-writing by women, see Eakin, *Lives Become Stories*, 46–53.

33. See also Schindler, "Nationalsozialismus als Bruch"; Sevin, "Frauenschicksal und Schreibprozeß."

In this feminist context, the fossilized phrases play a different role than they do in the father books. First, the narrators have to use them, repugnant as they are, because to eschew them would be to condemn their mothers to silence yet again. The mothers are almost completely subsumed by the social codes concretized in the phrases; they have no other resource for understanding or expressing their experience.[34] Handke reports, for instance, that when his mother returned to provincial Austria from Berlin, "she took to the native dialect again, though of course only in fun: she was a woman who had been ABROAD" (32) [Sie nahm wieder den heimischen Dialekt an, wenn auch nur spielerisch: eine Frau mit AUSLANDSERFAHRUNG (50)]. In the word "ABROAD," Handke signals his mother's satirical citation of the collective voice suspicious of her foreign experience—but she uses the word, nonetheless, and it is doubtful that this usage is only "in fun." The phrases' double voicing highlights the mothers' dependence on and the children's inflection of historically and ideologically colored language.[35]

Moreover, the mother's experience with her journals in Stefan's book shows that any attempts to construct an account of self outside that language must fail to be heard. The fossilized phrases show that the children, too, rely on it to make the mothers' stories accessible and relevant. Butler's antinarrativist mistrust of life stories derives partly from this necessary reliance: "The 'I' who begins to tell its story can only tell it according to recognizable norms of life narration . . . to the extent that it agrees, from the start, to narrative itself through these norms, it agrees to circuit its narration through an externality, and so to disorient itself in the telling."[36] This tension between individual and group has been seen as inherent to the historical project of representing the lives of "ordinary" women, of simultaneously doing justice to individual experience and making the individual story illustrative of a category of historical experience.[37] Handke's narrator clearly feels this tension and voices a mistrust akin to Butler's.[38] He does not want to make his mother

---

34. In "Freedom and Remembrance," Cecile Zorach sees the tension between ritualized public language and a private idiom as uniting Handke's reflections on his writing with the mother's biography. She reads the mother's final isolation as a result of her entirely abandoning the world of ritualized language that had defined her earlier life. I do not believe she ever escapes that language.

35. On polyvocality, ideology, and language, see Smith and Watson, *Reading Autobiography*, 80–81; Bakhtin, *Dialogic Imagination*, 282.

36. Butler, "Account of Oneself," 33.

37. Booth and Burton, "Critical Feminist Biography." On the tension between the exceptional and the representative in women's biography, see also Miller, "Representing Others," 16.

38. On this tension in Handke's text and its relationship to "classical" narrative style and biographical practice, see Rey, "Provokation durch den Tod," 298; Perry, "Kritik der Biographie."

mere fodder for "[a chain reaction of phrases and sentences like images in a dream], a literary ritual in which an individual life ceases to be anything more than a pretext" (28) [eine Kettenreaktion von Wendungen und Sätzen wie Bilder im Traum, ein Literatur-Ritual, in dem ein individuelles Leben nur noch als Anlaß funktioniert (44)].[39] At the same time, he relies on

> the already available formulations, the linguistic deposit of man's social experience . . . for only with the help of a ready-made public language was it possible to single out from all the irrelevant facts of this life the few that cried out to be made public. (29)[40]

> den bereits verfügbaren Formulierungen, dem gesamtgesellschaftlichen Sprachfundus . . . denn nur in einer nicht-gesuchten öffentlichen Sprache könnte es gelingen, unter all den nichtssagenden Lebensdaten die nach einer Veröffentlichung schreienden herauszufinden. (45)

Such extensive metanarrative commentary goes beyond the suggestions in *Doppelgänger* and *Stuffcake* that the silent oppressed (John, Hanna, and Valentine) should perhaps be able to tell their own stories. It questions how and if linguistic narrative can rescue the mothers as unique individuals from the mute invisibility that doomed them.[41] Handke's and Stefan's narrators use the fossilized phrases to mark their own representational difficulties, and to highlight their mothers' helpless reliance on the social expectations that crushed them.

These phrases also help the narrators protect themselves from the unremitting suffering and speechlessness that threaten to engulf them if they identify too closely with their mothers. In these texts, the mothers' inability to tell their life stories contributes to their vulnerability.[42] Handke's narrator avails himself of the formulae that construct "the orderliness of the usual

---

39. I have altered the parenthetical portion of the translation to fit the syntax of the sentence.

40. Ursula Love seems to suggest that the generalization serves to awaken interest for the mother's story. Love, "Identifizierung und negative Kreativität," 134. Christoph Parry maintains that she appears more as a representative of her generation than as an individual. Parry, "Vorzügen einer Fiktionalisierung," 90.

41. Similarly, Matthias Konzett contends in "Postideological Aesthetics" that Handke rejects the Frankfurt School's claim that the need to tell the story of one's own life amounts to nothing but *Kitsch* (46–47). Or, as one of Stefan's brothers believes, that the mother's desire to tell them her stories is "just a personal cult" (66) [doch nur Personenkult].

42. Cf. Hartwig, "Geschichtslosigkeit der Mütter," 48. Hartwig explains mothers' vulnerability as the result of a subjectivity that relies entirely on a dedication to giving unconditional love, rather than on stories.

biographical pattern" [die Ordentlichkeit eines üblichen Lebenslaufschemas] to escape the "horror" [Schreckensseligkeit] he feels when he identifies with his mother's feelings and speechlessness (31; 48).[43] In her epilogue, which contains the story of the story found in the frame of dynamic observer narratives, Stefan's narrator recounts in hindsight her struggle to work with the mother's desperate journals. She reports that she became physically ill trying to tell her mother's story from her mother's perspective. The breakthrough comes when she speaks with her mother in a dream. "I don't want my diaries to be published," says the mother. "I don't want that either, I answered, I'm eating your texts so that I can reproduce them in my own way" [Ich will nicht, daß meine Tagebücher veröffentlicht werden. Das will ich auch nicht, antwortete ich, ich esse deine Texte, um sie in meiner Form wiedergeben zu können (153)]. The chapter titles, each of which is an anagram of one of the mother's last statements, "It was a rich life" [es ist reich gewesen], are products of that process. Felicity Rash grants these anagrams positive force, claiming that they demonstrate the creativity of language and that, with their roots in the mother's words, they make Stefan's book the mother's book of her life.[44] But in reading them this way, Rash does not account for the desperate need for distance that prompted the narrator to begin this process of digestion and creation in the first place; after all, her life goal has been to escape "the tyranny of female weakness" [die Tyrannei weiblicher Schwäche (55)]. The calcified phrases that stud Stefan's prose are the indigestible remnants of this process. They are traces of the poisonous, debilitating maternal language that she must escape. In Stefan and Handke, the phrases serve a need for distance and autonomy that derives as much from the mother's suffering as from her belonging to a detested moral world.

At the same time, this suffering justifies—even demands—their attempts at reclamation. In these texts, "the project of finding an adequate language in which to articulate what makes the forbear worthy of attention is often closely related to the project of rearticulating the moral language(s) of this first interlocutor as a constitutive language(s) of self."[45] In other words, these narrators tell their mothers' stories to salvage what is salvageable. Handke's effort is particularly visible in the last several pages of his account. Here, where he recounts the aftermath of his mother's death, the narrative disintegrates into disjointed paragraphs and sentences; empty lines are all that link one brief statement to the next. Some of these reflect on the narrator's distraught and disoriented state. The others are anecdotes that capture, however

---

43. Manheim's translation slightly altered.
44. Rash, "Stefan Twenty Years On."
45. Parker, "Narratives of Autonomy," 151.

ambivalently, the mother's positive qualities: "The painful memory of her daily motions, especially in the kitchen. . . . When she was angry, she didn't beat the children; at the most, she would wipe their noses violently. . . . She was kindly" (68–69) [Die schmerzliche Erinnerung an sie bei den täglichen Handgriffen, vor allem in der Küche. . . . Im Zorn schlug sie die Kinder nicht, sondern schneuzte ihnen höchstens heftig die Nase. . . . Sie war menschenfreundlich (102, 104)]. The work of salvage is difficult. The memories are painful not only because she is gone, but because they remind the narrator of her enslavement to her domestic duties and of the warmth those duties never quite extinguished. At the same time, the lack of connections between the narrator's self-reflections and his memories of his mother indicate his ongoing inability, or unwillingness, to place himself in relationship to this self-sacrificing woman—a stance that echoes his ambivalence toward writing in the book's opening paragraphs.[46] This resistance contrasts sharply with the warm relationship that Stefan's narrator has achieved with her mother by the time she arrives at a narrative form, and Handke's conspicuous stylization in these pages, which differs markedly from the rest of the book, suggests an authorial distance toward the narrator that Stefan's implied author never assumes. Here, perhaps, Handke the author subtly criticizes his narrator's ideal audience—members of his own generation, his readers—who, as Michael Schneider charges of the postwar generation, refuse to implicate themselves in their parents' lives and who reciprocate the emotional unavailability they indict in their parents.[47]

Such authorial distance is missing when the narrator discusses the mother's experience of National Socialism. This lack of distance is remarkable, because while most postwar intergenerational autobiography has been seen as an attempt to condemn this era, the narrators of Sorrow and Rich Life try to reclaim something from it. In trying to remain faithful to his mother's experience and voice, Handke's narrator describes her life and the political backdrop of these years in largely neutral or positive terms. He often reproduces National Socialist rhetoric, perhaps assuming that it damns itself,[48] or perhaps merely reconstructing his mother's world; the page that reports Austria's annexation and Hitler's subsequent election presents without comment

---

46. The narrator's reluctance to represent himself as an actor in his mother's life manifests itself in other ways, too. Here and elsewhere, he writes of "children," rather than using a personal pronoun that would attach the narrating instance to the child who shared her experience (21, 31).

47. Schneider, "Fathers and Sons, Retrospectively."

48. Schlant's Language of Silence diagnoses and sharply criticizes this approach in the Väterliteratur (92).

what seem to be excerpts from National Socialist propaganda, along with a paragraph of entirely detached reporting (13). At other times, his critical perspective manifests itself. One brief paragraph employs fossilized phrases that signal his ironic stance, then shifts to his own postwar assessment of National Socialist political aesthetics:

> Demonstrations, torchlight parades, mass meetings. Buildings decorated with the new national emblem SALUTED; forests and mountain peaks DECKED THEMSELVES OUT; the historic events were represented to the rural population as a drama of nature. (14)

> Kundgebungen mit Fackelzügen und Feierstunden; die mit neuen Hoheitszeichen versehenen Gebäude bekamen STIRNSEITEN und GRÜSSTEN; die Wälder und die Berggipfel SCHMÜCKTEN SICH; der ländlichen Bevölkerung wurden die geschichtlichen Ereignisse als Naturschauspiel vorgestellt. (23)

In the end, however, he discounts the importance of the politics of National Socialism for his mother's story. Four pages detailing its political and social manifestations end with a long paragraph explaining his mother's lack of interest in politics and her failure to see the events taking place around her within a political framework: they were "something entirely different from politics—a masquerade, a newsreel festival, a secular church fair" (13–14) [alles andere—eine Maskerade, eine UFA-Wochenschau . . . , ein weltlicher Kirchtag (24)]. In saying that "politics" has nothing to do with "reality" for his mother, he exculpates her and patronizes her at the same time; she is incapable of understanding independently what is behind the empty words and symbols she has learned in school. The empty lines that follow this paragraph emphasize that the discussion of the mother's relationship to National Socialist politics is over.

Then, abruptly, the next sentence describes the National Socialist era as a release from the isolation, need, and narrow horizons that deformed the rest of his mother's life: "That period helped my mother to come out of her shell and become independent" (15) [Diese Zeit half meiner Mutter, aus sich herauszugehen und selbständig zu werden (25)]. Stephen Schindler calls this depiction a "scandal" for its misrepresentation of the realities of misogynist National Socialism,[49] but it also shifts the significance of the era away from the political: the paragraph goes on to trace this independence in

---

49. Schindler, "Nationalsozialismus als Bruch," 41.

the mother's personal relationships. She loses her fear of men and of physical contact, enjoys a feeling of familial belonging when she writes to her brother at the front, and surrenders to her first and only love. Political and social developments may provide the backdrop, but the real relevance of these years lies in their impact on her self-understanding and the personal relationships it facilitates. So does Handke present it, and so have scholars read it.[50] Such accounts and interpretations betray the blind spot that prevents mother literature from being read with father literature: the political emancipation that triggered the postwar generation's reevaluation of its fathers seems not to have affected its view of its mothers as private, rather than political, actors.[51] Handke's affirming summary sentence, and the shift it enacts between the political and the private realms, signals exactly this discrepancy. National Socialism is passed over as little more than the background condition for individual identity and personal relationships.

Stefan's text holds the mother accountable for her reactions to National Socialism more than Handke's does. The narrator notes the domestic responsibilities that prevented the mother from reflecting on "what is happening around her" [was rings um sie passiert (21)], but also reveals that she knew better. Her sister told her something of what was happening, and she feebly attempted to avoid the Nazi salute and declared herself, as a Swiss, independent of Hitler. Moreover, in the aftermath of the war, having been subjected to slave labor herself, she recognizes that she had deceived herself about the plight of the Jews, "because she hadn't looked closely enough, because she hadn't wanted to see anything" [weil sie nicht genau hingeschaut hat, weil sie nichts sehen wollte (27)]. Rather than turning the story of the war into a story of the mother's personal development and suffering, this account begins and ends its brief narration of the National Socialist years by highlighting what the mother failed to see.

50. Several commentators mention the National Socialist era in passing. See Nancy A. Kaiser, "Identity and Relationship," 50–51; Love, "Identifizierung und negative Kreativität," 133; Stoffel, "Antithesen," 45–46.

51. With the exception of Schindler's account, even those that focus on Handke's representation of National Socialism are colored by these gendered assumptions. Even Barry, who holds the mother responsible for her National Socialist enthusiasm, reads Handke as criticizing "a corrupt patriarchal discourse of the 'fathers,'" without explaining why Handke uses the *mother's* story for this critique. See Barry, "Nazi Signs," 303. Similarly, when Parry claims that Handke's later fiction fulfills the promise of the text's closing sentence to write more clearly later, he implicitly makes the relationship to the father the "real" story at stake. He reads this later fiction as constituting emotional, if not factual, *Väterliteratur;* the "more specific" treatment is not of Handke's mother's life but of the expected generational conflict. In conclusion, Parry claims "that Handke's processing of the fascist past and the representation of his relationship to his *fathers* is an incomplete project, of which *Wunschloses Unglück* is an integral part." Parry, "Vorzügen einer Fiktionalisierung," 99 (my emphasis).

Still, the primary legacy of the war is not guilt at this failure, but a fossilized phrase that the daughter adopts from the mother—the only one she makes her own. Later in her account, the daughter returns to her mother's internment in a cinema basement with hundreds of German women and children at the end of the war, where rape by Russian soldiers was a constant threat. The mother fended them off with a furiously spoken Swiss-German phrase: "*you damned pig!*" [*du verflüemerete Soucheib, du!* (66)]. The phrase appears in the italics of the calcified expression: the words have been repeated so many times so as to become legend. Decades later, her feminist daughter twice repeats these words when she feels threatened in her globe-trotting, independent life: "*you damned pig!*" (66). Five times in the space of a paragraph the daughter repeats this magical phrase, which protects her as it had protected her mother. The one scrap that Stefan can salvage from her mother's language to use in her own life comes from the war (or, at least, its immediate aftermath). In Stefan the era that is the grounds for rejection in the *Väterliteratur* opens a space of possibility. It is a threatened space, certainly: hunger, displacement, and the threat of rape make the war years dark and frightening. But the war also frees the mother from her husband and gives authority. In this one case, she can tell her own story, and others hear and acknowledge it:

> When she told that story, no one dared interrupt her.
> No one said:
>> Nonsense!
>> You're imagining it!
>> You don't understand!
>
> Bei der Geschichte hat niemand gewagt, sie zu unterbrechen.
> Niemand hat gesagt:
>> Unsinn!
>> Das bildest du dir ein!
>> Das verstehst du nicht! (21)

In Stefan the war is the only time when female words matter. What is more, the words that Stefan borrows from the war allow her and her mother to position themselves outside of the logic of perpetration and suffering: they are female words that resist male violence, and "neutral" Swiss-German words that resist the acts of war committed by the Germans and their enemies. Stefan's adoption of her mother's phrase is not a "solution" that *Mütterliteratur* offers to the problem of dealing with the National Socialist past. But it shows that understanding how the children of National Socialism have attempted to extricate themselves from the web of political, social, and gender identity that defined their parents—and how they remain bound to it—requires reading *Mütterliteratur* alongside *Väterliteratur*.

Both Handke's and Stefan's narrators present National Socialism and the war as crucial experiences in their mothers' lives. For both women, this era is filled with self-defining moments in the literal sense: their children see them as having taken control of their own lives and identities during this time. Both children accept—even implicitly celebrate—this self-definition; the mothers' response to National Socialism itself is secondary. This dynamic stands in complete opposition to the indictment of the fathers in the dominant paradigm of *Väterliteratur*. The fathers are seen as responsible for the language and the destruction it causes. Their presumed guilt compels their children to declare complete autonomy from them.[52] In contrast, the mothers are seen as victims of the moral language they speak. Their suffering drives the children to seek distance, for they want to neither contribute to it nor share it. At the same time, the children feel a need to acknowledge and understand this suffering, and, at least in Stefan's case, to reconnect her own life to her mother's.[53] National Socialism and the war do not provide the central thread in Handke's and Stefan's narratives, as they do in the narratives of *Väterliteratur*. Yet neither are they marginal. And the treatment of this period highlights the children's opposing assessments of their parents. The era is the source of the fathers' guilt, but in these mothers' stories, it acquires a positive aura because of the relief from suffering it brings.[54] The postwar generation works against its parents' corrupted moral language in both the father and the mother accounts, only in very different ways: in the father accounts by rejecting the dominant, violent voices that speak it, and in these two mother accounts by giving voice to those whom it silenced. Restoring gendered difference is a crucial part of telling a complete story of postwar generational relations.[55]

A Worthy, Wordy Forbear: Ortheil

In contrast to many other mother books, Ortheil's *Hedge* has been read almost solely within the context of *Väterliteratur*. Ortheil invites such a read-

---

52. Brandstädter calls this the "amputation paradigm." *Folgeschäden*, 124–30.

53. Brandstädter's "(re)construction and integration paradigm." Ibid., 131–36.

54. Parry highlights the way Maria Handke's suffering leads Handke to absolve her of historical responsibility. Parry, "Vorzügen einer Fiktionalisierung," 90–92.

55. There is more work to be done here. The effects of the gendered dynamics of mother-son and mother-daughter relationships on mother representations remain to be examined.

ing because, like the authors of the *Väterliteratur,* he zeroes in on the political and historical aspects of his mother's existence, portraying her not only as affected by them but also as a political actor. In addition, as all of the secondary literature notes, the dynamics of the narrator's relationship to his mother mirror those of the relationships between children and fathers in the *Väterliteratur.* The narrator tells the story of his mother's life in order to distance himself from her and from the language and mode of narration that she and her generation use to forget and obfuscate the National Socialist past. However, the linguistic and narrative self-reflection that permeate *Hedge* prompt Schlant and Helmut Schmitz to see Ortheil as having moved past the simple, judgmental stance of "classic" *Väterliteratur.* In terms that implicitly affirm the goal of using narrative to temporarily assume a foreign point of view,[56] they applaud Ortheil's quest to understand his mother's "experiential viewpoint" "on [her own] terms," and see his work as making "an exemplary contribution to a true *Vergangenheitsbewältigung.*"[57]

Hedge is a paradigmatic dynamic observer narrative and, despite its autobiographical basis, overtly fictionalized. In the texts of this chapter, then, fictionality is associated with dynamicism and life-writing with resolved memoir, although this association is not necessary. Authors willing to present themselves in the process of a writing that has not resolved instability (or cannot resolve it) can produce dynamic nonfiction.[58] *Hedge*'s opening paratexts mark its fictionality from the start: like many novellas, it declares itself a "narrative" [*Erzählung*], and it is dedicated to Mia, a figure who does not exist in the narrative world. Unlike the narrators of *Sorrow* and *Rich Life,* the narrator has negotiated a satisfactory relationship neither with his mother nor with her language; this process takes place only as he investigates and writes her story. That story, too, differs dramatically from those of the mothers in Handke and Stefan. As the daughter of a successful businessman, Katharina goes away to a boarding school and returns to her village full of self-confidence and curiosity about the wider world. She becomes church librarian, holding a recognized position in her community. When she refuses to cooperate with National Socialist control of the library, she is arrested and then loses her position. Years of increasing dissatisfaction with her life and desperation about the political situation follow, yet she becomes fascinated with the first young man of her acquaintance to join the SA. After a courtship

---

56. See the discussion of a literary "new ethics" in chapter 1.

57. Schmitz, "Family, Heritage," 74; Schlant, *Language of Silence,* 100; Aurenche, "L'assimilation du passé Nazi," 50.

58. Examples might be Joan Didion's *Year of Magical Thinking* (2005) and *Blue Nights* (2011), particularly the latter.

consisting largely of mutual attempts to change each other's political attitudes, she agrees to marry him when he shields her brother's induction to the priesthood from SA interference. Her family accepts this match readily, since it leads her to abandon her plan to study at the university, which they see as unfitting for a young woman. She moves with him to Berlin, where, for a short time, she revels in the freedom and variety the city offers. Soon, however, the war begins, and her primary experience of the city changes from excitement to fear. This fear is borne out when the terror of a bombing raid results in the stillbirth of her first son, and when she becomes pregnant again, her husband consents to her return to their village. A second son is born there, but this son is lost, too, a victim of the final moments of the war. The narrator, the third son, is born some years later and remains the couple's only child.

The narrator knows little of this story at the beginning, and his drive for an autonomous understanding of history, his mother, and himself provide the impetus for his investigation into her life. Like the narrators of the *Väterliteratur,* he must battle against his parent's dominant, mesmerizing voice to construct this account. Katharina has read a great deal, and she has a fluent, literate storytelling style that reassures her listeners: "her listeners feel secure, no matter how terrible the things she is reporting" [man fühlt sich geborgen, mag sie von noch so entsetzlichen Dingen berichten (24)]. Her stories appear inevitable and natural, and they never vary: "She will use the same words, mention the same details, keep the same evaluations. A story has an inviolate place in her memory" [Sie wird dieselben Worte benutzen, dieselben Details erwähnen, dieselben Wertungen beibehalten. Eine Geschichte hat in ihrer Erinnerung einen unumstößlichen Platz (24, 20)]. She participates in the same ritualized provincial language as the mothers of Handke and Stefan, and as the other people in her village: prejudice, stereotype, and an unwillingness to think or to empathize predetermine their stories (126–29). Yet Katharina is not erased or silenced by this language. On the contrary, she is an inexhaustible speaker and dominates her "conversations" (20). Moreover, she uses her stories to forget and erase the past, much like the fathers do; the narrator maintains that she "forgets by telling stories; but it is only by telling stories that she controls her forgetting" [vergißt, indem sie erzählt; aber nur indem sie erzählt, beherrscht sie ihr Vergessen (23)]. At the end of her stories, nothing of substance remains. They are comfortable, spellbinding performances that permit the kind of repression the postwar generation loathes.

Within this scheme, it is predictable that the narrator writes to counteract her repression of the past. He resists the position of "naïve listener" whose passive listening slowly immerses him in "the dreamy wave of forgetting" [einfältiger Zuhörer; die träumerische Woge des Vergessens (51)]. While his mother is on vacation, he interviews her friends and relatives and reads her old letters to reconstruct the story of what befell her during National Socialism. Here, too, the structure of the narrative largely reproduces the tropes of *Väterliteratur*. Her directly quoted letters appear to let her speak for herself.[59] The narrator reports having been enthralled by his mother's stories and language as a child and having achieved self-confidence by emulating her: "since language belonged to me, so did the world" [indem mir die Sprache gehörte, gehörte mir die Welt (24–26)]. The magic of his mother's language gives her an aura and a power much like that Meckel's father had for his young son, and it lasts from the moment she initiates him into the magical world of letters until the moment when a critical outside voice suddenly voids the power of his own "magic spells" [Zaubersprüche] and he realizes the emptiness of the ritualized incantations he has been mimicking (18, 26).

Following this disillusionment, the narrator goes through the same phases of relationship to his mother that marks the 68ers' relationship with their parents. First, as Michael Schneider had diagnosed, he becomes complicit in the silence about the National Socialist era[60] because he wants to dissociate himself from it entirely. He refuses to hear any stories about the past, no matter how innocuous or beautifying they may be. He refuses to see himself as the son, grandson, or descendant of the barbarians who had committed the unspeakable crimes, and he insists that his postwar birthdate grants him the "grace of belated birth" [Gnade der späten Geburt]: "the war—that was the time before I was born, a different time with no relationship and no connection to my experience" [der Krieg—das war die Zeit vor meiner Geburt, eine andere Zeit, die zu dem, was ich erlebte, in keinem Verhältnis und keiner Beziehung stand (37)]. Eventually, he makes the ultimate effort for autonomy, completely severing his relationship with his parents for a number of years. When he reestablishes ties and begins to pursue the story of his mother's past, he struggles to avoid repeating her fossilized stories; a page of his mother's direct speech about her arrest concludes with an ellipsis and the remark, "That's the way my mother tells it, and here I stop, so as not to repeat her stories" [ja, so erzählt meine Mutter, und ich breche hier ab, um ihre Geschichten nicht zu wiederholen (21–22)]. At the end of the book,

---

59. Mauelshagen suggests in *Schatten des Vaters* that the letters, journals, and recordings of the *Väterliteratur* constitute a gesture toward dialogue, allowing the father to "answer" to the child's account of his life (122). While they do allow the father to present his views—and, as Schlant contends, often go uncommented—the textual frames in which they appear clearly delegitimize his viewpoint.

60. Schneider, "Fathers and Sons, Retrospectively," 5–6.

having solved the riddles of his mother's past, he guards his interpretive independence by leaving her home before she returns from vacation. Ortheil's narrative seems to be a father book about a mother, where the son declares absolute autonomy from her self-protective view of the past and the powerful moral language that supports it.

In attempting to achieve autonomy from her voice, however, Ortheil's narrator establishes himself unquestionably as her son. Some father books depict men slowly yielding to the seductive language of National Socialism, but Ortheil's Katharina consistently strains against its pull, just as her son's narrative resists an abhorrent moral language. At first, she is somewhat troubled by her inability to incorporate herself into the jubilant masses. After hearing a triumphant newsreel pronouncement of the people's unity under Hitler, she tells her sister "that she wasn't a part of it, that she hadn't had the right words to belong to it, and, what was worst, that she couldn't even explain why" [daß sie nicht dazugehörte, daß ihr die richtigen Worte gefehlt hatten, um dabeizusein, und daß sie, was vielleicht das Schlimmste war, . . . nicht einmal erklären konnte, warum das so war (83)]. This reflection follows her terrifying arrest and interrogation for refusing to turn over library borrower lists to the SA. As church librarian, she is a recalcitrant guardian of long-term cultural memory who refuses the new regime's attempts to replace it with an instrumentalized collective memory of German identity and nation.[61] Predictably, she is promptly fired. Yet she continues to defend this culture and language under siege. When the list of banned books is published and the new librarian has removed them from the shelves for destruction, she claims that she needs to retrieve some belongings from the library, steals the books, and conceals them in her parents' attic. Each time she moves, she takes the books with her, a traveling repository of a language that she refuses to let the Nazis touch. Finally, she, like her traditional father, finds their language incomprehensible (60–61, 74, 214–15). She refuses to adjust her language to theirs, or, as her insistence on a public celebration of her newly ordained brother's first mass shows, to allow her moral orientation to shift in accordance with their values.

Her resistance to "the watchmen of words and laws" [die Wort- und Gesetzeshüter (245)] eventually assumes more drastic forms. After suffering a stillbirth in Berlin, she returns to her family's rural home, where she eventually gives birth to a healthy son. As he grows and learns to speak, her family realizes that she is initiating him into an idiosyncratic linguistic world

---

61. Jan and Aleida Assmann discuss cultural, collective, and communicative memory in a number of publications. For a brief account, see Assmann and Frevert, *Geschichtsvergessenheit*, 35–52.

separate from the one in which the rest of them live. Ortheil discusses not only the function of this language but also its texture and feel. She invents it to insulate her son from the violence that has irreversibly contaminated German, because "the language that everyone used had become irretrievably ugly, like a spirit of death, and the grumbles of the dying crouched behind each sound" [die Sprache, derer sich alle bedienten, sei für immer häßlich geworden, lemurenähnlich, und hinter jedem Laut hocke das Sterbegeme-cker der Toten (259)]. Morphologically, the language she speaks with him resembles German enriched by a collection of "wild sounds"; it is "strange and seductive," an "incessant singsong" full of "reassuring adages and magi-cal formulas" [wilde Lauten; sonderbar und verführerisch; unaufhörlicher Singsang; beruhigenden Sprüchen und zauberische Formeln (259)]. In the cocoon of this language, mother and son share an intimacy and interdepen-dence that far exceeds the already tight bonds between mother and young child. To protect her son, Katharina summons her resolve, her creativity, and the energy generated by fear to invent a new language. In this act, she could not be farther from the villagers, who spout predictably prejudiced stories; from Handke's and Stefan's mothers, who are imprisoned in traditional cli-chés; or even from her own postwar self, who relies on rehearsed, rote stories to hold the past at bay. Rejecting all of the moral languages that form the web of social life and social identity, she determines to provide her son with an entirely new and independent frame of moral reference.

In the end, however, the language she has invented for her son cannot protect him. As the Americans take control of the area around the farm where the family is staying, he is killed by shrapnel as she holds him in her arms. This devastating death brings about her final and most radical break with the world around her. After a scream "as from the eternal judgment" [wie aus der Ewigkeit des Gerichts (292)]—from outside the realm of human language and morality—she retreats into a silence and an isolation that no one can pen-etrate. She does not choose this state, but it is hard not to see in it a final act of separation from the brutality of life in the world that surrounds her. As the narrator presents it, the story of Katharina's life under National Socialism is a story of her steady dissociation from its language and community.

This pursuit of linguistic and moral autonomy proves fruitless, however.[62] Her son is killed, and the books that she has so assiduously shielded from being burned by the Nazis presumably burn, after all, when her village is

---

62. See also Schlant, *Language of Silence*, 111. She had brought them to Berlin after her marriage, and presumably brought them back to the village with the rest of their household goods as chaos in Berlin grew (225, 265–67). But, in the end, the village burned, too (282).

bombed. Still, tragedy is not language's weakness in the face of violence. Her tragedy is that, in her efforts to create an independent system of meaning, she repeats the abhorrent structural features of National Socialist language. Her suffering had begun with National Socialism's efforts to eradicate all competing moral languages and to provide the only framework for thought and decisions; when she invents a new language for her son, it is to shield him from violence by isolating him from all outside influences—including from his soldier father and her family (258). She pulls him from radio broadcasts and newspaper recitations and disappears with him for days into the woods, and the child becomes resistant to other words and other speakers, particularly his father (259–60). Eventually, her control over his language erodes, but in the emotionally intense final days of the war, she tries to draw him into this hermetic world again. Her linguistic efforts in this phase operate on the same principle of annihilation that was simultaneously destroying European Jewry; she insists that "certain words had to be entirely exterminated and winnowed out in time, before the victors' arrival" [bestimmte Worte müßten rechtzeitig vor dem Eintreffen der Sieger gänzlich vernichtet und aussortiert werden (287)].[63] Just as doggedly as the Nazis, she attempts to silence dissenting voices from within and without. Her attempt to protect her son amounts to an attempt to seal him hermetically from the world.

After the war, she is fearful and uncertain, increasingly so as two miscarriages make her fear that she will never have another healthy child. Her uncertainty disappears when the narrator is born. She determines again to protect her child from violence, suffering, and pain, but this time, protecting him means shielding him from the past, rather than the present. This determination produces the obfuscating language and avoidance that so frustrates the narrator. Again, her desire to protect her son misleads her into adopting a morally compromised language. This postwar language—which the mother shares with those who want to deny the past out of guilt—resembles National Socialist language even more clearly than her invented language had. As Schlant notes, the narrator uses the same expressions to characterize his mother's storytelling as she had used decades before to describe Hitler's speeches.[64] Moreover, his assertion that nothing of substance remains at the end of her stories echoes her observation that she can remember nothing of Hitler's speeches when they are over, "at most the final words" [höchstens die letzten Worte (215)].

---

63. See also Schlant, *Language of Silence.*

64. Schlant notes the dual use of "singsong." *Language of Silence,* 109–10. The narrator also uses the verb "(ver)streuen" [to scatter] to describe how both his mother and Hitler disseminate their messages to "das Volk" (24, 216).

The mother's insistence on autonomy throughout the war yields to an acceptance of the dominant moral language when it appears most suited to protecting her son. Eventually, the underlying poverty of this language and the intense and all-consuming relationship it weaves drive the narrator to wrest his independence from her, for only with such independence can he begin to recover from the effects her wartime trauma have had on him. These effects are profound.[65] He is apathetic, an insomniac, and incapable of having an intimate relationship with another woman—indeed, he rarely succeeds in maintaining human connections to anyone. Like she, he inhabits an unhappy isolation, insisting far too vehemently, "Oh, I like to be alone" [oh, ich bin gerne allein (8)]. Finally, he resents his lifelong efforts to assuage his mother's pain by being well, successful, and happy.[66] As in the *Väterliteratur*, the narrator appears emotionally stunted by the repercussions of the parent's past experience; he must escape her influence and work out a language of his own for understanding the past.

Because of its many similarities with *Väterliteratur*, *Hedge* has been interpreted solely within this frame of reference, but Schlant and Schmitz read it as a positive development in this tradition, emphasizing the narrator's attempt to understand his mother even as he struggles to distance himself from her and to grapple with how her experience has affected him.[67] Indeed, his account reveals that he reaffirms his relationship with her even as he makes himself independent of it. He gleans much of her story by talking with the people who are closest to her, reestablishing his own ties to them in the process. Staying in her house while she is away, he buys and plants dozens of beech trees to please her, a planting that suggests his own continuing and future rootedness there. Similarly, his construction of his own cabin on the land symbolizes his need to escape his mother's order, but also his desire to retain his attachment to the place that is, however ambivalently, still home. As he reads her letters to her husband and her brother, he finds himself questioning whether they understood her as he does—and concludes that only he has grasped what she was trying to communicate. Despite their material similarity to the documents investigated by the narrators of the *Väterliteratur*, then,

---

65. See Schlant, *Language of Silence*, 106; Schmitz, *On Their Own Terms*, 41–44.

66. In *On Their Own Terms*, Helmut Schmitz asserts that this "overburdening" of the child within "incestuous" parent-child relationships is a common symptom of the intergenerational transmission of war trauma in the postwar period (41). Thus, he, like Schneider, generalizes about the "psychopathology of postwar families" (41–44), but his twenty-first-century focus on German suffering and trauma lead him to conclusions very different than Schneider's.

67. Schlant, *Language of Silence*, 100; Schmitz, *On Their Own Terms*, 36–43, 49; Schmitz, "Family, Heritage," 74–75.

the letters play a very different role here. The narrator does not use them to indict his mother as she was and is, but to gain access and connect to a voice that has been lost.

The end of the text suggests that the narrator hopes to revive this voice in the present, as well. Although the story ends as he leaves her house to avoid seeing her, it also clearly expresses his desire to begin a new phase in their relationship. He asserts that he loves her and that he sees her as his "only understanding listener" [einzige verständnisvolle Zuhörerin (314)]. Finally, although he does not stay to talk to her, he begins a symbolic dialogue by shifting into direct address, and articulates the hope that this dialogue will continue, interrupting her desperate attempts to evade the past and helping heal its wounds (314–16). "I would so like to stay," he laments, "I hope we see each other soon" [Ich bliebe so gern; Ich hoffe, wir sehen uns bald wieder (315–16)]. In contrast to much of the *Väterliteratur,* he ends by seeking a new relationship with his mother, rather than a final break. Forging this relationship will be difficult, but it does not seem impossible—not least, because his mother is still alive, as many of the fathers of *Väterliteratur* are not. This real possibility for future conversation distinguishes the function of the direct address in this novel from that in many father books. There, the address to the deceased father testifies to his continuing influence on the child, and to the twin impulses to bring him back to life and to assert the self as a subject speaking against him.[68] In neither of these cases is the address a communicative gesture, but in Ortheil's novel the address is an invitation for a response, for the mother's answer to the narrator's reconstructed history. Instead of telling her story to finally silence her voice, the narrator tells it to be able to begin a conversation with her. Schmitz, Schlant, and Aurenche all valorize this approach to the mother's story and read Ortheil's mother book as an anomalous—and superior—father book as a result.

But such an understanding of the narrator, and of Ortheil's work, overlooks a crucial difference between *Hedge* and the contemporary father books. His book is different, not only because the narrator approaches his mother's story differently, but also because his mother is different. Schmitz implicitly equates her with the fathers; although he begins by talking about Ortheil's father and mother narratives, by the end the mother has disappeared:

---

68. On lyric apostrophe as rhetorical invocation, see Johnson, "Apostrophe"; Kacandes, *Talk Fiction,* ch. 4. On apostrophe as self-dramatizing gesture, see Culler, *Pursuit of Signs,* 135–54. Although Mauelshagen maintains that the narrators of some father books do seek to continue their emotional relationships with their fathers, she still reads instances of direct address as symptoms of the father's continuing influence on the narrator, rather than of intimacy. Mauelshagen, *Schatten des Vaters,* 120–22.

"The . . . incompatibility of the father's view of himself as victim and the son's focus on Auschwitz leaves the son literally displaced from genealogical and historical time."[69] Similarly, Schlant's emphasis on the resemblance between the mother's language and Hitler's seems to posit Katharina's historical position as structurally equivalent to that of the despised fathers. But it is not. She never collaborated with the Nazis. On the contrary, from the Nazi ascension to power to the war's end, she committed small acts of defiance: from defending the library and protecting its books, to attempting to dissuade her future husband from his pro-regime stance, to avoiding the obligatory Nazi salute, to organizing the public spectacle of her brother's first mass, to refusing optimism about the war and communicating her fears to her husband and family. Her son has to wrestle with her influence and with the way that National Socialism marked her. But he does not have to try to understand reasons for complicity, as the narrators of the father narratives do, or to come to terms with an awful culpability. Katharina has no guilt to hide. In this text the obfuscating language of the postwar period conceals only fear and suffering.

The narrator of this book approaches his mother's story differently because his mother's life demands a different story. She is not a guilty, recalcitrant tyrant. She is a woman of failed resistance and deep suffering whose efforts to protect her beloved children have unintended effects. These differences encourage the son's empathetic approach. He knows that she desires nothing but good for him, just as she desired only to protect his brother, and this knowledge softens his reaction to the havoc her desire wreaks. Similarly, his awareness that he suffers because her own suffering has been so great makes the inflicted pain easier to forgive. Finally, her attempts at resistance make her a worthy forbear. Her effort to establish autonomy stands as a precedent for his efforts to break with her language and find his own—his very determination to distance himself from her shows him to be the inheritor of her moral independence. This text shows clearly that "the project of 'finding an adequate language' is often closely related to the project of rearticulating the moral language(s) of these first interlocutors as constitutive language(s) of the self."[70] Katharina's moral language is not adequate. But it offers a point of departure for the narrator's own moral language and orientation. This narrator does not make himself his mother's heir only because *he* is willing and able. She offers him a linguistic and moral force that is worthy of inheritance.

---

69. Schmitz, "Family, Heritage," 74.
70. Parker, "Narratives of Autonomy," 142.

Conclusion

Stefan and Handke find less to inherit from their mothers, but they, too, work to understand their mothers' experience and to reckon with its influence on themselves. Within postwar German literary and cultural history, these family histories about the women of the war generation thus erode the paradigm of a *Vergangenheitsbewältigung* that demands absolute moral autonomy from the parents' generation. Indeed, acknowledging the contemporary existence of this competing paradigm in the 1970s and 1980s might have differentiated the response to the *Väterliteratur* over the years.[71] These different histories derive both from the mothers' differing experience and from the gendered frameworks of interpretation that the narrators use to understand it. In the best cases, the mothers embody a resistance to violence. Even when they appear as passive or complicit, however, their stories are not shaped by the normative narrative of German culpability that structures the second generation's narrative of the fathers. Instead, this behavior is interpreted within the "larger" story of their suffering as women and as mothers. Comparing these mother books to the dominant understanding of their father-book counterparts thus also highlights the gender-inflected nature of collective memory and of intergenerational autobiography.[72] The collective memory of guilt and responsibility seems not to determine the narrative of mothers as it does the narrative of fathers. The children are free to plumb the painful depths of their mothers' experiences as the narrators of the *Väterliteratur* perhaps were not— whether the mothers tolerated National Socialism, were themselves its victims, or occupied an ambiguous, ambivalent middle ground. Unencumbered by the dictates of *Vergangenheitsbewältigung,* the narrators here attribute widely divergent meanings to National Socialism. But in none of the narratives does that meaning relate to guilt. Instead, National Socialism is read with respect to its impact on the mother's suffering, either as an exacerbation of it, as a welcome temporary respite from it, or some combination of the two. In this focus, in fact, these narratives also trouble other common distinctions between postwar intergenerational narratives: between those of perpetrators

---

71. Again, Brandstädter's *Folgeschäden* is more differentiated. While earlier accounts sometimes include differentiated readings, their overall assessment of the genre often remains monolithic. See, for instance, Schneider, "Fathers and Sons, Retrospectively," 42.

72. In her development of the concept of postmemory, Marianne Hirsch emphasizes the role that gender plays in shaping subsequent generations' reconstructions of the past. In "Generation of Postmemory," she cautions that the danger of postmemory lies in its reliance on the "preformed screen images" that can distort the view of the past and its actors (120). Conceptions of gender contribute substantially to these images. From the perspective of autobiography studies, see Miller, "Representing Others," 17.

and of victims, and between those of the second and third generations.[73] In addressing this suffering, the narrators explore autonomy and relationality just as intergenerational autobiographies of many kinds do. German generational writing as a whole did not follow a *Sonderweg* in the postwar period.

I do not claim to define a *Mütterliteratur* with clearly identifiable boundaries and characteristics; it, like *Väterliteratur*, appears in many guises. But even as their narratives seek to enact a critical break with the discredited moral language of the past, the narrators in this group of mother books are acutely aware of the influence that language still has on their identities and moral orientation, and they acknowledge the continuing relation with their mothers that this persistent language signals. In *Doppelgänger* the narrator is astonished to find that his native dialect remains buried within him, but he does not recognize that the beliefs of his childhood persist with it; the narrators of these books know only too well that the two endure together. Second, as their extensive metanarrative reflections and strategies of double voicing show, all of these narrators tell their stories to recognize their mothers' individual experience and humanity and to make their mothers' submerged, historically inflected voices audible. In this effort, they explicitly undertake the project that implicitly motivates Storm's and Raabe's narrators, and that will dictate Sebald's. These mother books, then, are paradigmatic examples of the ambivalence of reckoning with the past and of the assumptions about the ethical potential of telling another person's story that characterize many dynamic observer narratives on both sides of the fiction/nonfiction divide. Their stylized, self-reflective approach to these concerns marks them as products of the linguistic turn, second-wave feminism, and the New Subjectivity. Their concern about the nexus of narrative, identity, ethics, and a reckoning with the past clearly belongs within the tradition of the dynamic observer narrative, however, and their positions along the continuums between life-writing and fiction and between memoir and dynamic narrative help bring the form more sharply into focus.

---

73. Sigried Weigel challenges generation-based distinctions in "Generation." In theorizing postmemory as a condition that may affect the descendants of both perpetrators and victims, Hirsch bridges the divide between these groups. "Generation of Postmemory," 105–7, 15. In addition, my reading of the mother books suggests that the "new paradigm" of generational literature that has been characterized as emerging in third-generation narratives around the turn of the millennium is not so new. See Byram, "Challenging" (under review). On this new paradigm, see Fuchs, "Generational Memory Contests"; Holdenried, "Zum Aktuellen Familienroman"; Eigler, *Gedächtnis und Geschichte*.

seven

A Footnote to History

German Trauma and the Ethics of
Holocaust Representation in W. G. Sebald's *Austerlitz*

> I think we are well advised to keep on nodding terms with the people we used
> to be, whether we find them attractive company or not. Otherwise they turn
> up unannounced and surprise us, come hammering on the mind's door at 4
> a.m. of a bad night and demand to know who deserted them, who betrayed
> them, who is going to make amends.
>
> —Joan Didion, *Slouching toward Bethlehem*

W. G. *Sebald* (1944–2001), the German expatriate professor whose melancholy prose has fascinated readers since the late 1990s, talked extensively about his narrators and their role in his approach to representing the tragedies of twentieth-century history. "I think it's important to know the point of view from which these tales are told, the moral makeup of the teller," he explained in October 2001. "That's why my narrator has such a presence."[1] He affirmed that he always approached the topic of the Holocaust obliquely,[2] or in a mediated fashion: "That is intentional, because I fear a slide into melodrama, even if that melodrama is based on historical circumstances. Aesthetic authenticity—which is tied to the ethical in a subterranean, intimate way— gets lost then. . . . There are always reminders that [the story] is told this way by somebody, that it has gone through the filter of the narrator."[3] I begin this last chapter with the historical author's statements about his narrators, because in this chapter, even more than in my discussion of Grass, my topic is

---

1. Baker, "Q&A."
2. Jaggi, "Last Word."
3. Doerry and Hage, "Ich fürchte das Melodramatische."

as much the discursive field in which his work operates as it is the work itself. My focus is Sebald's final novel, *Austerlitz,* and the ethical frameworks that underlie his narrative strategies in this text. I argue that tracing the narrator's story shows Sebald challenging the two distinct paradigms that dominate thinking about the proper role of narrative in representing the Holocaust, but that the challenge is masked by the expectations that the paradigms themselves awaken.

The first paradigm applies to survivor narratives and is closely related to the field of trauma studies. In this highly narrativist approach, narrative testimony about the Holocaust is seen as the victims' path to integrating their traumatic experience into a broader self-understanding and, hence, to achieving a modicum of healing. These stories also allow the outside world to acknowledge the victims by hearing, preserving, and communicating their stories. The other paradigm applies to representations by nonsurvivors. Those who did not experience the historical disaster directly are enjoined to avoid falsely totalizing or granting meaning to it and to maintain an appropriate distance. They should not pretend to comprehend the incomprehensible, identify with victims, evoke sentimentality or falsely transfiguring emotion, or try to directly depict the worst of the horrors. Many of the injunctions and vocabulary used within this paradigm resonate strongly with antinarrativist approaches to understanding identity.

Somewhat paradoxically, *Austerlitz* has emerged as an exemplar of both paradigms. Both feature prominently in discussions of the title character's story, and, while the tension between them lies at the root of some critical disagreements, readers seem to have had little difficulty reconciling them in this context. The situation becomes trickier when the narrator becomes the focus of inquiry, however. This chapter takes up that focus, contending that the narrator is key to the work, not only as a teller of Austerlitz's story but also as a historical figure with a story of his own. I argue that the text presents the narrator's behavior and his relationship to Austerlitz as structured by psychological trauma,[4] and pursue the implications this psychological state bears for his story of self, both the way he tells it and the way it is received. As I pursue the implied author's story about the narrator, I read Sebald the historical author as challenging the ethical guidelines of Holocaust representation, even as he consistently signals their importance. In the end, I question the ethics of Sebald's novel, but I do not indict him; instead, I use his novel to show that neither narrative nor antinarrative form can guarantee ethical soundness.

---

4. Katja Garloff's "Task of the Narrator" and Claire Feehily's "Surest Engagement" also interpret the narrator as suffering from trauma.

The Discursive Background of *Austerlitz*'s Reception

Both representational paradigms share a fundamental tenet: the central story of the Holocaust is one of Jewish suffering. In his introduction to the 1992 collection *Probing the Limits of Representation: Nazism and the "Final Solution,"* Saul Friedlander argues that in representations of the Holocaust "some claim to 'truth' appears particularly imperative. . . . There are limits to representation *which should not be but can easily be transgressed,"* and most people have a sense of "obligation" to preserve a "master-narrative" about these truths.[5] While Friedlander maintains that defining the components of this "master-narrative" is very difficult, it would seem that there is a central and crucial truth of the Holocaust: Jews and other groups suffered catastrophe, loss, and pain at the hands of Germans under National Socialism. Sebald's novel privileges a reading that conforms to this central tenet. The Jewish Austerlitz's story comprises the text's central narrative and claims 333 of the book's 421 pages. The book places his story at its core, flanking it with the anonymous narrator's account of the circumstances of his meetings with Austerlitz. It then further wraps Austerlitz's story within short accounts of other victims of German National Socialist violence: at the beginning that of the torture victims Gastone Novelli and Jean Améry, and at the end that of the Jews murdered in the Lithuanian city of Kaunus and the nearby Fort IX. Finally, and as if to dispel any doubt about the text's subject, the title points to Austerlitz as its topic and its goal. Most criticism has followed the discursive expectations and the book's overt cues. Austerlitz's story assumes central importance, and most of those who discuss the German narrator focus on how he presents Austerlitz's story and assess the ethical status of this presentation. The narrator is read as a listener of and conduit for Austerlitz's historically victimized voice, and the ethical status of the narrator and of the work as a whole is seen as turning on this relationship.[6]

Initially, the fictional memoir of a Jewish man's suffering and dislocation as a result of the Holocaust received overwhelmingly positive reviews in the

---

5. Friedlander, "Introduction," 3. Friedlander's claim rejects the perspectival, postmodernist abandonment of the idea of "truth" in history and the concomitant effort to resist historical "master narratives." In particular, he rejects Hayden White's argument that historians can tell different stories about the same historical facts depending on the historical narrative frames they choose to employ and insists that there are constraints on such relativism in the context of the Holocaust (10). For White's articulation of the role of emplotment in historiography, see White, "Question of Narrative."

6. See Fuchs, *Schmerzensspuren der Geschichte*, 32, 141–42; Long, "History, Narrative, and Photography," 125; Wolff, *Sebald's Hybrid Poetics*, 189–91.

United States, from the *New York Times* to *Newsweek*.[7] Critics attributed a "harrowing emotional power" to the story of Jacques Austerlitz and deemed Sebald's treatment of the Holocaust through that story a "small but significant miracle."[8] Lukewarm responses from the United States and Great Britain tended to criticize the book on literary and stylistic grounds rather than historical or political ones.[9] Some German reviewers did express reservations about the book's historiographical implications; Iris Radisch, for instance, charged that it diminishes the horror of the Holocaust by making it just another exhibit in Sebald's historical "museum of lost things."[10] Still, the vast majority of immediate responses lauded the book, almost entirely disregarding the narrator as they did so. The *New York Times* reviewer Michiko Kakutani went so far as to complain about the "gratuitous device of the narrator."[11]

Much of the scholarship on Sebald has been as celebratory as the journalistic reviews,[12] and the early scholarship, in particular, focuses on the character Austerlitz and treats the narrator as a marginal figure. Many discuss the narrator primarily in terms of his relationship to Sebald, taking a position on whether one should read the figure as an autobiographical representation or as a fictional character.[13] Early considerations of his function usually remained brief, even when he was assigned substantial importance. Sigrid Löffler, for instance, calls the narrator in Sebald's texts the actual protagonist, but she never discusses the figure in depth.[14] Thomas Wirtz and Amir Eshel go further

---

7. Examples of strongly positive reviews include Baker, "Remembering to Forget," and Annan, "Ghost Story." The Canadian *Maclean's* also published an enthusiastic review: Bethune, "Look Back in Melancholy." Mark McCulloh provides additional references to and summaries of reviews in *Understanding W. G. Sebald,* 183–84.

8. Kakutani, "No Man's Land"; Jones, "Blending Fact with Fiction," 60.

9. See Eder, "Excavating a Life"; Bernstein, "Melancholy Baby"; Beckett, "Long and Winding River"; Markovits, "What Was It?"

10. Radisch, "Waschbär der falschen Welt," 56. See also Steinfeld, "Wünschelrute in der Tasche." Arthur Williams remarks on and offers an explanation for the fact that no secondary literature accuses Sebald's fiction of historical relativization. Williams, "Holistic Approach," 104–5.

11. Kakutani, "No Man's Land."

12. In his introduction to a special issue of *Germanic Review,* Mark Anderson opens by saying that the journal "adds its voice to a chorus of praise" for Sebald's work (155). For other examples of explicitly celebratory work, see Bigsby, *Remembering and Imagining;* Blackler, *Reading W. G. Sebald;* Schütte, *W. G. Sebald.*

13. Gray Kochhar-Lindgren takes the narrator unproblematically as Sebald in "Charcoal," 371. Sigrid Löffler's "Melancholie" reads the narrator as a fictional character who shares traits with and, thus, remains close to his creator. McCulloh calls the narrator "Sebald" or "the narrator" by turns. See, for example, *Understanding W. G. Sebald,* 110, 19. Amir Eshel's "Power of Time" argues that the text encourages this uncertainty as part of its project to thematize the "tension between fact and fiction" (76).

14. Löffler, "Melancholie," 107–8.

in acknowledging and analyzing the narrator as a character, but their examinations still remain cursory.[15]

The spectrum of opinions about the novel's ethical status has widened in the successive waves of criticism, and the narrator has attracted more attention, often in the form of questions about his ethical status. Some have continued to read Sebald's work as a paradigm of ethical representation of the Holocaust. Jan Ceuppens views ethical representation as the fundamental goal of Sebald's writing and maintains that Sebald's fiction seeks a mode of representation that would respect the other by maintaining "the appropriate distance with regard to the object under scrutiny."[16] Deane Blackler's book on Sebald devotes a chapter to his narrators, arguing that the texts position the narrator as an authority to be questioned and use the figure to encourage an ethically positive "disobedient" reading.[17] Lynn L. Wolff discusses the narrator as a feature of Sebald's "literary historiography," which aims to provide "restitution" for past events by establishing circuits of testimony that can generate empathy for individuals and their stories.[18] But others ask whether the narrator infringes on the central truth of Jewish suffering by identifying with Austerlitz or blurring the line between Jewish suffering and the German's response to it. Katja Garloff, for instance, sees the novel as acknowledging "the encrypted wish to be able to speak for [the victims] . . . which remains an arrogation as much as an obligation." In the end, however, she argues that Sebald uses the narrator figure to critique narrative appropriation and to illustrate the impossibility of ever adequately understanding or representing the victim's story.[19] Stuart Taberner begins by casting doubt on the motives of the narrator in Sebald's earlier *Die Ausgewanderten,* but he sees *Austerlitz*'s narrator as self-conscious about the dangers of identifying with the victim whose story he tells. The narrator of the later novel eschews identification and foregrounds his mediation of Austerlitz's life story.[20] And Anne Fuchs, while admitting some uneasiness about Sebald's fictional project and the impulse to identification it contains, maintains that his unrelenting self-reflexivity carefully "marks the divide between self and other."[21] Even many initially critical studies, then, eventually affirm the narrator's engagement with Austerlitz's

15. See Wirtz, "Schwarze Zuckerwatte," 531–33; Eshel, "Power of Time," 80.

16. Ceuppens, "Transcripts," 254. He makes this statement in the context of discussing Sebald's earlier text *The Emigrants* [*Die Ausgewanderten*].

17. Blackler, *Reading W. G. Sebald.*

18. Wolff, *Sebald's Hybrid Poetics,* 189–91, 205–15.

19. Garloff, "Task of the Narrator," 169.

20. Taberner, "German Nostalgia?" 198–99.

21. Fuchs, *Schmerzensspuren der Geschichte,* 32. Fuchs discusses the narrator on 32–35 and her ambivalence on Sebald's work on 16–17.

story as self-aware and ethically sound; while giving voice to Austerlitz, he resists the temptation to blur the line between himself and his protagonist.[22] Read in this way, Sebald's text becomes a fictional counterpart to the proliferation of Holocaust history told through personal memory and testimony; it joins the Holocaust Museum in Washington, D.C., the USC Shoah Foundation, and documentaries such as the BBC's *Into the Arms of Strangers* in relating Holocaust history by telling stories of its victims. Other scholars, however, take a more critical stance. Silke Horstkotte finds that the narrator displays a disturbing lack of empathy as he confronts the tragedies of the past.[23] Brad Prager reaches a diametrically opposed position, diagnosing the narrator as displaying a deep empathy but questioning the ethical appropriateness of such a German figure; he concludes that "despite his attempts to let victims speak for themselves—to allow their voices to emerge—Sebald's work at times blurs important differences between the speaker and the listener."[24]

As these brief summaries show, even those studies that analyze the narrator extensively tend to focus on the way he represents Austerlitz's story, rather than on the way he presents his own. Many explicitly refer to the assumption that the victims of the Holocaust should be given room to "speak for themselves." One of their main concerns in assessing the ethical status of this representation is whether or not the narrator properly "disidentifies" with Austerlitz in doing so—whether or not he both acknowledges and shows empathy for the man's experience and resists the temptation to blur the line between himself and his subject.[25] As I discuss later, these readings are strongly cued by the text, but they also align with thinking about the proper mode for engaging with Holocaust victims and experience. Dominic LaCapra, for instance, valorizes this kind of careful empathy as a "virtual, not vicarious, experience" of emotion and of historical trauma.[26]

The novel presents itself as transmitting the (fictional) victim's voice, but, in accordance with norms for nonsurvivor accounts, it does not pretend to offer an unmediated account of events. Scholarly responses to it have applauded this approach, as they have its adherence to other norms: that nonsurvivor representations should resist a totalizing urge that would impose coherence on historical events; that they should refrain from ascribing meaning, especially moral meaning, to victims' experience and suffering;

22. See also Schlant, *Language of Silence*, 230–34; Williams, "Remembrance and Responsibility," 75; Wolff, *Sebald's Hybrid Poetics*, 57, 63, 66, 175.

23. Horstkotte, *Nachbilder*, 251–52.

24. Prager, "Good German as Narrator," 101.

25. See chapter 1 for a discussion of disidentification.

26. LaCapra, *Writing History*, 40.

that they should be wary of narrative conventions used for inciting emotion, because these facilitate a slide into false sentimentality or identification; and that they should refrain from providing direct images of the atrocities themselves.[27] Many of these injunctions would seem to rule out a narrativist approach to the events of the Holocaust and the lives they interrupted or severed. The Holocaust, these scholars would argue, constituted a radical break that disrupts the possibility of constructing a life story in a narrativist framework. No story could or should repair the radical loss of continuity, of socially supported identity, of moral orientation that these events caused.

In his essay in Friedlander's volume, for instance, Hayden White advocates representing stories of the Holocaust in a "modernist style, that was developed in order to represent the kind of experiences which social modernism made possible."[28] Citing White, Todd Presner argues that, instead of trying to represent historical disaster as a realist would, erasing "experiential and historical gap[s]" and using "meaning-making strategies" to generate a coherent, stable story, Sebald takes a "modernist" approach that undermines the illusion of a complete, authoritative account of meaningful events.[29] In this description that contrasts a "realist" approach with a "modernist" one, one that aims to create wholeness with one that emphasizes breaks and gaps, a preference for an antinarrativist approach to history and identity manifests itself. Claudia Öhlschläger, too, reads Sebald as rejecting a historiographical approach that seeks coherence and consensus; implicitly, she associates that approach with realism, as she places Sebald "between the modern and the postmodern" and describes his writing in terms such as "fragmentary, blurry, incoherent."[30] Sebald's narrative ethics consists of "the narration of the gaps, holes, and tears that the history of destruction has left behind."[31] Fuchs

---

27. Ibid., 52–55, 98–99. These are "norms" within cultural theory and the academy; popular representations often transgress these norms and are criticized for it in critical discourse. The reactions to *Schindler's List*, for instance, including Sebald's comments on the film, offer an example of this phenomenon. On the debate about *Schindler's List*, see ibid., 99, n. 12, and many of the essays in Loshitzky, *Spielberg's Holocaust*. For Sebald's comments about the film, see Jaggi, "Recovered Memories."

28. White, "Historical Emplotment," 52.

29. Presner, "Synoptic and Artificial View." White emphasizes that while modernism rejected the genre of realism as it had developed in the late nineteenth century, it was still centrally concerned with historical reality. White, "Historical Emplotment," 50–51. A new reality demanded new modes of artistic representation. Not all unequivocally embrace such an approach, however. The editors of the volume *After Testimony* note that while such techniques aim to do justice to the experience of the events, the interpretive difficulties they engender raise questions about the ethical status of the relationship between text and audience. See Lothe et al., "Introduction."

30. Öhlschläger, *Beschädigtes Leben*, 11.

31. Ibid., 248.

contends that "because for Sebald history can no longer be narrated as the story of causal chains of development, but only as a network of fates, in his prose it always leads out of the present and into that 'encyclopedic cosmos of memory and research' that grips both his narrators and his readers."[32] In critical writing on nonsurvivor representations of the Holocaust, there is a strong preference for discontinuity, incoherence, and the contingency of history and the lives it touches: for antinarrativist approaches to history and identity. Sebald's fictional writing appeals to this preference.[33]

Some scholars have noted the tension between the narrativist and antinarrativist paradigms as they apply to Austerlitz's story. Fuchs questions the compatibility of a therapeutic model of narration based on trauma theory and a historical approach that resists reaching any kind of satisfying conclusions.[34] She reconciles these opposing tendencies by associating one approach with Austerlitz and the other with the narrator; while the therapeutic model holds for the victim, outsiders cannot indulge in this closure but must resist it.[35] John Zilcosky argues that, despite Sebald's protestations to the contrary and his clear narrative efforts to avoid it, *Austerlitz* is a traditionally narrative melodrama. "If history is so unrecoverable," he asks, "then why has Austerlitz just been able to discover all the major details of his past?"[36] Kathy Behrendt resolves the tension between the two paradigms by revising the antinarrativist position to accommodate the novel's focus on memory. *Austerlitz*, she contends, is an antinarrative that shows that memory is not dispensable when personal memory is connected to historical memory; the antinarrativist position needs to acknowledge the painful necessity of memory.[37] Behrendt accepts the novel's "narrative skepticism" without question,[38] locating

---

32. Fuchs, *Schmerzensspuren der Geschichte*, 53–54.

33. See also Feehily, "Surest Engagement"; Wolff, "H. G. Adler."

34. Fuchs, *Schmerzensspuren der Geschichte*, 32.

35. Cf. Bettina Mosbach, "Superimposition." Mosbach reverses these assumptions, asserting that while Austerlitz cannot restore a chronological sense of self, the narrator creates "meaningful correspondences" and "continuity" through analogy and superimposition (407). Mosbach's assessment of the narrator's creation is also problematic; while she criticizes the narrator's analogies as "the product[s] of a mind confused" that are superimposed on Austerlitz's story (402), she concludes that it is the narrator's "systematic confusion of its 'true' chronology that paradoxically puts A's story in 'proper order'" (407). Given that Austerlitz has departed, however, he could not benefit from this "proper order," which he had sought.

36. Zilcosky, "Lost and Found," 692.

37. Kathy Behrendt, "Scraping Down the Past," 398–99, 405–7. She also says that the narrativist position must recognize that memory and a coherent story are not always grounds for optimism. I disagree with her conclusions about the ultimate results of memory, since I think that the end of the novel suggests a positive outlook for Austerlitz, if with a melancholy tone. See also Zilcosky, "Lost and Found."

38. Kathy Behrendt, "Scraping Down the Past," 394.

the tension about memory within the antinarrative position, rather than in the book's combination of the two modes.

I think, though, that both modes are clearly visible. In Austerlitz's story, the tension between them has been unproblematic because Sebald uses them according to convention and the norms of ethical representation. Most readers have unconsciously resolved the tension as Fuchs does: the narrativist arc that corresponds to trauma theory is associated with Austerlitz's voice, and the antinarrativist tendencies and strategies are emphasized as the German narrator's and/or author's efforts to maintain appropriate distance. Sebald and his critical readers seem to be in accord about who should tell what kinds of stories about the Holocaust.

I assert, however, that both the narrativist and antinarrativist paradigms can also be applied to the narrator's implicit story about *himself*. And in that context, they become much more contentious. In talking about his narrator, Sebald, like his readers, emphasized his role as a mediator: "I think it's important to know the point of view from which these tales are told, the moral makeup of the *teller*. That's why my narrator has such a presence."[39] The narrator in *Austerlitz* does have a palpable presence. Of the 421-page book, 79 pages take place outside of Austerlitz's memories. While many of these reproduce Austerlitz's architectural monologues, the remainder consists of the narrator's accounts of his meetings with Austerlitz and of the personal experiences he associates with those meetings. These accounts allow the reader to infer a great deal about his identity and his relationship to Austerlitz. They suggest that as a German, he has been traumatized indirectly by the events of the Holocaust, and that this trauma determines the nature of his relationship to Austerlitz and his story. Both Garloff and Taberner pursue aspects of this interaction between the narrator's identity and his representation of Austerlitz's history. But the narrator's story is not present simply to inflect Austerlitz's, or even to explore the problem of narrating the Jewish "other's" story. The narrator's story, or the position that it assumes in relation to Austerlitz's, is an essential part of the story about postwar identity and history that the text tells. The shape that the German narrator's story takes is crucial, yet even those studies that focus on the narrator do not consider this shape.[40]

I think that the narrator appears as a victim of trauma who needs a therapeutic story but whose need is thwarted because of discursive constraints: German suffering does not belong to the "master-narrative" of the Holocaust.

---

39. Baker, "Q&A" (my emphasis).

40. See, for instance, Garloff, "Task of the Narrator"; Taberner, "German Nostalgia?"; Prager, "Good German."

The issue of German suffering during the war at large has been a recurring topic of great controversy in Germany. Memory and historical fact both provide ample proof of German civilian hardship, but while some argue that these stories must be heard, others object that they distract attention from, and even seek to ameliorate German culpability for, the National Socialist massacre of the Jews. Thus, from the television miniseries *Heimat* to Ronald Reagan's and Helmut Kohl's visit to the military cemetery at Bitburg, from the *Historikerstreit* [historians' debate] to the international arguments about the proposed museum for documenting the plight of German refugees after World War II,[41] representations of the German experience of the war have sparked public controversy on a scale few topics in contemporary Germany can. The *feuilleton* flurry surrounding Sebald's own *On the Natural History of Destruction* [*Luftkrieg und Literatur*], in which he laments the supposed dearth of literary writing about the bombing of Germany, also owes its intensity to this dynamic. Andreas Huyssen rejects the charge that this text relativizes the German past and argues that the taboo on discussing German suffering must weaken,[42] but Sebald's delivery of the original lectures in Zürich in 1997 and their subsequent publication in 2001 began a heated debate about the possibility of discussing German suffering without relativizing German crimes.[43] Strangely, despite the strong responses to these lectures, the issue of German suffering has rarely been raised in connection with Sebald's fiction. Or perhaps it is not so strange. After all, whereas the lectures treat the firebombings, the fiction treats the Holocaust. In this realm, the idea of German suffering and trauma is even more out of place. And yet, I believe that both German suffering at the Holocaust and the discursive constraints placed on representing it—its decisive "out-of-placeness"—are central components of Sebald's text.

---

41. Edgar Reitz's *Heimat* (1984) treats German history, including National Socialism and World War II, by following the experiences of a fictional family and village from 1919 to 1982. Reagan's and Kohl's 1985 ceremonial visit to Bitburg became controversial after it was revealed that members of the *Waffen-SS* were buried there alongside army soldiers. In the *Historikerstreit*, which played out largely in newspapers, historians and philosophers contested the interpretation of Germany's World War II history (were Nazi crimes singular, or comparable to those of other authoritarian regimes?) and its implications for postwar German identity and policy. The Center against Expulsions [*Zentrum gegen Vertreibungen*] was first proposed in 1999. After public and political debates, the Federal Foundation Flight, Expulsion, Reconciliation [*Bundesstiftung Flucht, Vertreibung, Versöhnung*] was founded in 2008 with a broader mission of commemorating all the refugees generated by National Socialist policies, World War II, and their aftermath.

42. Huyssen, "Rewritings and New Beginnings," 81.

43. Gerald Fetz's online review of *Luftkrieg und Literatur* (2003) credits Sebald's lectures and text with having touched off the flood of writing and documentation about the bombings in Germany.

The Narrator's Trauma

Sebald's narrator has a strong presence, but he offers little concrete information about himself. He spent his childhood in the town of W., probably sometime in the 1940s, since he was a university student in the mid-1960s. He studied in England, during which time he made several trips to Belgium, and after a brief return to Germany in 1975, he made England his permanent home in 1976. There, he teaches at a university. He comes to London only rarely; one of his visits is prompted by a frightening disruption in the vision of his right eye. Even such a spare biography is difficult to assemble; the reader must glean bits of information from the narrator's comments on his meetings with Austerlitz and, particularly, on the experiences that are temporally close to and that he associates with those meetings.

The Footnote

I believe that the key for deciphering this information resides in a passage that has been almost entirely overlooked: the book's single, anomalous footnote. This footnote opens the door to understanding the narrator's preoccupations and fascination with Austerlitz, the narrative style that effaces the differences between him and his subject, and the relationship that the text suggests between the story the narrator tells about Austerlitz and his own history. The footnote signals the repressed German trauma that constitutes the text's second story line.

Reviewing his manuscript and Austerlitz's discussion of the Lucerne train station, the narrator remembers, as if he had forgotten it until then, his own experience of that spot. The narrator visits Lucerne and, thinking of Austerlitz's comments, observes the train station from a bridge. A few hours later, as he is sleeping, the building catches fire and burns to the ground. The news images of the burning building remain in his mind for weeks, and he says that these visions cause him to feel "that I had been to blame, or at least one of those to blame, for the Lucerne fire" (11) [daß ich der Schuldige oder zumindest einer der Mitschuldigen sei an dem Luzerner Brand (20)]. Vivid dreams of the fire haunt him for years thereafter. In this footnote, the German narrator expresses his unease and anxiety at the thought of a conflagration that spun out of control and destroyed an old and venerable building; despite his physical distance from the event, he cannot help but feel himself to be guilty. His response to this fire thus mirrors a common German response to the historical event that bears the name of such a fire: the Holocaust.

The connection to the Holocaust is intensified by the narrator's use of the word "Mitschuldige" [accessory], a term common in postwar discussions of German guilt, to refer to his inexplicable feeling of culpability.[44] The narrator feels guilty about the fire simply by virtue of his temporal and spatial proximity to its location; it actually occurs only "long after I was fast asleep in my hotel room in Zurich" (10) [als ich längst wieder in tiefstem Schlaf in meinem Züricher Hotelzimmer lag (19)]. Similarly, any guilt he experiences about the Holocaust can be only of a proximate nature, since he is too young to bear any direct responsibility for its events.

The footnote's form and content suggest that the narrator is marked not only by guilt, however, but also by trauma. For the reader who follows the star that marks the footnote and who reads the note as it extends across three pages, the subordinated text arrests and interrupts the main narrative, much as mental reenactments of traumatic events are said to intrude into and interrupt normal experience. And the footnote's content describes the narrator's haunting by the events that traumatize him: "In my dreams, even years later, I sometimes saw the flames leaping from the dome and lighting up the entire panorama of the snow-covered Alps" (11) [Noch viele Jahre später habe ich manchmal in meinen Träumen gesehen, wie die Flammen aus dem Kuppeldach schlugen und das gesamte Panorama der Schneealpen illuminierten (20)]. With respect to the Lucerne fire, the narrator exhibits the classic signs of trauma. He could not fully experience the horror of the event at the time or construct a narrated and structured memory of it, since he was in bed and unaware. But after seeing news footage of the blaze, he relives it time and again in his dreams; the image is engraved in his mind.[45] Even as he experiences guilt for the event, it traumatizes him.

This mixture of guilt and trauma is symptomatic of the relationship the text suggests between the narrator and National Socialist violence. Even the way he learns of the traumatizing Lucerne fire links his experience of it to a common German experience of the Holocaust; Aleida Assmann posits that Germans have been traumatized by the Holocaust through the photos and newsreels they saw of its horrors after they "slept through" the events them-

---

44. Wirtz, in "Schwarze Zuckerwatte," and Garloff, in "Task of the Narrator," also note the narrator's feeling of guilt. Wirtz interprets it as a manifestation of the "black narcissism" that binds the narrator to Austerlitz (533), and Garloff mentions it in passing as an instance of the narrator's "occasional guilt feelings," which "indicate that he also feels responsible for the violence he recounts" (161).

45. This idea of an "unexperienced" experience being replayed by the trauma victim belongs to a conception of trauma that Ruth Leys terms the "mimetic paradigm." Leys, *Trauma: A Genealogy*, 1–17. For an example of such a conception, see Caruth, "Introduction," 153.

selves.[46] As Garloff puts it, "the narrator is rather carefully construed as both similar to and different from the protagonist, and as both a victim and an accomplice of past violence."[47] Although the narrator's relation to the Holocaust diverges completely from Austerlitz's, the text depicts both as suffering trauma from it. This trauma marks both men; "they [have] become themselves the symptom of a history that they cannot entirely possess."[48]

Traumatic Traces

The remainder of the narrator's account of his own experiences supports the idea that he suffers from a trauma originating in the Holocaust, and this supposition explains oddities in both his character and his narration. The overarching structure of the text, for instance, reflects the trauma victim's compulsion to repeat, a common element of the theory of trauma from Freud's anecdote of his grandson's "fort/da" game in "Beyond the Pleasure Principle" to contemporary psychological writings on post-traumatic stress syndrome. The narrator's text reveals his inability to turn from the topic of Jewish suffering during the Holocaust. He leads into his discussion of Austerlitz's life through the story of the victim Jean Améry, and when he closes Austerlitz's tale, it is only to embark on a narrative about Dan Jacobson's Jewish forefathers. This narrative constitutes the text's inconclusive end; the narrator finishes Jacobson's book and returns to Mechelen, the site from which Belgian Jews were deported to the death camps in the East.

Not only does the narrator return explicitly to stories of the Holocaust's victims, but his descriptions of the few places he visits exhibit uncanny connections to them and to the events that claimed them. The most striking of these resemblances surfaces when the narrator relates Austerlitz's discussion of the Antwerp train station. Standing beneath the huge clock that usurps the traditional place of the emperor in the pantheon, Austerlitz comments on its omnipotent power:

> The movements of all travelers could be surveyed from the central position occupied by the clock in Antwerp Station, and conversely all travelers had to look up at the clock and were obliged to adjust their activities to its demands. (12)

---

46. Assmann and Frevert, *Geschichtsvergessenheit*, 117.
47. Garloff, "Task of the Narrator," 160.
48. Caruth, "Introduction," 5.

Von dem Zentralpunkt, den das Uhrwerk im Antwerpener Bahnhof ein-
nehme, ließen sich die Bewegungen sämtlicher Reisender überwachen,
und umgekehrt müßten die Reisenden alle zu der Uhr aufblicken und
seien gezwungen, ihre Handlungsweise auszurichten nach ihr. (22)

The clock and its regulation of time assume the all-powerful position of an
upstart dictator. The next sentence both relates this dictator directly to Hitler and identifies the narrator as the source of this uncanny connection; it
refers to universal time's final triumph over the world in the nineteenth century as "Gleichschaltung," the term used to describe Hitler's consolidation
of power in 1933 and a German word that must originate with the narrator,
rather than with the French-speaking Austerlitz.[49] This same clock doubles
as an eerie concentration camp guard, as its guarantee and slogan "Endracht
maakt macht" (12) [Unity makes power],[50] echoes the infamous "Arbeit macht
frei" [Work makes free] of the Auschwitz gates.

Likewise, the narrator's association of the people in the train station with
the animals of the nocturnal zoo locates the novel's association between
train stations and the Holocaust with him. Entering the station, he sees it as
"another Nocturama" (6) [zweites Nocturama (13)] and its people as the zoo's
animals. He is overtaken by the

> passing thought, nonsensical in itself, that they were the last members of a
> diminutive race which had perished or been expelled from its homeland,
> and that because they alone survived they wore the same sorrowful expres-
> sion as the creatures in the zoo. (7)

> an sich unsinnigen Gedanken, es handle sich bei ihnen um die letzten
> Angehörigen eines reduzierten, aus seiner Heimat ausgewiesenen oder
> untergegangenen Volks, um solche, die, weil nur sie von allen noch über-
> lebten, die gleichen gramvollen Mienen trugen wie die Tiere im Zoo. (14)

Like the Jews to be found in train stations during the final years of the Third
Reich, the figures know themselves to be the sad and final members of a
doomed people.[51] The narrator's comparison of them with animals even recalls

---

49. Translation plays a key role in both revealing and obscuring the narrator's trauma. The
narrator's translation of Austerlitz's French narration into German allows the text to resonate
with German discussions of the Holocaust and National Socialism. The English translation
often removes these traces, and perhaps also words that lend strong emotional coloring to the
narrator, from the text. In this case, Bell writes that the clocks were "standardized" (12).

50. My translation. Bell leaves the phrase untranslated, as it is in the original.

51. Of course, the connection between train stations and the Holocaust underlies Austerlitz's own fascination and engagement with train stations throughout the novel. See Öhlschläger,

uncannily the propaganda that proclaimed the Jews to be subhuman. And the next sentence identifies Austerlitz, whose story will shortly reveal him as the last of his line, to be one of these people.

But this passage also reveals the narrator's resistance to recognizing consciously the connections his mind makes. He dismisses the image as a "passing thought, nonsensical in itself," refusing to recognize its relevance for the story he is telling. The passage that perhaps most strongly suggests his own traumatic relationship to the World War II past indicates that he also avoids the connection between these historical events and himself. Here, he describes his reactions to the fortress of Breendonk, a building in which Jewish victims were imprisoned and tortured. During his visit, the rooms of the fortress remind him of his home and his childhood. The first of these associations seems innocuous: massive carts that the prisoners had pushed recall to his mind the farmers' wheelbarrows of his hometown. But the associations become progressively more sinister as he penetrates deeper into the fortress. He next sees the recreation room of the SS men and easily imagines the men who spent their time there: "After all, I had lived among them until my twentieth year" (23) [denn unter ihnen hatte ich ja gelebt bis in mein zwanzigstes Jahr (37–38)]. Finally, he reaches the torture chamber. There, looking at the floor of the pit that seems to fall away into oblivion and the iron hooks on which the victims were tortured, he is assaulted by childhood memories that arise out of "the abyss": the washhouse, the butcher cleaning away the bloody remains of his work, his father using the disliked word "scrubbing brush" (25) [Wurzelbürste (41)]. Upon reaching the place in the fort most terribly representative of Jewish trauma, he is overcome by memories of his own, contemporaneous childhood, of determined and painful efforts to wash away dirt and blood stains. And he begins to faint. Still, he professes not to understand why the location should call forth these upsetting childhood memories: "No one can explain exactly what happens within us when the doors behind which our childhood terrors lurk are flung open" (25) [Genau kann niemand erklären, was in uns geschieht, wenn die Türe aufgerissen wird, hinter der die Schrecken der Kindheit verborgen sind (41)].[52]

The narrator thus exhibits the opposing tendencies of the trauma victim that Freud identifies. On one level, he seeks repetition of the event. On another, his behavior conforms to Freud's observation that trauma victims' waking energies are spent less in trying to remember the traumatic event

---

Beschädigtes Leben, 111–16. The description here is the narrator's, however, rather than Austerlitz's.

52. The German "aufgerissen" suggests a more violent act in opening the doors to memory than does the English "flung."

than in trying not to think about it.[53] During the upsetting flood of childhood memories at Breendonk, the narrator speaks of them as being hidden behind closed doors that must forcibly be torn open. In contrast, Austerlitz's fascination with closed doors leads him to imagine what they hide. He recalls a dream in which he catches a glimpse of what lies inside: "I still remember how, in my half-conscious state, I tried to hold fast to my powdery gray dream image . . . and to discover what it concealed" (194) [Ich weiß noch, wie ich im Halbschlaf versuchte, das pulvergraue . . . Traumbild festzuhalten und zu erkennen, was in ihm verborgen war (280–81)]. The narrator behaves quite differently. He reports that when he first visits Breendonk, he shrinks from passing through its dark entrance. Once in the fort, each step into the interior increases his panic and his perception of lack of air and of weight pressing down until he almost cannot make the final descent into the torture chamber. Much of the visit has "darkened" in his mind, possibly "because I did not really want to see what it had to show" (23) [weil ich nicht wirklich sehen wollte, was man dort sah (38)]. On his second visit to Breendonk, after Austerlitz completes his story, he cannot enter the fort's "dark gate" at all (296). Instead, he sits down on the bank of the moat to read Jacobson's story, unable or unwilling to reenter the place where his memories had assaulted him before.

Trauma and Identification

Reading the text as a product of the narrator's traumatic relationship to the Holocaust accounts for much of his strangeness as a character and a storyteller. On a psychological level, it provides grounds for his devotion to Austerlitz's story. On the level of poetics, it explains both his narrative style and the text's structure. The interaction of these two levels raises questions about the historical, political, and ethical implications of his story and the text's representation of it. The narrator's trauma provides an unspoken justification for breaking the injunction against identification with the victims and, at the same time, implies his own need for a narrative of healing.

The narrator's final look at the fortress highlights the symbolic role this recurring image plays, a role that parallels the novel's narrative structure. Just as fortresses were built with multiple lines of defense to protect against assault from without, the narrator uses others' stories to shield himself from assault from within. His repeated engagement with others' stories facilitates his effort

---

53. Freud, "Beyond the Pleasure Principle," 13.

to keep his own buried, a practice that Eric Santner terms "narrative fetishism." By telling others' stories, he avoids "the need for mourning by simulating a condition of intactness, typically by situating the site and origin of loss elsewhere."[54] The layers upon layers of narration—Austerlitz's citing of others' words in his own telling, Jacobson's text on his family's history, Claude Simon's relation of Gastone Novelli's life story—act as defensive walls that shield the narrator's own story. During his first conversation with the narrator in Antwerp, Austerlitz remarks on the irrational and futile nineteenth-century efforts to protect the old fortifications around cities by ringing them with layers of new walls. He sees these projects as proof of the human tendency "to forge ahead with our projects far beyond any reasonable bounds" (18) [unsere Unternehmungen voranzutreiben weit über jede Vernunftgrenze hinaus (31)]. Certainly, the unconscious efforts to protect oneself from remembering traumatic events thwart all reason; LaCapra holds that remembering and narrating the traumatic event offers the only hope for mourning and working through it to some degree.[55] But reason does not enter the equation. In fact, the narrator's unconscious engagement with his trauma resembles the behavior of the only animal he remembers from the Nocturama. His repeats others' stories much as the raccoon incessantly washes his apple,

> as if it hoped that all this washing, which went far beyond any reasonable thoroughness, would help it to escape the unreal world in which it had arrived, so to speak, through no fault of its own. (4)

> als hoffe er, durch dieses, weit über jede vernünftige Gründlichkeit hinausgehende Waschen entkommen zu können aus der falschen Welt, in die er gewissermaßen ohne sein eigenes Zutun geraten war. (10–11)

Reading the narrator as a trauma victim employing narrative fetishism to protect himself explains his obsession with Austerlitz. From the beginning, his interaction with Austerlitz exhibits a curious one-sidedness. During their first meeting in the Antwerp train station, Austerlitz's descriptions of train station architecture consume hours. Once Austerlitz has begun telling the narrator his life story, a postcard with a date and address is enough to bring the narrator scurrying to London to listen silently to the next installment. Long intervals between such summons generate anxiety in the narrator; the first time it occurs, he expresses fear that he might have said something to offend

---

54. Santner, "Representation of Trauma," 144.
55. LaCapra, *History and Memory*, 10–12.

Austerlitz and, thus, to prevent him from continuing with his story. The narrator's need to hear Austerlitz's story results in a relationship based neither in the equal exchange of friendship nor on the standard therapeutic model of doctor and patient. A victim of trauma himself, the narrator remains oddly passive in his role as interlocutor for Austerlitz's narration of his traumatic memories. He does not fulfill the role Dori Laub outlines for someone who is helping a trauma victim excavate and witness his experience of the traumatic events; while the narrator remains "unobtrusive [and] nondirective," he fails spectacularly to be "active, in the lead" as Austerlitz tells his story.[56] This passivity is, perhaps, a symptom of his desire for the complete obliteration of his own story. After all, it is after the first installment of Austerlitz's story has consumed eighty pages of text in which the narrator disappears almost completely that the hotel doorman's friendly "good night" appears to the narrator "almost an absolution or a blessing" (97) [eine Freisprechung beinahe oder ein Segen (145)].[57] He desperately needs the self-forgetfulness that Austerlitz's story offers.

The entire text bears the traces of the narrator's desire to erase himself from the story he tells, a desire that derives both from his trauma and from the ethical imperative to give voice to the Jewish experience of suffering. At the same time, the trauma forces a continual return to his own connection to the events, and the ethical demands require that the narrator *mediate* the victim's voice, rather than disappear into it. In other words, the text shows a constant tension between the narrator's self-erasure and the insistent need, both psychological and ethical, to insert himself into the story. His strategy for reporting Austerlitz's story provides an obvious example. As Eduard does in *Stuffcake,* Sebald's narrator presents himself as a simple scribe, transparently recording the facts of his meetings and conversations with Austerlitz. His text consists of an ostensibly verbatim reconstruction of the conversations; the tag "he said," followed by direct speech, recurs constantly. Eventually, however, the ubiquitous tags foreground the story's mediated nature even as they insist on the narrator's role as mere reporter. This mediation becomes particularly visible when he reports Austerlitz's report of another's speech, resulting in passages such as, "in the Šporkova, Vera said to me, said Austerlitz" [in der Šporkova, sagte mir Věra, sagte Austerlitz (262)].[58] Many critics cite these tags as evidence of Sebald's care to approach the victim's

---

56. Laub, "Bearing Witness," 71.

57. In these eighty pages, the narrator surfaces only in the numerous "he said" phrases and in a single mention of a slight pause in Austerlitz's narration.

58. My translation.

story in a mediated, ethical way.[59] It seems that Sebald intended them to be read in this way: "I try to let people talk for themselves, so the narrator is only the one who brings the tale but doesn't install himself in it. . . . I content myself with the role of the messenger."[60] Disidentification happens here. The narrator recognizes Austerlitz's experience, but he avoids the dangerous trap of identifying with him.

Still, the danger of the German narrator's inappropriate identification with the Jewish Austerlitz looms large in interpretations such as Taberner's and Garloff's,[61] and I think that many interpretations argue against its presence precisely because the novel pushes the bounds. Even as the tags and other stylistic features foreground distance, other characteristics of the narrator's style work toward eliding the boundaries between himself and Austerlitz. He forgoes quotation marks for demarcating individuals' speech, instead using a combination of the German special subjunctive to indicate indirect quotations and lexical markers such as "he said" to mark direct quotations. The combination of indirect and direct citation can create the impression of a gradual slide from the narrator's voice to the voice that he attributes to Austerlitz and back. These slides often occur at the beginning of one of Austerlitz's monologues, when the narrator's relation of the events surrounding the two men's conversation gradually yields to Austerlitz's voice. One passage, for instance, begins with the narrator's direct speech and self-reference; then shifts to the special subjunctive as Austerlitz begins to speak; and then presents direct speech from an "I" that it identifies as Austerlitz only after a long sentence of uncertainty.[62]

---

59. Garloff, "Task of the Narrator," 166–69; Taberner, "German Nostalgia?" 196–99; Feehily, "Surest Engagement," 188; Fuchs, *Schmerzensspuren der Geschichte*, 32; Dubow and Steadman-Jones, "Mapping Babel," 25–26; Wolff, *Sebald's Hybrid Poetics*, 63.

60. Jaggi, "Recovered Memories."

61. The problem of improper identification is one of Taberner's central concerns in "German Nostalgia?" Garloff begins "Task of the Narrator" with her contention that in *Austerlitz*, Sebald sets out to work against the improper identification with the Jewish victims of National Socialism (157–58).

62. The slides produce their full effect only in the German, as English has no way of rendering the German special subjunctive. In her translation, Bell shifts immediately to Austerlitz's direct speech:

> As we walked down to Greenwich, Austerlitz told me that a number of artists had painted the park in past centuries. Their pictures showed . . . [two long sentences, more than a half page, of indirect speech; the narrator is the speaker, but uses verb mood to indicate that he is reproducing Austerlitz's speech]. I believe I first saw an example of these panoramas of Greenwich in one of the dilapidated country houses which, as I mentioned yesterday, I often visited with Hilary when I was studying at Oxford. I clearly remember, said Austerlitz . . . ." (102–3)

Other passages waver between the two forms, as if the narrator cannot quite decide whose voice should dominate. When Austerlitz tells the narrator of his gradually intensifying disgust at his own writing, for instance, a single sentence of indirect speech appears between two "directly quoted" statements:

> I was increasingly overcome by a sense of aversion and distaste, said Austerlitz, at the mere thought of opening the bundles of papers and looking through the endless reams I had written in the course of the years. Yet reading and writing had always been his favorite occupation. How happily, said Austerlitz, have I sat over a book in the deepening twilight. (121–22)[63]

> Aber je größer die Mühe, die ich über Monate hinweg an dieses Vorhaben wandte, desto kläglicher dünkten mich die Ergebnisse und desto mehr ergriff mich, schon beim bloßen Öffnen der Konvolute und Umwenden der im Laufe der Zeit von mir beschriebenen ungezählten Blätter, ein Gefühl des Widerwillens und des Ekels, sagte Austerlitz. Und doch sei das Lesen und Schreiben immer seine liebste Beschäftigung gewesen. Wie gerne, sagte Austerlitz, bin ich nicht bei einem Buch gesessen bis weit in die Dämmerung hinein. (179–80)

Perhaps most striking are those few passages when an unusual use of deictics makes identifying the subject and object of speech difficult. In the middle of a passage in which Austerlitz describes his retirement in first-person direct speech, the following sentence appears: "I might perhaps, Austerlitz said to me, have had some idea since our first conversations in Antwerp of the extent of his interests" (120) [Ich hätte ja, so sagte Austerlitz zu mir, vielleicht seit unseren ersten Antwerpener Gesprächen schon eine Ahnung von der Weitläufigkeit seiner Interessen (178)]. Suddenly and without warning, the "I" is the narrator, not Austerlitz.

Compare to the German original:

> Beim Hinabgehen nach Greenwich erzählte mir Austerlitz, daß der Park in den vergangenen Jahrhunderten oft gemalt worden sei. Man sehe auf diesen Bildern . . . Ich glaube, ich habe ein solches Greenwich-Panorama zum ersten mal in einem der vom Untergang bedrohten Landsitze gesehen, die ich, wie ich gestern schon erwähnte, während meiner Oxforder Studienzeit gemeinsam mit Hilary oft aufsuchte. Ich weiß noch genau, sagte Austerlitz . . . ." (153–54)

63. Though the "his" of the English translation does signal a shift back to the narrator's voice, Bell includes the tag "he added," which attributes the middle sentence to Austerlitz and dampens the effect. I have removed this tag here.

Other elements also contribute to the blurring between the voices and identities of the narrator and his subject. Prager notes the afflictions of sight that plague both Austerlitz and the narrator and concludes that "Sebald's work at times blurs important differences between the speaker and the listener," so that the narrator sometimes appears as a kind of "doppelgänger."[64] And there are many other ways in which they coincide. Among the novel's recurring motifs and images are half-light and the soft, blurred colors often accompanying it. Both "the narrator" and "Austerlitz" paint the background for the events they relate as an atmosphere that hovers between darkness and light.[65] Similarly, both figures are often surrounded by silent spaces empty of other people. Sitting in a hotel late at night, the narrator writes in a quiet broken only by the inhuman clacking of the heating and an occasional funereal black taxi on the street outside (97). This quiet reappears in the narrator's description of Austerlitz's house, which lies on a "remarkably quiet street" (117) [auffallend stille Gasse (174)] leagues away in atmosphere from the geographically adjacent, busy Mile End junction. Similarly, Austerlitz's accounts feature the silence of abandoned, unpeopled spaces, which he encounters in the empty streets of Terezin and the silent rooms of the Theresienstadt and veterinary museums (188–89, 198, 265). The narrator has blurred the distinctions between himself and his subject to the extent that the reader can determine no clear voice for either one.

In other words, despite Sebald's clear emphasis on maintaining distance between the narrator and Austerlitz, the text undermines that distance in many ways. Prager calls the narrator's getting closer to Austerlitz empathy; Ralf Jeutter holds that the narrator appropriates Jewish stories to discover "his own truth which converges with the truth of his subjects."[66] In either case, such readings question whether the narrator really does what so many praise him for doing: fulfilling the imperative to give the Holocaust victim voice while emphasizing the distance between the victim and the narrator (or author, painter, filmmaker, etc.). Instead, the narrator's mode of approach appears to be one that corresponds to what Michael Geyer sees as a common kind of German memory practice. He contends that the tension of wanting both to feel German and to acknowledge the disaster of the Holocaust has led Germans to emphasize repentance, reconciliation, and pity when dealing with the past. This emphasis, in turn, has fostered a German identification

64. Prager, "Good German," 99, 101.

65. For instances where Austerlitz is the speaker, see 45, 125, 145, 156–57. For examples by the narrator, see 3–4, 6, 31, 39, 298.

66. Prager, "Good German"; Jeutter, "Am Rand der Finsternis," 170.

with Jewish victims, rather than an unearthing of German memory.[67] Despite the text's emphasis on the narrator as a mediator, I do not think that the narrator can be absolved of trying to identify with Austerlitz in order to avoid confronting his own past.

Evaluating the Text's Ethics

The question, then, becomes how to evaluate both the narrator who seeks this identification and the text that presents him as seeking it. In other words, my concern in this last section is to investigate how an understanding of the narrator as traumatized affects ethical judgments of the text on two different levels: the level of the narrative audience, within the logic of the storyworld; and that of the authorial audience, which sees the storyworld as a construction.[68] I argue that these judgments are very different, and that their differences have repercussions both for understanding the novel, and for the claims of the narrativist and antinarrativist paradigms. Other recent studies have also pointed to the differences of interpretation that these two levels of reading yield. Richard Crownshaw has roundly criticized studies that read Austerlitz's trauma and the text's traumatic engagement with readers as *real,* rather than as authorial reflections *on* trauma.[69] Targeting studies that view Sebald as an ethical model, Prager asserts that, while a nonfiction account similar to the novel might be ethically laudable, a *fictional* empathetic German listener is not appropriate to the topic: "*Were the work not ultimately a well-orchestrated work of fiction,* it would appear that Sebald's intention is to make room for testimony, or to allow the victims to speak for themselves."[70] As a work of fiction, however, it does not achieve this ethical goal. Horstkotte maintains that Austerlitz's reluctance to face the reality of Auschwitz is psychologically motivated, but the *novel's* retreat from that reality conjures Auschwitz as an "unreal or mythical place that bears no consequence for the characters' lives and no relation to the present."[71] In its refusal to approach Auschwitz, the novel denies its violence any relevance to Austerlitz, the narrator, or the present world. My reading of the narrator's story runs in a similar vein: while it is unproblematic on the narrative level, I find it unsettling on the authorial one. In this case, then, the distances of ethical and interpretive judgment are

67. Geyer, "Politics of Memory," 188.
68. Rabinowitz's "Truth in Fiction" provides a typology of audiences.
69. Crownshaw, "On Reading Sebald Criticism."
70. Prager, "Good German," 92 (my emphasis).
71. Horstkotte, *Nachbilder,* 253.

not located between the ideal narrative and narrative audiences within the fictional world, as Rabinowitz has argued; instead, the fact of fictionality that separates narrative and authorial audience generates the disjuncture in ethical judgment.[72]

Evaluating the Narrator's Need for His Story

NARRATIVE AUDIENCE. Read from the perspective of the narrative audience, as a bystander within the fictional world, the idea that the narrator suffers from a trauma originating with the events of the Holocaust discourages judging his mode of encounter with the past: he is a man who suffers because he cannot tell his story. As I noted at the outset, many have argued that the novel is highly antinarrative. Behrendt, for instance, reads its emphasis on mediation, discontinuity, and uncertainty as indicating Sebald's antinarrativist approach to Austerlitz's story, and to identity and history in general. Such stories should not be coherent.[73] Bettina Mosbach, too, sees narrative as inadequate to Austerlitz's plight; he cannot recreate a coherent life story because the Holocaust is a fissure that cannot be bridged.[74] No narrative can generate a sense of *idem*-identity, of sameness over time, across that break.[75] The little Czech boy and the English professor can never be united.

Yet the trauma theory that underlies the novel values narrative differently, and the novel's overall logic suggests that assembling a life story can restore a sense of self. From Freud to recent psychological and humanist accounts, trauma theorists have emphasized the therapeutic value of testimony, often in the form of narrative.[76] The novel's narrative arc suggests that for Austerlitz, self-narration has had a therapeutic effect. As Zilcosky argues, while the novel's discourse and mode of representation *assert* that "coming home" is impossible, its progression tells a different story.[77] Austerlitz identifies himself, finds his mother, regains his childhood language, and embarks on a search for his father. Most significant, I think, he intends to undertake that trip with

---

72. Cf. Rabinowitz, "Truth in Fiction," 135.

73. Kathy Behrendt, "Scraping Down the Past."

74. Mosbach, "Superimposition," 402–3.

75. Paul Ricoeur attributes such a bridging function to narrative. See *Oneself as Another* (122, 48) and my discussion in chapter 2.

76. Felman and Laub, *Testimony*; Freud, "Beyond the Pleasure Principle," ch. 3; Freud, "Erinnern, Wiederholen und Durcharbeiten," 214–15; LaCapra, *Writing History*, 67; Laub, "From Speechlessness to Narrative"; Judith Lewis Herman, *Trauma and Recovery*, 3; Kacandes, *Talk Fiction*, ch. 3.

77. Zilcosky, "Lost and Found," 696.

another living person. In the grip of his crippling past, he had fled from his love interest Marie and the life in the present that she represents. At the end of the book, he goes to look for her. Despite the novel's emphasis on the discontinuities and destroyed connections of Austerlitz's life, his encounter with the listening narrator has allowed him to construct a coherent life story and to move forward into the future.

That encounter provides no ray of hope for the narrator, however. Zilcosky believes that the narrator, too, finds his "point of origin" and the possibility of a "recuperated self" at the end of the book. Having returned to Mechelen, the narrator reads Dan Jacobson's account, in which he finds Sebald's birthdate (and, presumably, his own) in a list of victims' identifying data; Zilcosky discounts the narrator's return to "nomadism" in the novel's final sentence as holding within it the promise of "reorientation."[78] I think that the narrator's situation is very different, however. Claire Feehily observes that "the narrator's psychological journey overarches the plot" of the novel.[79] While Austerlitz's story remains encapsulated within the novel and attains a degree of closure, the narrator's story neither begins nor ends with Austerlitz's. At the book's end, Austerlitz is still searching, but when the search for his father is complete, his quest will reach its logical end, an end where the hope of life, as represented by Marie, awaits. But the narrator leaves Austerlitz's story only to delve into and lose himself in the next. And there is no end to the victims' stories. Nor, despite his discovery of his birthdate, can he ever really find himself there. The "point of origin" he finds can never be his own.

Cathy Caruth sees the experience of trauma shared through testimony as leading to an "encounter with another" and the potential of an ethical "awakening" to the real.[80] But the relationship between Austerlitz and the narrator belies the implicit optimism of this view of trauma and its articulation. Unable to speak his trauma himself, the German narrator perpetually seeks voices, victims, who can. Continually projecting this loss on others allows him to avoid narrating and processing his own trauma—but this avoidance of memory and mourning wins only the certainty that the trauma will persist.[81]

---

78. Ibid., 696–97.

79. Feehily, "Surest Engagement," 191.

80. Caruth, *Unclaimed Experience*, 8–9, 97–112. Other theorists have criticized the broad understanding of trauma and its relationship to history that Caruth and others have articulated. The objection to expanding the term to ever-new situations, including those of perpetrators, is a driving force of Leys's genealogy of the term in *Trauma: A Genealogy* (1–2, 305). In *Writing History, Writing Trauma*, LaCapra warns against conflating history and trauma (xi), or sacralizing it by granting it redemptive power (23).

81. LaCapra, *History and Memory*, 10.

The text's close indicates that, for the narrator, the experience of the Holocaust remains traumatic indeed.

The narrator's failure to address and narrate his own trauma carries another consequence. LaCapra holds that "witnessing is a necessary condition of agency" and that, for trauma victims, it may be the only activity that can release them from shock and help them interact with others in the present time.[82] The narrator, who cannot tell his story because postwar discursive constraints prevent him from doing so, remains a nonentity with no apparent ties to the world. He seems to have no country, no relationships other than that with Austerlitz, and no connection to the present day. Instead, his story emerges from the silent corners where the past persists: the fort-become-museum, the cemetery, the quiet house and photographs that offer the only proof and remembrance of Austerlitz's past life. Prisoner to his trauma, the narrator comes running whenever Austerlitz sends a postcard, and then inherits Austerlitz's house, a place dedicated to memory and the past that the narrator cannot escape. While Austerlitz goes out to meet the world at the end of the book, the narrator retreats from it; in the last scene, he returns to Mechelen and the stories of Holocaust victims.[83]

The footnote's structure, too, appears symptomatic of the narrator's traumatic relationship to the past. Readers are likely to accept its form as a footnote unthinkingly, since a note appears entirely appropriate to its contents: neither forwarding Austerlitz's story, nor providing information about the narrator's encounters with him, those contents belong in a subordinated relationship to the rest of the text, if they belong there at all. In fact, the reader may be tempted to skip over what the text presents (literally) as marginally relevant commentary; the sizeable chunks of three successive pages that the footnote takes up appear a tedious interruption of the narrative. In fact, however, this interruptive nature highlights the traumatic character of the memory. The narrator states that he remembers the occurrences in Lucerne "on looking through these notes" (10) [bei der Durchsicht dieser Aufzeichnungen (18)]; that is, the memory of this event breaks into what otherwise seems to be a completed, coherent, and linear history. Narratively and typographically, the memory disturbs the ordered and, while painful and distressing, accepted story of twentieth-century Jewish suffering. Such a disruption corresponds to the concept of history Shoshana Felman develops in *The Juridical Uncon-*

---

82. Ibid., 12. See also van Alphen, *Caught by History*, 13.

83. Focusing on the way the narrator presents Austerlitz's tale, Taberner views this difference as the final evidence that the text refuses to equate the narrator with Austerlitz ("German Nostalgia?" 99).

scious. Based on her interpretation of Benjamin's writings on history, she concludes that history actually "consists in chains of traumatic interruptions."[84] Rather than acknowledging these traumatic interruptions, however, history works to repress them. It first denies the defeated and traumatized access to history, silencing the direct expression of this trauma within the historical record, and then refuses to include the story of those traumatized within the official "victor's history," erasing any secondary mention of these traumatic breaks. This "historical unconscious" remains, however, with the result that the speechless silence of trauma lies at the heart of any history.[85] Even if the narrator identifies himself with Austerlitz, his unacknowledged trauma prevents him from profiting from that identification. His trauma seems to justify his mode of engagement with the past.

AUTHORIAL AUDIENCE. Reading the narrator as a figure in a deliberately constructed story changes this assessment, however. Read on the level of the narrative audience, the footnote is symptomatic. But read on the level of the authorial audience, it is symbolic. It seems to represent the interruption of coherent history by this historical unconscious, the momentary expression of what remains silenced at the heart of Sebald's text. In this interruptive capacity, it functions very much like the photographs that punctuate the text from beginning to end;[86] indeed, the two photographs that appear on the page parallel the footnote's effects. The footnote betrays what the main body of the text represses: the story of the narrator's buried traumatic relationship to the events that drive Austerlitz's story, the events of the Holocaust. Similarly, the thumbnail photograph of the fire that accompanies it, which depicts the scene from a distance, tells the story behind the narrator's haunting much as a journalistic photo might. By relegating this relationship and story to the footnote, the text encourages the reader to skim over it. But at the same time, its placement in the footnote, in subscript underneath the main narrative of Austerlitz, draws attention to its subordination. In fact, the footnote and its photo are dwarfed by a large photograph of the inside of the dome, presumably taken by Austerlitz, whose fragmentary and tilted perspective reproduces his own feeling of skewed disorientation.[87] In this text, the German narrator is a traumatized victim of a history that has been silenced in favor of the Jewish

---

84. Felman, *Juridical Unconscious*, 33.

85. Ibid., 34.

86. Eshel's "Power of Time" argues that the photos act as Benjaminian "genuine images" to mark that which remains absent from it (91, 94). Carolin Duttlinger's "Traumatic Photographs" asserts that in *Austerlitz*, Sebald posits a "structural analogy" between trauma and photography.

87. I thank James van Dyke for drawing my attention to the very different characteristics of these two photos.

victims' story. As a result, the narrator cannot hope to process his trauma or to experience a healing release from it. He is the unrecognized victim of the past that haunts Austerlitz.

While reading *Austerlitz* this way goes against the dominant grain of interpretations of Sebald's fiction, it is very much in keeping with the concerns that Sebald raised in *On the Natural History of Destruction,* where he decries the failure of postwar German literature to offer an adequate account of German suffering during the war. And as Huyssen notes in relation to the nonfictional text, the novel may be concerned not only with the "psychic repression" associated with trauma, but also subliminally with the "political repression" that memory politics and the discursive constraints associated with them have imposed.[88] The novel, like the lectures and the book they produced, argues that Germans must be able to tell the story of their own suffering if they are to be able to come to terms with the past, inhabit the present, and move forward into the future. Yet the paradigms of Holocaust representation dictate that their stories be subordinated, even silenced, in favor of other victims' stories.

Evaluating the Narrator's Evasion of His Story

The novel represses the narrator's story and his need for it, because his story does not accord with the paradigms of Holocaust representation to which the novel otherwise so scrupulously adheres. Sebald demotes the narrator's story to the margins and presents it in splintered fragments out of deference to the Jewish victim's story—and highlights that demotion, a move that simultaneously reinforces and questions the paradigm that demands it.

This demotion might be seen not only as self-effacing, however, but also as self-serving for the narrator. As in all of the other fictional texts I have discussed, the narrator resists giving his life a narrative form that would unify his experience and his identity over time; in so doing, he evades the connection between his present self and the past that torments him. If readers imagine themselves among the narrative audience, as contemporaries of Jacques Austerlitz and his unnamed biographer, then the narrator's opposing need for and evasion of his own story are psychologically motivated by his trauma.

---

88. Huyssen, "On Rewritings," 85. In his discussions of *Luftkrieg und Literatur,* Wilfried Wilms pursues the idea that politically driven discursive norms contributed not only to the dearth of representations of German suffering but also to Sebald's attribution of this dearth to purely psychic causes. According to Wilms, these norms so conditioned Sebald's perception that he failed to perceive them as he contemplated the topic of the Allied bombings. See "Taboo and Repression" and "Speak No Evil."

In this case, the evasion is understandable. Behrendt conceives of Austerlitz's antinarrative impulses in this way and interprets the novel as showing that such avoidance, while it may be understandable, cannot be *desirable*. When personal and historical memory are so entwined as to be inseparable, she argues, "certain strands of historical memory are morally imperative for all concerned."[89] A similar argument can be made about the narrator, as Behrendt does not. The end of the novel shows the effects of his resistance to connecting past and present. His failure to reckon with his past makes him a nonentity in the present, an empty figure with no relation to or ability to act in the world he inhabits. Fuchs's assessment of Sebald's relationship to the present applies to his narrator's, as well: his historical engagement consists entirely of the memory of loss, with no notion that an awareness of this loss might call for critical—and potentially transformative—action in the present.[90] The narrator's existence is not, it seems to me, an ethically desirable one.

I know that my evaluations thus far present a catch-22: the narrator is damned if he (wants to) tell his story, and damned if he doesn't. There seems to be no acceptable way for the German narrator to represent his own history. In fact, reading from within the authorial audience, I think this predicament is the point. Sebald exposes the narrator's personally and ethically undesirable dilemma: the novel diagnoses the German plight as an inability to inhabit the present because of an unprocessed obsession with the past, an obsession that can take no acceptable form. This reading draws credibility from the openness with which the novel presents the narrator's obsession with and desire for identification with Austerlitz, his evasion of his own past, and his hopeless future. On a more general level, this predicament exposes the inadequacy of approaches that proclaim either narrativist or antinarrativist approaches to identity and history as inherently superior.[91] In its adherence to expectations as it presents Austerlitz's story, the novel makes both appear viable: survivors have a right to narrativist self-understanding, while nonsurvivors should resist narratively constructed meaning when they represent survivors' histories. Conversely, neither the depiction of the narrator's narrativist need as repressed nor his antinarrativist self-presentation seems adequate. Either approach *might,* under certain circumstances, but neither *does.* Neither a narrativist nor an antinarrativist paradigm guarantees ethical soundness, in

---

89. Kathy Behrendt, "Scraping Down the Past," 401.

90. Fuchs, *Schmerzensspuren der Geschichte,* 167–68. For Fuchs, Sebald's seeming valuation of the past over the present is perhaps the most problematic aspect of his work (169–76).

91. In a similar vein, Wolff claims that Sebald work follows the "principle of simultaneously thematizing and problematizing narration—narration not only as story-telling but also as story-making—all while remaining within the narrative process." Wolff, *Sebald's Hybrid Poetics,* 198.

Holocaust representations or elsewhere. Nor does either preclude it. Whether or not a representation is ethical depends on the identities in question and the circumstances under which they are recalled, represented, and understood. Such a novel seems to me an important contribution to discussions about appropriate modes for engaging with the Holocaust, and with history more generally. It seeks to acknowledge and give voice to the German experience, making the German plight visible. It illuminates the impossible corner into which the narrativist and antinarrativist paradigms have driven the German narrator—and, perhaps, also the melancholy, expatriate Sebald.

This understanding of the narrator and Sebald's presentation of him complements accounts like Wolff's recent and compelling book, which focuses primarily on the author and Austerlitz as it argues that Sebald's oeuvre as a whole searches for an ethical, literary approach to the past.[92] Still, I have to close by relativizing my enthusiasm for Sebald's achievement. This novel has always made me uneasy. In part, this uneasiness may stem from my own internalization of the norms that Sebald challenges: the idea that a survivor has a right to and need for a story, while the (child of a) perpetrator does not. The same interpretive framework that has discouraged many people from even *perceiving* the narrator's story affects my judgment of it. In essence, we are the narrator's ideal audience. We take him at face value, allowing him to hide in plain sight, because our own perceptual limitations make us blind to his situation. We are captivated by, and captives of, the lyric state that Sebald conjures. We have not yet become the authorial audience, one that can recognize and accept the novel as a book about Austerlitz *and* the narrating protagonist. We are the audience the implied author wants to expose; we should feel uneasy, because the book challenges our frameworks of interpretation.

But I think that my uneasiness also has another source. It is not just the narrator who directs attention to Austerlitz while he retreats, unconsciously presenting his story as suppressed by Jewish experience. Sebald, too, represents the book as a Jewish story, and consciously so. Paratexts like the title, cover photo, and interviews signal Austerlitz's story not just as the more important one but, implicitly, as the only one. The German is "only" the narrator. "Hiding" the narrator's story is part of Sebald's point: discursive norms demand that such stories hide. But I have never been able to shake the suspicion that Sebald is hiding a bit, himself. Perhaps he was hiding from undesired controversy like that he experienced after the *Luftkrieg und Literatur* [*Natural History of Destruction*] lectures. Perhaps he feared that the story he wanted to tell about Austerlitz and the children's transports

---

92. Wolff, *Sebald's Hybrid Poetics*.

would be overshadowed or lost if such controversy ensued. Or, perhaps, he was moved by considerations about what his flesh-and-blood readers would bear.

I value the novel's depiction of both Austerlitz's plight and the narrator's. I value the story it tells about how narratives can and cannot reconcile past and present. I value its diagnosis of the limitations that the narrativist and antinarrativist paradigms impose on individuals' ability to tell their stories, and to be heard telling their stories, and to be understood as they tell them. Despite my appreciation for its achievements, however, my uneasiness persists about the way Sebald presents the two stories that he tells. Perhaps time will tell if that uneasiness is the product of my own limitations as an audience or of Sebald's construction and presentation of his book. For now, I know only that it has been productive. It prompted me to investigate how narrative reckoning with the past functions in novels such as these—how dynamic observer narratives both present narrative as a means for reconciling past and present identities and cast doubt on its ability to achieve that aim.

conclusion

If you think you can grasp me, think again:
my story flows in more than one direction
a delta springing from the riverbed
with its five fingers spread
  —Adrienne Rich, "Delta"

What's your story? It's all in the telling. Stories are compasses and architecture; we navigate by them, we build our sanctuaries and our prisons out of
them, and to be without a story is to be lost in the vastness of a world that
spreads in all directions like arctic tundra or sea ice. To love someone is to put
yourself in their place, we say, which is to put yourself in their story, or figure
out how to tell yourself their story.
  —Rebecca Solnit, *The Faraway Nearby*

fter Galen Strawson's 2004 attack on narrative conceptions of identity, James Phelan, champion of narrative theory, confessed to being a
"recovering Diachronic." No longer able to conceive of his life in terms of a
single, (honest) overarching narrative that would stitch its parts into a meaningful whole, he disavowed a narrativist self-understanding in favor of an episodic or multiple view: mini-narratives, he said, can integrate no more than
a few years of his experience, and even within this span, several stories might
compete with each other.[1] In this book, I have read dynamic observer narratives as exploring a position similar to that Phelan asserts to occupy. Faced
with the discontinuity of self that is the condition of human existence in the
ever-changing modern world, the narrators of these books evince a desire for
a story that forges a comprehensible and acceptable connection between past

---

1. Phelan, "Who's Here?" 209.

and present. (They are recovering Diachronics.) At the same time, all show an uneasy awareness that these stories are often self-deceptive, or ethically suspect, or simply inadequate to the task. (They are recovering Diachronics.)

Chapter 1 provided an extensive account of the narrativist assumptions that underlie these dynamic observer narratives, so I will not cover this ground again here. In brief: modern human self-understanding relies on narrative. "How was it? Where do you come from? Where do I come from?" (*Rich Life* 42) [Wie ist es gewesen? Wo kommst du her? Wo komme ich her?]. The answers are stories: stories that explain who their tellers are in relation to others. These stories both help the teller position herself with respect to others and, sometimes, give the great gift of human recognition. In fact, it is sometimes in giving this great gift of recognition that the individual can most satisfactorily position herself. By telling another person's story, she establishes herself as an ethical individual. Whether self- or other-focused, stories have great performative potential. This belief in the ethical power of narrative informs political, psychological, philosophical, and sociological theories of reckoning with the past and also undergirds practices such as the South African Truth and Reconciliation Commission.

My examination of literary narratives of reckoning with the past has traced an evolution in this faith in stories, however. The changing narrative strategies of dynamic observer narratives suggest that, over time, the requirements for an ethically sound story have shifted, from telling a "good" story *for* another to enabling another to tell her own tale. This shift is neither necessary nor universal. It plays no role in *Cat and Mouse*, for instance. Still, a trend is visible in the books I have examined, and my discussions of these books have suggested that their approaches are often representative of the views of their times. In Textor's *Paul Roderich* the narrator is moved not by benevolence at all, but by a (largely self-interested) desire to accurately represent what had become a vilified position: a republican belief in democracy and individual freedom. Storm's narrator, on the other hand, aims to compensate for his own past prejudice by acknowledging John Hansen's humanity. Despite their differences, both Textor's and Storm's narrators retain clear control of their protagonists' stories as they seek to rehabilitate their reputations. Raabe's Eduard can no longer take such control. His victim, the previously bullied Schaumann, insists on telling his own story. Indeed, forcing Eduard to listen to him tell that story is an act of revenge. At the same time, Schaumann's wife displays resentment at his co-opting of her story. Raabe's novel presents characters who fight to control the stories of their lives, and the conflict between these characters determines the book's structure. A tension between voices also characterizes the mother books of the 1970s to the early 1990s. There, however, the narrators struggle to make their mothers' voices audible. While Raabe's novel *depicts* individuals who want to control their own stories, the mother books show a deliberate attempt to cede (some) narrative control to these individuals by incorporating their (often distasteful) historical voices into the text. Sebald's *Austerlitz* undertakes a related effort to make a historical victim's voice heard. Unlike in the mother books, however, this ethical aim remains entirely unremarked. I believe that this silence reflects the degree of unspoken acceptance that the principle of doing justice by giving voice has attained. In the age of truth commissions, Holocaust video archives, and even National Public Radio's StoryCorps mission "to provide Americans of all backgrounds and beliefs with the opportunity to record, share, and preserve the stories of our lives," much of contemporary society holds this truth to be self-evident: that "every voice matters."[2]

This movement toward valuing narratives that transmit other voices does not, however, correspond clearly to a trajectory of development within narrative strategies. Representations of the protagonists' direct speech, for instance, play a key role in Textor, Raabe, Ortheil, and Sebald. But while the mechanism remains the same, the function shifts. In Textor and Ortheil, direct speech is documentary; in Raabe, a device to make the contest of voices visible; in Sebald, an effort both to honor the victim's historical experience and to recede behind it. The device of direct speech itself possesses no independent predictive value. Nor does a shared conviction in the importance of letting the other's voice be heard entail a shared approach to representing it. Handke's, Stefan's, and Sebald's texts show the clearest commitment to this principle, yet their narrative approaches are diametrically opposed. Handke's and Stefan's narrators highlight their mothers' inability to be heard by carefully avoiding direct speech and using obtrusive stylistic techniques. In contrast, Sebald's narrator naturalizes his ubiquitous direct citation of Austerlitz's speech and deemphasizes transitions between the two voices. One can argue, of course (and I have), that this ploy of transparency is ostentatious in its own way. The fact remains, however, that there is no simple equation between the strength of the conviction that a story about a person's life should strive to make that person's voice heard and the strategies used to achieve that end. As I indicated in the introduction, the relationship between narrative form and cultural history is messy. The significance of narrative devices and strategies must be analyzed within their particular historical and cultural contexts, because they carry different valences depending on the interpretive frameworks within which they are employed.

2. StoryCorps, "About Us."

Despite the evolving views of voice, the history of dynamic observer narratives is not a simple story of an advancing faith in the positive power of stories. Although all of the narrators respond to disturbances in their self-understanding with narratives, very few arrive at one that reconciles their past and present selves, or yields a clearly positive sense of self in the present. Certainly, the narrators in Raabe, Grass, Handke, and Sebald find no resolution through the stories they tell. Their failures might be attributed, in part, to the fact that they route their "self"-examinations through stories about others, largely avoiding a confrontation with their own lives and development. They do not really tell stories about themselves; hence, they arrive at no self-understanding. Such a reading would align with narrativist views that having a story of self is requisite to having a good life. Such a reading would also overlook the stories the narrators have to tell, however. Many of these narrators choose to tell stories about their protagonists rather than themselves, because the stories they could tell about themselves would not be "good" ones—they would be stories of prejudice, or cruelty, or thoughtlessness—while the stories they tell about others allow them to appear as "good," because they acknowledge the other person's experience. Pilenz may want to confess, but he also wants to avoid admitting acts of which he is ashamed. Handke's narrator wants to expose the oppressive environment that poisoned his mother's life, but he shies from confronting his own role in her situation. Apparently benevolent narratives serve selfish ends.

The dynamic observer narrative emphasizes the necessarily selfish—or, at least, self-centered—nature of telling stories. All narrators narrate from a specific time and place, from within a specific framework of understanding. This positioning bears two consequences. First, as I discussed in chapter 2, a narrator always reveals something about her position and identity through her telling. In fact, if stories are understood to be performative, she not only *reveals* something about herself but *enacts* a certain self. All narrators, then, are subject to the pull of self-interest. Second, the character narrators of the dynamic observer form expose the inherent interpretive limitations imposed by a narrator's historical position and her associated moral framework. In all of the texts I have discussed, these interpretive frameworks prevent the narrators from entirely relinquishing their old, inadequate stories about their protagonists and themselves. They try to tell new stories that account for those protagonists' self-understanding, but they remain partially bound to the assumptions and language that informed their earlier worldview. Storm's narrator purports to abandon his middle-class prejudices and to divine the experience and emotions of his working-class, ex-convict protagonist, but textual clues reveal the middle-class ideals and attitudes that continue to shape his understanding of the man. All of the texts bear traces of the tug-of-war of perspectives that plagues the narrators' efforts to reinterpret the past. As Taylor contends, a shift in interpretive framework and self-understanding is "not necessarily a once-for-all affair. The older condemned goods remain; they resist; some seem ineradicable from the human heart. So that the struggle and tension continues."[3] The dynamic observer narratives make this struggle and tension visible. No matter how intently the narrators train their (and their readers') attention on John Glückstadt's story, or Schaumann's, or Mahlke's, or the mother's, or Austerlitz's, the narrators' own words, own experience, and own story frame the stories they tell.

These dynamic observer narratives, then, simultaneously put their faith in benevolent narrative as an ethical force, and question whether benevolent narration is ever attainable. Narrators can never entirely abandon either their self-interest or the limitations that their historical and cultural position impose. This impossibility afflicts fictional narrators and less fictional ones alike—as well as authors. Bakhtin may have seen the true author's voice as transcending the limitations of ideology,[4] but this view is hardly viable today. That the author is constrained by linguistic and interpretive frameworks need not mean her death, however. As it draws attention to the act of authorship, the dynamic observer narrative simply draws attention to the limitations any author confronts. And, in cases where the narrator resembles the historical author, it seems designed to raise questions about that author's historical limitations. Perhaps Grass has been asking to be recognized as ashamedly evasive all along; only readers' sophisticated refusal to associate narrator with author has prevented that recognition. Dynamic observer narratives dramatize the impossibility of a historically positioned teller ever fully assuming another person's perspective or, in the terms of Dorothy Hale's summary of the "new ethicists" in narrative theory, of "submitting" to another perspective for the duration of the story.[5]

---

3. Taylor, *Sources of the Self*, 65.

4. Bakhtin, *Dialogic Imagination*, 314–15.

5. Hale, "Fiction as Restriction." Interestingly, this limitation of the historically bound reading subject is oddly absent in the readerly ethics that Hale describes. While many of the theorists she discusses emphasize the social and discursive constraints on the oppressed "other," they often assume that the producer or consumer of the story can choose to submit to temporarily yield to the other's radically different point of view. In "Values of Difficulty," for example, Butler advocates refraining from judging others because "translating" from the language of one social group to another is sometimes impossible, but she never questions what conditions allow one to see that translation is necessary. Lynne Huffer's "'There Is No Gomorrah'" argues that the reader should be aware of the norms of language, identity, and narration that allow her to speak (18), but she fails to note that these same norms may inhibit the reader from comprehending the difference between self and other or from seeing a very different other as deserving of recognition.

In these texts, history matters. It matters because the narrators' stories are a response to the impact of history on self-understanding. It matters because both their ability to narrate reliably and their capacity to reinterpret stories of the past from another's point of view are constrained by the interpretive frameworks forged within their historical moment and experience. It matters because the very idea of what a "good" story about someone else is changes with history. And it matters because neither a narrativist nor an antinarrativist approach to giving an account of a life provides any guarantees about that account's ethical soundness; historical circumstances always affect its adequacy.

Given my emphasis on the importance of history, I should perhaps say a word about why dynamic observer narratives selected from two centuries of German-language literature permit any kind of generalizations about the narrative form beyond those historical boundaries. They do not, necessarily. Nor, as I specified in the introduction, do they allow generalizations about *all* German-language narratives in which a character narrator tells a story about another figure. I suspect, however, that the form does share similar characteristics and fulfill similar functions in other traditions. In English-language literature, canonical works like Joseph Conrad's *Heart of Darkness,* Willa Cather's *My Antonia,* Herman Melville's *Moby Dick,* and F. Scott Fitzgerald's *Great Gatsby* all share some of the same concerns and narrative strategies, as do recent works like Art Spiegelman's *Maus* or Téa Obreht's *The Tiger's Wife.* Perhaps future examinations of texts from other times and places will elucidate the particular shapes the form assumes in these contexts, explain other correspondences between cultural history and narrative forms, or even, in their differences, further illuminate the German tradition I have explored.

If I have given the impression that this is an unraveling tradition, I have failed in my task. Dynamic observer narratives may expose narrative's shortcomings as a ground for identity or the ethical treatment of others, but as chapter 7 showed for the relatively recent *Austerlitz,* antinarrative accounts of self are not a clearly preferable alternative; antinarrative resistance to connecting the dots of one's history can also be a form of evasion. In other words, the narrativist theories I discussed in chapter 1 were not mere straw men to be knocked down. On the contrary, new dynamic observer narratives continue to appear, showing the persistence of the desires and impulses that have animated their narrators for more than two hundred years: to understand who one is by connecting one's past and present selves, and to trace that route through the story of another person whose path has intersected with one's own.

Perhaps it is particularly in the presence of antinarrativist doubts that dynamic observer narratives continue to be written—after all, as Annie Dillard writes about religion, "doubt and dedication often go hand in hand."[6] (And if stories of self are accounts of evolving morality and identity, perhaps this comparison is not inapt.) Rebecca Solnit's new book, *A Faraway Nearby*, is labeled a "memoir/anti-memoir." Solnit resists the neat Diachronic story of progress that books labeled memoirs tend to serve up; such books, she says, grant "a kind of assurance about the self that doesn't work for me: that the author knows who she herself is, and who others are, and that people are consistent."[7] She strains against the notion of narratives that claim to provide stable, definitive accounts of either the author or her subjects. Like Butler and Strawson, she wants to hold the self open: "Part of my endeavor to describe a more nebulous, metamorphic, and open self is this one that our stories change all the time and there is no definitive version."[8] And yet, the idea that our stories change over time entails the conviction that people live and understand themselves through stories. Being changeable doesn't mean not having a story. It means reinterpreting that story in the face of new experiences, or new engagement with others and their stories. Solnit's book, in fact, is in part an account of her mother's decline due to Alzheimer's: it is a narratively self-reflexive story about someone telling a story about someone else. Because, as Solnit writes, "We don't live our whole lives in our own skin. We live through stories and for a little while we're someone else. Those other stories feed our lives and guide them; we learn through stories and they become part of us."[9]

---

6. Dillard, *For the Time Being*, 146.
7. Biggins, "Interview with Rebecca Solnit."
8. Ibid.
9. Ibid.

bibliography

Adorno, Theodor. "What Does Coming to Terms with the Past Mean?" Translated by Timothy Bahti and Geoffrey Hartman. In *Bitburg in Moral and Political Perspective*, edited by Geoffrey Hartman. 114–29. Bloomington: Indiana University Press, 1986.

Agamben, Georgio. *Remnants of Auschwitz: The Witness and the Archive*. Translated by Daniel Heller-Roazen. Brooklyn, NY: Zone Books, 1999.

Ahlberg, Sofia. "Günter Grass as Literary Intellectual: Memory, Ambiguity, and Constructive Conflict." *Studies in the Humanities* 35, no. 2 (2008): 216–30.

Altbach, Edith Hoshino. "The New German Women's Movement." *Signs* 9, no. 3 (1984): 454–69.

Anderson, Mark. "Introduction." *Germanic Review* 79, no. 4 (2004): 155–62.

Annan, Gabriele. "Ghost Story." *New York Review of Books*, November 1, 2001, 26–27.

Ashley, Keith Allen. "Intersubjectivity in Narration: The Peripheral-Subject Situation in Jean Paul, Franz Grillparzer, Christa Wolf." In *Dissertation Abstracts International*, 2053A: Ohio State University, 1996.

Assmann, Aleida, and Ute Frevert. *Geschichtsvergessenheit, Geschichtsversessenheit: Vom Umgang mit deutschen Vergangenheiten nach 1945*. Stuttgart: Deutsche Verlags-Anstalt, 1999.

Aulls, Katharina. *Verbunden und gebunden: Mutter-Tochter-Beziehungen in sechs Romanen der siebziger und achtziger Jahre*. Frankfurt: Peter Lang, 1993.

Aurenche, Emmanuelle. "Contribution à l'assimilation du passé Nazi: Hecke de Hanns-Josef Ortheil." *Cahier d'études germaniques* 21 (1991): 41–50.

Austin, J. L. *How to Do Things with Words*. Edited by J. O. Urmson and Marina Sbisà. 2nd ed. Cambridge, MA: Harvard University Press, 1975.

Baker, Kenneth. "Q&A: W. G. Sebald: Up against Historical Amnesia." *San Francisco Chronicle*, October 7, 2001.

——. "Remembering to Forget." Review of *Austerlitz*, by W. G. Sebald. *San Francisco Chronicle*, October 7, 2001.

Bakhtin, M. M. *The Dialogic Imagination.* Translated by Caryl Emerson and Michael Holquist. Edited by Michael Holquist. Austin: University of Texas Press, 1981.

Bal, Mieke. *Narratology: Introduction to the Theory of Narrative.* 2nd ed. Toronto: University of Toronto Press, 1997.

Barkan, Elazar, and Alexander Karn. "Group Apology as an Ethical Imperative." In *Taking Wrongs Seriously: Apologies and Reconciliation,* edited by Elazar Barkan and Alexander Karn. 3–30. Stanford, CA: Stanford University Press, 2006.

Barry, Thomas F. "Nazi Signs: Peter Handke's Reception of Austrian Fascism." In *Austrian Writers and the Anschluss: Understanding the Past, Overcoming the Past,* edited by Donald G. Daviau. Studies in Austrian Literature, Culture, and Thought (SALCT), 298–312. Riverside, CA: Ariadne, 1991.

Bartoleit, Ralf. "Das Verhältnis von Ferdinand Tönnies' 'Gemeinschaft und Gesellschaft' zu Theodor Storms Erzählwerk : Über die Fragwürdigkeit einer naheliegenden Interpretation." *Schriften der Theodor-Storm-Gesellschaft* 36 (1987): 69–82.

Battersby, James L. "Narrativity, Self, and Self-Representation." *Narrative* 14, no. 1 (2006): 27–44.

Beckett, Andy. "Long and Winding River." Review of *Austerlitz*, by W. G. Sebald. *Guardian*, September 29, 2001. http://www.guardian.co.uk/books/2001/sep/29/fiction.reviews3.

Behrendt, Johanna E. "Auf der Suche nach dem Adamsapfel: Der Erzähler Pilenz in Günter Grass' Novelle *Katz und Maus.*" *Germanisch-Romanische Monatsschrift* 50 (1969): 313–26.

Behrendt, Kathy. "Scraping Down the Past: Memory and Amnesia in W. G. Sebald's Anti-Narrative." *Philosophy and Literature* 34, no. 2 (2010): 394–408.

Bernstein, Michael André. "Melancholy Baby." Review of *Austerlitz,* by W. G. Sebald. *Los Angeles Times*, October 14, 2001.

Bethune, Brian. "Look Back in Melancholy." Review of *Austerlitz,* by W. G. Sebald. *Maclean's*, January 2002, 1.

Biese, Alfred. "Theodor Storm." *Preussische Jahrbucher* 60 (1887): 219–28.

Biggins, Walter. "An Interview with Rebecca Solnit." *Bookslut,* June 2013.

Bigsby, Christopher. *Remembering and Imagining the Holocaust: The Chain of Memory.* Cambridge: Cambridge University Press, 2006.

Bird, Stephanie. "Scham, Beschämung und Gesellschaftskritik in Gottfried Kellers *Martin Salander* und Wilhelm Raabes *Stopfkuchen.*" *Jahrbuch der Raabe-Gesellschaft* 49 (2008): 48–65.

Blackler, Deane. *Reading W. G. Sebald: Adventure and Disobedience.* Rochester, NY: Camden House, 2007.

Blustein, Jeffrey. *The Moral Demands of Memory.* Cambridge: Cambridge University Press, 2008.

Booth, Marilyn, and Antoinette Burton. "Critical Feminist Biography II." *Journal of Women's History* 21, no. 4 (2009): 8–12.

Booth, Wayne. *The Rhetoric of Fiction.* Chicago: University of Chicago Press, 1961.

Böttger, Fritz. *Theodor Storm in seiner Zeit.* Berlin: Verlag der Nation, 1958.

Brandstädter, Mathias. *Folgeschäden: Kontext, narrative Strukturen und Verlaufsformen der Väterliteratur 1960 bis 2008.* Würzburg: Königshausen & Neumann, 2010.

Braun, Frank X. "Theodor Storm's 'Doppelgänger.'" *Germanic Review* 32 (1957): 267–72.

Braun, Rebecca. *Constructing Authorship in the Work of Günter Grass*. Oxford Modern Languages and Literature Monographs (OMLLM). Oxford: Oxford University Press, 2008.

———. "'Mich in Variationen erzählen': Günter Grass and the Ethics of Autobiography." *Modern Language Review* 103, no. 4 (2008): 1051–66.

Breger, Claudia. *An Aesthetics of Narrative Performance: Transitional Theater, Literature, and Film in Contemporary Germany*. Columbus: Ohio State University Press, 2012.

Brewster, Philip J. "Onkel Ketschwayo in Neuteutoberg: Zeitgeschichtliche Anspielungen in Raabes *Stopfkuchen*." *Jahrbuch der Raabe-Gesellschaft* (1983): 96–118.

Brooks, Cleanth, and Robert Penn Warren. *Understanding Fiction*. New York: F. S. Crofts, 1943.

Bruce, James C. "The Equivocating Narrator in Günter Grass's *Katz und Maus*." *Monatshefte* 58 (1966): 139–49.

Bruffee, Kenneth. *Elegiac Romance: Cultural Change and Loss of the Hero in Modern Fiction*. Ithaca, NY: Cornell University Press, 1983.

Bruner, Jerome. *Acts of Meaning*. Cambridge, MA: Harvard University Press, 1990.

———. "Life as Narrative." *Social Research* 54 (1987): 11–32.

Bürner-Kotzam, Renate. *Vertraute Gäste—Befremdende Begegnungen in Texten des bürgerlichen Realismus*. Heidelberg: C. Winter, 2001.

Burns, Barbara. "'Vorbestraft': Differing Perspectives on Reintegration and Recidivism in Narratives by Storm and Fallada." *Neophilologus* 86, no. 3 (2002): 437–53.

Butler, Judith. *Excitable Speech: A Politics of the Performative*. New York: Routledge, 1997.

———. "Giving an Account of Oneself." *Diacritics* 31, no. 4 (2001): 22–40.

———. "Values of Difficulty." In *Just Being Difficult? Academic Writing in the Public Arena*, edited by Jonathon Culler and Kevin Lamb. 199–216. Palo Alto, CA: Stanford University Press, 2003.

Byram, Katra. "Mother Books and the Myths of Generational Memory Culture." Unpublished manuscript, last modified October 30, 2014.

———. "Colonialism and the Language of German-German Relations in Raabe's *Stopfkuchen*." In *Wilhelm Raabe: Global Themes, International Perspectives*, edited by Dirk Göttsche and Florian Krobb. Oxford: Legenda, 2009.

———. "German Realism's Proximal Others: Franz Grillparzer's *The Poor Fiddler* and Theodor Storm's *Ein Doppelgänger*." In *Realism's Others*, edited by Eva Aldea and Geoffrey Baker. 49–67. Newcastle upon Tyne: Cambridge Scholars, 2010.

Caruth, Cathy. "Introduction." In *Trauma: Explorations in Memory*, edited by Cathy Caruth. 3–12. Baltimore: Johns Hopkins University Press, 1995.

———. *Unclaimed Experience: Trauma, Narrative, and History*. Baltimore: Johns Hopkins University Press, 1996.

Cavarero, Adriana. *Relating Narratives: Storytelling and Selfhood*. Translated by Paul A. Kottman. Edited by Andrew Benjamin. London: Routledge, 2000.

Ceuppens, Jan. "Transcripts: An Ethics of Representation in *The Emigrants*." In *W. G. Sebald: History—Memory—Trauma*, edited by Mark McCulloh and Scott Denham. 251–64. Berlin: de Gruyter, 2006.

Cooper, Frederick, and Ann Laura Stoler. "Between Metropole and Colony: Rethinking a Research Agenda." In *Tensions of Empire: Colonial Cultures in a Bourgeois World*, edited by Frederick Cooper and Ann Laura Stoler. 1–56. Berkeley: University of California Press, 1997.

Croft, Helen. "Günter Grass's *Katz und Maus*." *Seminar* 9 (1973): 253–64.

Crownshaw, Richard. "On Reading Sebald Criticism: Witnessing the Text." *Journal of Romance Studies* 9, no. 3 (2009): 10–22.

Culler, Jonathon. *The Pursuit of Signs: Semiotics, Literature, Deconstruction.* Ithaca, NY: Cornell University Press, 2002.

———. *Structuralist Poetics.* Ithaca, NY: Cornell University Press, 1975.

Cunliffe, W. G. "Günter Grass: *Katz und Maus*." *Studies in Short Fiction* 3 (1966): 174–85.

Dawson, Paul. "Real Authors and Real Readers: Omniscient Narration and a Discursive Approach to the Narrative Communication Model." *Journal of Narrative Theory* 42, no. 1 (2012): 91–116.

Detroy, Peter. *Wilhelm Raabe: Der Humor als Gestaltungsprinzip im* Stopfkuchen. Bonn: H. Bouvier, 1970.

Di Maio, Irene Stocksieker. "The 'Frauenfrage' and the Reception of Wilhelm Raabe's Female Characters." In *Wilhelm Raabe: Studien zu seinem Leben und Werk,* edited by Leo A. Lensing and Hans-Werner Peter. 406–13. Braunschweig: Pp-Verlag, 1981.

Dillard, Annie. *For the Time Being.* New York: Knopf, 1999.

Doerry, Martin, and Volker Hage. "Ich fürchte das Melodramatische." *Der Spiegel,* March 12, 2001.

Downing, Eric. *Double Exposures: Repetition and Realism in Nineteenth-Century German Fiction.* Stanford, CA: Stanford University Press, 2000.

Dubow, Jessica, and Richard Steadman-Jones. "Mapping Babel: Language and Exile in W. G. Sebald's *Austerlitz.*" *New German Critique* 115 (2012): 3–26.

Dunker, Axel. "'Gehe aus dem Kasten': Modell einer postkolonialen Lektüre kanonischer deutschsprachiger Texte des 19. Jahrhunderts am Beispiel von Wilhelm Raabes Roman *Stopfkuchen.*" In *(Post-)Kolonialismus und deutsche Literatur: Impulse der angloamerikanischen Literatur- und Kulturtheorie,* edited by Axel Dunker. 147–60. Bielefeld: Aisthesis, 2005.

Durzak, Manfred. "Entzauberung des Helden: Günter Grass, *Katz und Maus* (1961)." In *Deutsche Novellen,* edited by Winfried Freund. 265–77. Munich: Wilhelm Fink, 1993.

Duttlinger, Carolin. "Traumatic Photographs: Remembrance and the Technical Media in W. G. Sebald's *Austerlitz.*" In *W. G. Sebald: A Critical Companion,* edited by Anne Whitehead and J. J. Long. 155–71. Seattle: University of Washington Press, 2004.

Dye, Elizabeth. "'Weil die Geschichte nicht aufhört': Günter Grass's *Im Krebsgang.*" *German Life and Letters* 57, no. 4 (2004): 472–87.

Eakin, Paul John, ed. *The Ethics of Life Writing.* Ithaca, NY: Cornell University Press, 2004.

———. *How Our Lives Become Stories.* Ithaca, NY: Cornell University Press, 1999.

———. "Narrative Identity and Narrative Imperialism: A Response to Galen Strawson and James Phelan." *Narrative* 14, no. 2 (2006): 180–87.

Eder, Richard. "Excavating a Life." Review of *Austerlitz,* by W. G. Sebald. *New York Times Book Review,* October 28, 2001.

Eigler, Friederike. *Gedächtnis und Geschichte in Generationenromanen seit der Wende.* Berlin: Erich Schmidt, 2005.

Eisele, Ulf. *Der Dichter und sein Detektiv: Raabes* Stopfkuchen *und die Frage des Realismus.* Tübingen: Max Niemeyer, 1979.

"Das Ende einer moralischen Instanz." *General-Anzeiger,* August 14, 2006, 14.

Enzensberger, Hans Magnus. "Poesie und Politik." In *Einzelheiten,* edited by Hans Magnus Enzensberger. 334–52. Frankfurt: Suhrkamp, 1962.

Eshel, Amir. "Against the Power of Time: The Poetics of Suspension in W. G. Sebald's *Austerlitz.*" *New German Critique* 88 (2003): 71–96.

Fechner, Rolf, ed. *Der Dichter und der Soziologe: Zum Verhältnis zwischen Thedor Storm und Ferdinand Tönnies.* Hamburg: Rolf Fechner Verlag, 1987.

Feehily, Claire. "'The Surest Engagement with Memory Lies in Its Perpetual Irresolution': The Work of W. G. Sebald as Counter-Monument." In *W. G. Sebald: Schreiben ex patria/Expatriate Writing,* edited by Gerhard Fischer. Amsterdam: Rodopi, 2009.

Felman, Shoshana. *The Juridical Unconscious: Trials and Traumas in the Twentieth Century.* Cambridge, MA: Harvard University Press, 2002.

Felman, Shoshana, and Dori Laub. *Testimony: Crises of Witnessing in Literature, Psychoanalysis, and History.* New York: Routledge, 1992.

Fetz, Gerry. "Review of Winfried G. Sebald, *Luftkrieg und Literatur.*" *H-German,* November 2003. http://www.h-net.org/reviews/showrev.php?id=8364.

Fickert, Kurt J. "The Use of Ambiguity in *Cat and Mouse.*" *German Quarterly* 44, no. 3 (1971): 372–78.

Fludernik, Monika. "Defining (In)Sanity: The Narrator of *The Yellow Wallpaper* and the Question of Unreliability." In *Grenzüberschreitungen: Narratologie im Kontext / Transcending Boundaries: Narratology in Context,* edited by Walter Grünzweig and Andreas Solbach. 75–95. Tübingen: Narr, 1999.

———. "Metanarrative and Metafictional Commentary: From Metadiscursivity to Metanarration and Metafiction." *Poetica* 35 (2003): 1–39.

Freud, Sigmund. "Beyond the Pleasure Principle." In *Standard Edition of the Complete Psychological Works of Sigmund Freud,* edited by James Strachey. 7–64. London: Institute of Psychoanalysis, 1955.

———. "Erinnern, Wiederholen und Durcharbeiten." In *Studienausgabe,* edited by Alexander Mitscherlich, Angela Richards, and James Strachey. 205–15. Frankfurt: S. Fischer, 1975.

Freudenburg, Rachel. "Fictions of Friendship in Twentieth-Century German Literature: Mann's *Doktor Faustus,* Grass's *Katz und Maus,* Bernhard's *Der Untergeher,* and Wolf's *Nachdenken über Christa T.*" PhD Diss., Harvard University, 1995. UMI (9538908).

Friedlander, Saul. "Introduction." In *Probing the Limits of Representation: Nazism and the "Final Solution,"* edited by Saul Friedlander. 1–21. Cambridge, MA: Harvard University Press, 1992.

Friedman, Norman. *Form and Meaning in Fiction.* Athens: University of Georgia Press, 1975.

Friedman, Susan Stanford. "Women's Autobiographical Selves: Theory and Practice." In *The Private Self: Theory and Practice of Women's Autobiographical Writings,* edited by Shari Benstock. 34–62. Chapel Hill: University of North Carolina Press, 1988.

Friedrichsmeyer, Sara, Sara Lennox, and Susanne Zantop, eds. *The Imperialist Imagination: German Colonialism and Its Legacy.* Ann Arbor: University of Michigan Press, 1998.

Fuchs, Anne. *Die Schmerzensspuren der Geschichte: Zur Poetik der Erinnerung in W. G. Sebalds Prosa.* Cologne: Böhlau, 2004.

———. "'Ehrlich, du lügst wie gedruckt': Günter Grass's Autobiographical Confession and the Changing Territory of Germany's Memory Culture." *German Life and Letters* 60, no. 2 (2007): 261–75.

———. "From 'Vergangenheitsbewältigung' to Generational Memory Contests in Günter Grass, Monika Maron and Uwe Timm." *German Life and Letters* 59, no. 2 (2006): 169–86.

———. "The Tinderbox of Memory: Generation and Masculinity in *Väterliteratur* by Christoph Meckel, Uwe Timm, Ulla Hahn, and Dagmar Leupold." In *German Memory Contests: The Quest for Identity in Literature, Film, and Discourse since 1990*, edited by Anne Fuchs, Mary Cosgrove, and George Grote. 41–65. Rochester, NY: Camden House, 2006.

Gall, Lothar. "'Ich wünschte ein Bürger zu sein . . . ': Das Selbstverständnis des deutschen Bürgertums im 19. Jahrhundert." *Historische Zeitschrift* 245 (1987): 601–23.

Garloff, Katja. "The Task of the Narrator: Moments of Symbolic Investiture in W. G. Sebald's *Austerlitz*." In *W. G. Sebald: History—Memory—Trauma*, edited by Mark McCulloh and Scott Denham. 157–70. Berlin: de Gruyter, 2006.

Genette, Gérard. *Narrative Discourse: An Essay in Method*. Translated by Jane E. Levin. Ithaca, NY: Cornell University Press, 1980.

Geyer, Michael. "The Politics of Memory in Contemporary Germany." In *Radical Evil*, edited by Joan Copjec. 169–200. London: Verso, 1996.

Goldammer, Peter. "Einführung." In *Theodor Storm: Sämtliche Werke*. Edited by Peter Goldammer. Vol. 1, 3–107. Berlin: Aufbau-Verlag, 1967.

Göttsche, Dirk. "Der koloniale 'Zusammenhang der Dinge' in der deutschen Provinz. Wilhelm Raabe in postkolonialer Sicht." *Jahrbuch der Raabe-Gesellschaft* (2005): 53–73.

———. *Zeit im Roman: Literarische Zeitreflexion und die Geschichte des Zeitromans im späten 18. und im 19. Jahrhundert*. Munich: Wilhelm Fink, 2001.

———. *Zeitreflexion und Zeitkritik im Werk Wilhelm Raabes*. Würzburg: Königshausen & Neumann, 2000.

Graf, Johannes, and Gunnar Kwisinski. "Heinrich Schaumann, ein Lügenbaron? Zur Erzählstruktur in Raabes *Stopfkuchen*." *Jahrbuch der Raabe-Gesellschaft* (1992): 194–213.

Grass, Günter. *Cat and Mouse*. In *The Danzig Trilogy*, 467–556. Translated by Ralph Manheim. San Diego: Harcourt Brace Jovanovich, 1987.

———. *Crabwalk*. Translated by Krishna Winston. New York: Harcourt, 2002.

———. "Günter Grass—Nobel Lecture: Fortsetzung folgt . . ." Nobelprize.org, http://www.nobelprize.org/nobel_prizes/literature/laureates/1999/lecture-g.html. Translated by Michael Henry Heim as "Günter Grass—Nobel Lecture: To Be Continued . . ." Nobelprize.org, http://www.nobelprize.org/nobel_prizes/literature/laureates/1999/lecture-e.html.

———. *Peeling the Onion*. Translated by Michael Henry Heim. New York: Harcourt, 2007.

———. "Was gesagt werden muss." *Süddeutsche Zeitung*, April 10, 2012. http://www.sueddeutsche.de/kultur/gedicht-zum-konflikt-zwischen-israel-und-iran-was-gesagt-werden-muss-1.1325809. Translated by Breon Mitchell as "What Must Be Said," *Guardian*, April 5, 2012. http://www.guardian.co.uk/books/2012/apr/05 /gunter-grass-what-must-be-said? intcmp=239.

———. *Werke*. 12 vols. Göttingen: Steidl, 2007.

Grimm, Gunter. "Theodor Storm: *Ein Doppelgänger*." In *Romane und Erzählungen des Bürgerlichen Realismus: Neue Interpretationen*, edited by Horst Denkler. 325–46. Stuttgart: Reclam, 1980.

"Günter Grass gilt den meisten weiter als glaubwürdig." *Associated Press Worldstream*, August 17, 2006.

Hale, Dorothy J. "Fiction as Restriction: Self-Binding in New Ethical Theories of the Novel." *Narrative* 15, no. 2 (November 10, 2007): 187–206.

Hall, Katharina. "Günter Grass's 'Danzig Quintet.'" In *The Cambridge Companion to Günter Grass*, edited by Stuart Taberner. 67–80. Cambridge: Cambridge University Press, 2009.

Handke, Peter. *Wunschloses Unglück*. Frankfurt: Suhrkamp Taschenbuch, 1974. Translated by Ralph Manheim as *A Sorrow beyond Dreams* (New York: Farrar, Straus & Giroux, 1974).

Hansen, Per Krogh. "Reconsidering the Unreliable Narrator." *Semiotica* 165 (2007): 227–46.

Hartwig, Ina. "Die Geschichtslosigkeit der Mütter." *Kursbuch* 132 (1998): 45–52.

Hasselbach, Ingrid. *Katz und Maus*. Munich: Oldenbourg, 1990.

Hebbel, Christa. *Die Funktion der Erzähler- und Figurenperspektiven in Wilhelm Raabes Ich-Erzählungen*. 1960. Microform.

Hell, Julia. "Wilhelm Raabes *Stopfkuchen*: Der ungleichzeitige Bürger." *Jahrbuch der Raabe-Gesellschaft* (1992): 165–93.

Herman, David. "Introduction: Narratologies." In *Narratologies: New Perspectives on Narrative Analysis*, edited by David Herman. 1–30. Columbus: Ohio State University Press, 1999.

Herman, Judith Lewis. *Trauma and Recovery*. New York: Basic Books, 1992.

Hirsch, Marianne. "The Generation of Postmemory." *Poetics Today* 29, no. 1 (2008): 103–28.

Holdenried, Michaela. "Zum aktuellen Familienroman als erinnender Rekonstruktion." *Le Texte Étranger* 8 (January 2011). http://www.univparis8.fr/dela/etranger/pages/8 /holdenried.html.

Hollington, Michael. *Günter Grass*. London: Marion Boyars, 1980.

Hoppe, Karl. "Stopfkuchen." In *Wilhelm Raabe: Sämtliche Werke*, edited by Karl Hoppe. 419–63. Göttingen: Vandenhoeck & Ruprecht, 1963.

———. *Wilhelm Raabe: Beiträge zum Verständnis seiner Person und seines Werkes*. Göttingen: Vandenhoeck & Ruprecht, 1967.

Horstkotte, Silke. *Nachbilder: Fotografie und Gedächtnis in der deutschen Gegenwartsliteratur*. Cologne: Böhlau, 2009.

Huffer, Lynne. "'There Is No Gomorrah': Narrative Ethics in Feminist and Queer Theory." *differences* 12, no. 3 (2001): 1–32.

Huyssen, Andreas. "On Rewritings and New Beginnings: W. G. Sebald and the Literature about the *Luftkrieg*." *Zeitschrift für Literaturwissenschaft und Linguistik* 124 (2001): 72–90.

Jaggi, Maya. "The Last Word." *Guardian*, December 20, 2001.

———. "Recovered Memories." *Guardian*, September 21, 2001.

Jaspers, Karl. *The Question of German Guilt*. Translated by E. B. Ashton. New York: Fordham University Press, 2000.

Jehmüller, Wolfgang. *Die Gestalt des Biographen bei Wilhelm Raabe*. Munich: Wilhelm Fink, 1975.

Jeutter, Ralf. "'Am Rand der Finsternis': The Jewish Experience in the Context of W. G. Sebald's Poetics." In *Jews in German Literature since 1945: German-Jewish Literature?*, edited by Pól O'Dochartaigh. 165–79. Amsterdam: Rodopi, 2000.

Johnson, Barbara. "Apostrophe, Animation, and Abortion." *Diacritics* 16, no. 1 (1986): 28–47.

Jones, Malcolm. "Blending Fact with Fiction." Review of *Austerlitz*, by W. G. Sebald. *Newsweek*, November 5, 2001.

Jückstock-Kießling, Nathali. *Ich-Erzählen: Anmerkungen zu Wilhelm Raabes Realismus*. Göttingen: Vandenhoeck & Ruprecht, 2004.

Kacandes, Irene. *Daddy's War: Greek American Stories*. Lincoln: University of Nebraska Press, 2009.

———. *Talk Fiction: Literature and the Talk Explosion*. Lincoln: University of Nebraska Press, 2001.

———. "'When Facts Are Scarce': Authenticating Strategies in Writing by Children of Survivors." In *After Testimony: The Ethics and Aesthetics of Holocaust Narrative for the Future*, edited by Jakob Lothe, James Phelan, and Susan Rubin Suleiman. 179–97. Columbus: Ohio State University Press, 2012.

Kafalenos, Emma. *Narrative Causalities*. Columbus: Ohio State University Press, 2006.

Kaiser, Gerhard. *Günter Grass: Katz und Maus*. Munich: Wilhelm Fink, 1971.

Kaiser, Nancy A. "Identity and Relationship in Peter Handke's *Wunschloses Unglück* and *Kindergeschichte*." *Symposium* 40, no. 1 (1986): 41–58.

Kakutani, Michiko. "In a No Man's Land of Memories and Loss." Review of *Austerlitz*, by W. G. Sebald. *New York Times*, October 26, 2001.

Keil, Lars-Broder. "Kritik und Verständnis für Grass' späte Enthüllung." *Die Welt*, August 14, 2006.

Kernmayer, Hildegard. "Wie der Brief ins Feuilleton kam: Gattungspoetologische Überlegungen zu Ludwig Börnes *Briefen aus Paris*." In *Poetik des Briefromans: Wissens- und mediengeschichtliche Studien*, edited by Gideon Stiening and Robert Vellusig. 295–315. Berlin: de Gruyter, 2012.

Klepper, Nathalie. *Theodor Storms späte Novellen: bürgerliche Krisenerfahrungen im Umbruch zur Moderne*. Marburg: Tectum, 2008.

Klopfenstein, Eduard. *Erzähler und Leser bei Wilhelm Raabe: Untersuchungen zu einem Formelement der Prosaerzählung*. Bern: Paul Haupt, 1969.

Knaller, Susanne. "Der italienische Briefroman im Kontext von Subjektivitäts- und Mimesispoetiken des 18. und 19. Jahrhunderts." In *Poetik des Briefromans: Wissens- und mediengeschichtliche Studien*, edited by Gideon Steining and Robert Vellusig. 279–92. Berlin: de Gruyter, 2012.

Kochhar-Lindgren, Gray. "Charcoal: The Phantom Traces of W. G. Sebald's Novel-Memoirs." *Monatshefte* 94, no. 3 (2002): 368–80.

Kocka, Jürgen. "Bürgertum und bürgerliche Gesellschaft im 19. Jahrhundert: Europäische Entwicklungen und deutsche Eigenarten." In *Bürgertum im 19. Jahrhundert: Deutschland im europäischen Vergleich*, edited by Jürgen Kocka. 11–76. Munich: Deutscher Taschenbuch Verlag, 1988.

Kokora, Michel Gnéba. "Die Ferne in der Nähe: Zur Funktion Afrikas in Raabes *Abu Telfan* und *Stopfkuchen*." *Jahrbuch der Raabe-Gesellschaft* (1994): 54–69.

König, Helmut, Michael Kohlstruck, and Andreas Wöll, eds. *Vergangenheitsbewältigung am Ende des zwanzigsten Jahrhunderts*. Wiesbaden: Westdeutscher Verlag, 1998.

Konzett, Matthias. "Cultural Amnesia and the Banality of Human Tragedy: Peter Handke's *Wunschloses Unglück* and Its Postideological Aesthetics." *Germanic Review* 70, no. 2 (1995): 42–50.

Koonz, Claudia. *Mothers in the Fatherland: Women, the Family, and Nazi Politics*. New York: St. Martin's, 1987.

Krebs, Sandra. "'Das Weiße zwischen den Worten': die Erzählbarkeit des Ich zwischen Realismus und Moderne am Beispiel von Wilhelm Raabes *Die Akten des Vogelsangs* und Max Frischs *Stiller*." In *Signaturen realistischen Erzählens im Werk Wilhelm Raabes*, edited by Dirk Göttsche and Ulf-Michael Schneider. 231–52. Würzburg: Königshausen & Neumann, 2010.

Krobb, Florian. *Erkundungen im Überseeischen: Wilhelm Raabe und die Füllung der Welt*. Würzburg: Königshausen & Neumann, 2009.

Kunz, Barbara. "Von der Rebellion zur Emanzipation: Zürcher 68erinnen erinnern sich." *Schweizerische Zeitschrift für Geschichte* 53, no. 3 (2007): 272–95.

Laage, Karl Ernst. "Ein Doppelgänger." In *Theodor Storm: Sämtliche Werke,* edited by Karl Ernst Laage. 999–1027. Frankfurt: Deutscher Klassiker, 1987.

LaCapra, Dominick. *History and Memory after Auschwitz.* Ithaca, NY: Cornell University Press, 1998.

———. *Writing History, Writing Trauma.* Baltimore: Johns Hopkins University Press, 2001.

Ladenthin, Volker. "Erinnerndes Erzählen: Ein Beitrag zur Interpretation der Novelle *Ein Doppelgänger* von Theodor Storm." *Literatur für Leser* 2 (1994): 77–83.

———. *Gerechtes Erzählen: Studien zu Thomas Manns Erzählung 'Das Gesetz,' zu Theodor Storm und Ernst Toller.* Würzburg: Königshausen & Neumann, 2010.

Lanser, Susan Snaider. *Fictions of Authority: Women Writers and Narrative Voice.* Ithaca, NY: Cornell University Press, 1992.

———. *The Narrative Act: Point of View in Prose Fiction.* Princeton, NJ: Princeton University Press, 1981.

Laub, Dori. "Bearing Witness or the Vicissitudes of Listening." In *Testimony: Crises of Witnessing in Literature, Psychoanalysis, and History,* edited by Dori Laub and Shoshana Felman. 57–74. New York: Routledge, 1992.

———. "From Speechlessness to Narrative: The Cases of Holocaust Historians and of Psychiatrically Hospitalized Survivors." *Literature and Medicine* 24, no. 2 (2005): 253–65.

Le Vaillant, François. *Anecdotes in Travels, from the Cape of Good Hope into the Interior Parts of Africa. From the French of M. Vaillant.* London: W. Darton & Co., 1790.

Lejeune, Philippe. *On Autobiography.* Translated by Katherine M. Leary. Minneapolis: University of Minnesota Press, 1989.

Leonard, Irène. *Günter Grass.* New York: Barnes & Noble Books, 1974.

Leuschner, Brigitte. "Erfinden und Erzählen: Funktion und Kommunikation in autothematischer Dichtung." *Modern Language Notes* 100, no. 3 (1985): 498–513.

Levi, Primo. *Survival in Auschwitz.* Translated by Stuart Woolf. New York: Touchstone, 1996.

Leys, Ruth. *Trauma: A Genealogy.* Chicago: University of Chicago Press, 2000.

Liebrand, Claudia. "Wohltätige Gewalttaten? : zu einem Paradigma in Raabes *Stopfkuchen.*" *Jahrbuch der Raabe-Gesellschaft* (1997): 84–102.

Linke, Angelika. *Sprachkultur und Bürgertum: Zur Mentalitätsgeschichte des 19. Jahrhunderts.* Stuttgart: J. B. Metzler, 1996.

Löffler, Sigried. "Melancholie ist eine Form des Widerstands: Über das Saturnische bei W. G. Sebald und seine Aufhebung in der Schrift." *Text + Kritik* 158 (2003): 103–11.

Long, J. J. "History, Narrative, and Photography in W. G. Sebald's *Die Ausgewanderten.*" *Modern Language Review* 98, no. 1 (2003): 117–37.

Loshitzky, Yosefa, ed. *Spielberg's Holocaust: Critical Perspectives on Schindler's List.* Bloomington: Indiana University Press, 1997.

Lothe, Jakob, Susan Rubin Suleiman, and James Phelan. "Introduction." In *After Testimony: Holocaust Representation and Narrative Theory,* edited by Jakob Lothe, Susan Rubin Suleiman, and James Phelan. 1–22. Columbus: Ohio State University Press, 2012.

Love, Ursula. "'Als sei ich . . . ihr GESCHUNDENES HERZ': Identifizierung und negative Kreativität in Peter Handkes Erzählung *Wunschloses Unglück.*" *Seminar* 17, no. 2 (1981): 130–46.

MacIntyre, Alasdair. *After Virtue*. Notre Dame, IN: University of Notre Dame Press, 1984.

Margalit, Avishai. *Ethics of Memory*. Cambridge, MA: Harvard University Press, 2002.

Markovits, Benjamin. "What Was It That So Darkened Our World?" Review of *Austerlitz*, by W. G. Sebald. *London Review of Books*, October 18, 2001.

Mason, Ann. *The Skeptical Muse: A Study of Günter Grass' Conception of the Artist*. Bern: Herbert Lang, 1974.

Mason, Mary G. "The Other Voice: Autobiographies of Women Writers." In *Autobiography: Essays Theoretical and Critical*, edited by James Olney. 207–35. Princeton, NJ: Princeton University Press, 1980.

Mauelshagen, Claudia. *Der Schatten des Vaters: Deutschsprachige Väterliteratur der siebziger und achtziger Jahre*. Frankfurt: Peter Lang, 1995.

Maurer, Susanne. "Gespaltenes Gedächtnis? '1968 und die Frauen' in Deutschland." *L'Homme* 20, no. 2 (2009): 118–28.

McCulloh, Mark. *Understanding W. G. Sebald*. Columbia: University of South Carolina Press, 2003.

McGlothlin, Erin. *Second-Generation Holocaust Literature: Legacies of Survival and Perpetration*. Rochester, NY: Camden House, 2006.

Meckel, Christoph. *Suchbild: Über meinen Vater*. Düsseldorf: Claassen, 1980.

Mein, Georg. "'. . . beim letzten Droppen Dinte angekommen?' Raabes *Stopfkuchen* als Projekt einer poetologischen Selbstvergewisserung." In *"Die Besten Bissen vom Kuchen": Wilhelm Raabes Erzählwerk*, edited by Søren R. Fauth, Rolf Parr, and Eberhard Rohse. 115–29. Göttingen: Wallstein Verlag, 2009.

Meyer, Herman. "Raum und Zeit in Wilhelm Raabes Erzählkunst." In *Raabe in neuer Sicht*, edited by Hermann Helmers. 98–129. Stuttgart: W. Kohlhammer, 1968.

Meyer, Jürgen. "'Of Our Time Distinc(t)ly': Joseph Conrads *Heart of Darkness* und Wilhelm Raabes *Stopfkuchen*." *Germanisch-romanische Monatsschrift* 60, no. 2 (2010): 181–201.

Meyer-Krentler, Eckhardt. *Der Bürger als Freund: Ein sozialethisches Programm und seine Kritik in der neueren deutschen Erzählliteratur*. Munich: Wilhelm Fink, 1984.

Midgley, David. "Günter Grass, *Im Krebsgang*: Memory, Medium, and Message." *Seminar* 41, no. 1 (2005): 55–67.

Miller, Nancy K. *But Enough about Me: Why We Read Other People's Lives*. New York: Columbia University Press, 2002.

———. "Representing Others: Gender and the Subjects of Autobiography." *Differences* 6, no. 1 (1994): 1–27.

Minden, Michael. "'Even the Flowering of Art Isn't Pure': Günter Grass's Figures of Shame." In *Changing the Nation: Günter Grass in International Perspective*, edited by Rebecca Braun and Frank Brunssen. 23–35. Würzburg: Königshausen & Neumann, 2008.

Mitscherlich, Alexander, and Margarete Mitscherlich. *The Inability to Mourn: Principles of Collective Behavior*. Translated by Beverley R. Placzek. New York: Grove, 1975.

Mosbach, Bettina. "Superimposition as a Narrative Strategy in *Austerlitz*." In *Searching for Sebald: Photography after W. G. Sebald*, edited by Lise Patt and Christel Dillbohner. 390–411. Los Angeles: Institute of Cultural Inquiry, 2007.

Neuhaus, Volker. *Günter Grass*. 2nd ed. Stuttgart: J. B. Metzler, 1993.

Neumann, Christian. "Ein Text und sein Doppelgänger: Eine plurale Lektüre von Theodor Storms Novelle *Ein Doppelgänger.*" *Schriften der Theodor-Storm-Gesellschaft* 52 (2003): 53–73.

Niewerth, Hans-Peter. "Theodor Storm." In *Handbuch der deutschen Erzählung,* edited by Karl Konrad Polheim. 303–18. Düsseldorf: Bagel, 1981.

"The Nobel Prize in Literature 1999." Nobelprize.org, http://www.nobelprize.org/nobel_prizes/literature/laureates/1999/.

Nolte, Detlef. *Vergangenheitsbewältigung in Lateinamerika.* Frankfurt: Vervuert, 1996.

Norberg, Jakob. "'Haushalten': The Economy of the Phrase in Peter Handke's *Wunschloses Unglück.*" *German Quarterly* 81, no. 4 (2008): 471–88.

Nünning, Ansgar. "Narratology and Cultural History: Tensions, Points of Contact, New Areas of Research." *Wider Scope of English* (2006): 154–85.

———. "On Metanarration: Studies in Anglo-American Narratology." In *The Dynamics of Narrative Form,* edited by John Pier. 11–57. Berlin: de Gruyter, 2004.

———. "Unreliable, Compared to What? Towards a Cognitive Theory of 'Unreliable Narration.'" In *Grenzüberschreitungen: Narratologie im Kontext / Transcending Boundaries: Narratology in Context,* edited by Walter Grünzweig and Andreas Solbach. 53–73. Tübingen: Gunter Narr, 1999.

———. "*Unreliable Narration* zur Einführung: Grundzüge einer kognitiv-narratologischen Theorie und Analyse unglaubwürdigen Erzählens." In *Unreliable Narration: Studien zur Theorie und Praxis unglaubwürdigen Erzählens in der englischsprachigen Erzählliteratur,* edited by Ansgar Nünning, Carola Surkamp and Bruno Zerweck. 3–40. Trier: Wissenschaftlicher Verlag Trier, 1998.

Nünning, Vera. "Unreliable Narration and the Historical Variability of Values and Norms: *The Vicar of Wakefield* as a Test Case of a Cultural-Historical Narratology." *Style* 38, no. 2 (2004): 236–52.

Nussbaum, Martha. *Poetic Justice: The Literary Imagination and Public Life.* Boston: Beacon Press, 1995.

Ó Dochartaigh, Pól. "Günter Grass's *Im Krebsgang* as a German Memory Contest without Jews." *German Life and Letters* 63, no. 2 (2010): 194–211.

Ohl, Hubert. "Eduards Heimkehr oder Le Vaillant und das Riesenfaultier: Zu Wilhelm Raabes *Stopfkuchen.*" In *Raabe in neuer Sicht,* edited by Hermann Helmers. 247–78. Stuttgart: W. Kohlhammer, 1968.

Öhlschläger, Claudia. *Beschädigtes Leben. Erzählte Risse: W. G. Sebalds poetische Ordnung des Unglücks.* Freiburg: Rombach, 2006.

Ortheil, Hanns-Josef. *Hecke.* Frankfurt: S. Fischer, 1983.

Palmer, Alan. *Social Minds in the Novel.* Columbus: Ohio State University Press, 2010.

Parker, David. "Narratives of Autonomy and Narratives of Relationality in Auto/Biography." *A/B: Auto/Biography Studies* 19, no. 1–2 (2004): 137–55.

Parry, Christoph. "Von den Vorzügen einer Fiktionalisierung: Peter Henischs und Peter Handkes Elternbiographien und die Suche nach einer adäquaten literarischen Form der Wahrheitsfindung." *Jahrbuch für internationale Germanistik* 33, no. 2 (2001): 81–100.

Pastor, Eckart. *Die Sprache der Erinnerung: Zu den Novellen von Theodor Storm.* Frankfurt: Athenäum, 1988.

Perry, Petra. "Peter Handkes *Wunschloses Unglück* als Kritik der Biographie: Geschichte und Geschichten." *Orbis Litterarum* 39 (1984): 160–68.

Pezold, Klaus. "*Im Krebsgang* und *Danziger Trilogie*—Weiterführung oder Zurücknahme?" In *Literatur—Grenzen—Erinnerungsräume*, edited by Bernd Neuman, Dietmar Albrecht, and Andrzej Talarczyk. 189–94. Würzburg: Königshausen & Neumann, 2004.

Phelan, James. "Bonding and Estranging Unreliability and the Ethics of *Lolita*." *Narrative* 15, no. 2 (2007): 222–38.

———. *Experiencing Fiction: Judgments, Progressions, and the Rhetorical Theory of Narrative.* Columbus: Ohio State University Press, 2007.

———. *Living to Tell about It: A Rhetoric and Ethics of Character Narration.* Ithaca, NY: Cornell University Press, 2004.

———. *Narrative as Rhetoric: Techniques, Audiences, Ethics, Ideology.* Columbus: Ohio State University Press, 1996.

———. "Rhetorical Literary Ethics and Lyric Narrative: Robert Frost's 'Home Burial.'" *Poetics Today* 25, no. 4 (2004): 627–51.

———. "Who's Here? Thoughts on Narrative Identity and Narrative Imperialism." *Narrative* 13, no. 3 (2005): 205–10.

Pickar, Gertrud B. "Intentional Ambiguity in Günter Grass' *Katz und Maus*." *Orbis Litterarum* 26 (1971): 232–45.

Pietsch, Timm. "*Wer hört noch zu?*" *Günter Grass als politischer Redner und Essayist.* Essen: Klartext, 2006.

Pizer, John. *Ego–Alter Ego: Double and/as Other in the Age of German Poetic Realism.* Chapel Hill: Univerity of North Carolina Press, 1998.

Plagwitz, Frank. "Die Crux des Heldentums: Zur Deutung des Ritterkreuzes in Günter Grass' *Katz und Maus*." *Seminar* 32, no. 1 (1996): 1–14.

Plumpe, Gerhard. "Gedächtnis und Erzählung: Zur Ästhetisierung des Erinnerns im Zeitalter der Information." In *Theodor Storm und die Medien: Zur Mediengeschichte eines poetischen Realisten,* edited by Harro Segeberg and Gerd Eversberg. 67–80. Berlin: Erich Schmidt, 1999.

Prager, Brad. "The Good German as Narrator: On W. G. Sebald and the Risks of Holocaust Writing." *New German Critique* 96 (2005): 75–102.

Pratt, Mary Louise. *Imperial Eyes: Travel Writing and Transculturation.* London: Routledge, 1992.

Preisendanz, Wolfgang. "Erzählstruktur als Bedeutungskomplex der *Akten des Vogelsangs*." *Jahrbuch der Raabe-Gesellschaft* (1981): 210–24.

———. *Humor als dichterische Einbildungskraft: Studien zur Erzählkunst des poetischen Realismus.* Munich: Eidos, 1963.

Presner, Todd Samuel. "'What a Synoptic and Artificial View Reveals': Extreme History and the Modernism of W. G. Sebald's Realism." *Criticism* 46, no. 3 (2004): 341–60.

Raabe, Wilhelm. *Sämtliche Werke.* Edited by Karl Hoppe. 20 vols. Göttingen: Vandenhoeck & Ruprecht, 1951–68.

———. *Tubby Schaumann: A Tale of Murder and the High Seas.* Translated by Barker Fairley. In *Wilhelm Raabe: Novels,* edited by Volkmar Sander. 155–311. New York: Continuum, 1983.

Rabinowitz, Peter J. "Truth in Fiction: A Reexamination of Audiences." *Critical Inquiry* 4, no. 1 (1977): 121–41.

Radisch, Iris. "Der Waschbär der falschen Welt: W. G. Sebald sammelt Andenken und rettet die Vergangenheit vom Vergehen." Review of *Austerlitz*, by W. G. Sebald. *Die Zeit*, April 5, 2001.

Rash, Felicity. "Verena Stefan Twenty Years On: Aesthetic and Linguistic Innovation in *Wortge-treu ich träume* and *Es ist reich gewesen.*" In *Whose Story? Continuities in German-language Literature*, edited by Arthur Williams, Stuart Parkes, and Julian Preece. 269–89. Bern: Peter Lang, 1998.

Reddick, John. *The "Danzig Trilogy" of Günter Grass*. New York: Harcourt Brace Jovanovich, 1974.

———. "Eine epische Trilogie des Leidens? *Die Blechtrommel, Katz und Maus, Hundejahre.*" *Text + Kritik* 1, no. 1 (1971): 38–51.

Reents, Edo. "Er hätte sagen sollen: 'Hier hätte ich auch liegen können'—Erich Loest über Günter Grass." *Frankfurter Allgemeine Zeitung*, August 15, 2006.

Rey, William H. "Provokation durch den Tod: Peter Handkes Erzählung *Wunschloses Unglück* als Modell stilistischer Integration." *German Studies Review* 1 (1978): 285–301.

Richards, Anna. "The Era of Sensibility and the Novel of Self-Fashioning." In *German Literature of the Eighteenth Century: The Enlightenment and Sensibility*, edited by Barbara Becker-Cantarino. 223–43. Rochester, NY: Camden House, 2005.

Richter, Frank. *Die zerschlagene Wirklichkeit: Überlegungen zur Form der Danzig-Trilogie von Günter Grass*. Bonn: Bouvier, 1977.

Richter, Frank-Raymund. *Günter Grass: Die Vergangenheitsbewältigung in der Danziger-Trilogie*. Bonn: Bouvier, 1979.

Richter, Hans Werner, ed. *Deine Söhne, Europa: Gedichte deutscher Kriegsgefangener*. Munich: Deutscher Taschenbuch Verlag, 1985.

Ricoeur, Paul. *Oneself as Another*. Translated by Kathleen Blamey. Chicago: University of Chicago Press, 1992.

Riehl, Wilhelm. *Die bürgerliche Gesellschaft*. Stuttgart: J. G. Cotta, 1861.

Roberts, David. "The Cult of the Hero: An Interpretation of Katz und Maus." *German Life and Letters* 29 (1976): 307–22.

Roebling, Irmgard. *Wilhelm Raabes doppelte Buchführung: Paradigma einer Spaltung*. Tübingen: Max Niemeyer, 1988.

Rothberg, Michael. "Progress, Progression, Procession: William Kentridge and the Narratology of Transitional Justice." *Narrative* 20, no. 1 (2012): 1–24.

Ruhleder, Karl H. "A Pattern of Messianic Thought in Günter Grass' *Cat and Mouse.*" *German Quarterly* 39, no. 4 (1966): 599–612.

Said, Edward. *Orientalism*. New York: Random House, 1978.

Sammons, Jeffrey L. *Wilhelm Raabe: The Fiction of the Alternative Community*. Princeton, NJ: Princeton University Press, 1987.

Santner, Eric L. "History beyond the Pleasure Principle: Some Thoughts on the Representation of Trauma." In *Probing the Limits of Representation: Nazism and the "Final Solution,"* edited by Saul Friedlander. 143–54. Cambridge, MA: Harvard University Press, 1992.

Sauder, Gerhard. *Empfindsamkeit*. Vol. 1. Stuttgart: Metzler, 1974.

Schaal, Gary S., and Andreas Wöll, eds. *Vergangenheitsbewältigung: Modelle der politischen und sozialen Integration in der bundesdeutshen Nachkriegsgeschichte*. Baden-Baden: Nomos, 1997.

Schaumann, Caroline. *Memory Matters: Generational Responses to Germany's Nazi Past in Recent Women's Literature*. Berlin: de Gruyter, 2008.

Schechtman, Marya. *The Constitution of Selves*. Ithaca, NY: Cornell University Press, 1997.

Schiller, Friedrich. *Werke und Briefe*. Vol. 4, Wallenstein. Frankfurt: Deutscher Klassiker, 2000.

Schindler, Stephen K. "Der Nationalsozialismus als Bruch mit dem alltäglichen Faschismus: Maria Handkes typisiertes Frauenleben in *Wunschloses Unglück.*" *German Studies Review* 19, no. 1 (1996): 41–59.

Schirrmacher, Frank, and Hubert Spiegel. "Eine deutsche Jugend: Günter Grass spricht zum ersten Mal über sein Erinnerungsbuch und seine Mitgliedschaft in der Waffen-SS." *Frankfurter Allgemeine Zeitung,* August 12, 2006.

Schlant, Ernestine. *The Language of Silence: West German Literature and the Holocaust.* New York: Routledge, 1999.

Schmitz, Helmut. "Family, Heritage, and German Wartime Suffering in Hanns-Josef Ortheil, Stephan Wackwitz, Thomas Medicus, Dagmar Leupold, and Uwe Timm." In *Germans as Victims in the Literary Fiction of the Berlin Republic,* edited by Stuart Taberner and Karina Berger. 70–85. Rochester, NY: Camden House, 2009.

———. *On Their Own Terms: The Legacy of National Socialism in Post-1990 German Fiction.* Birmingham: University of Birmingham Press, 2004.

Schneider, Michael. "Fathers and Sons, Retrospectively: The Damaged Relationship between Two Generations." Translated by Jamie Owen Daniel. *New German Critique* 31 (1984): 3–51.

Schnell, Ralf. *Geschichte der deutschsprachigen Literatur seit 1945.* 2nd ed. Stuttgart: J. B. Metzler, 2003.

Schunicht, Manfred. "Theodor Storm: *Ein Doppelgänger.*" In *Wege der Literaturwissenschaft,* edited by Jutta Kolkenbrock-Netz, Gerhard Plumpe, and Hans Joachim Schrimpf. 174–83. Bonn: Bouvier, 1985.

Schuster, Ingrid. "Storms *Ein Doppelgänger* und Brechts *Der gute Mensch von Sezuan:* Eine Gegenüberstellung." In *"Ich habe niemals eine Zeile geschrieben, wenn sie mir fern war."* 199–206. Berlin: Peter Lang, 1998.

Schütte, Uwe. *W. G. Sebald.* Göttingen: Vandenhoeck & Ruprecht, 2011.

Searle, John. *Speech Acts.* Cambridge: Cambridge University Press, 1969.

Searle, John, and Daniel Vanderveken. "Speech Acts and Illocutionary Logic." In *Logic, Thought, and Action,* edited by Daniel Vanderveken. 109–32. Berlin: Springer, 2005.

Sebald, W. G. *Austerlitz.* Frankfurt: Fischer Taschenbuch, 2003. Translated as *Austerlitz* by Anthea Bell. New York: Random House, 2001.

Sedgwick, Eve Kosofsky. *Epistemology of the Closet.* Berkeley, CA: University of California Press, 2008.

Seeba, Hinrich C. "Erfundene Vergangenheit: Zur Fiktionalität historischer Identitätsbildung in den Väter-Geschichten der Gegenwart." *Germanic Review* 66, no. 4 (1991): 176–81.

Segeberg, Harro. "Ferdinand Tönnies' *Gemeinschaft und Gesellschaft* und Theodor Storms Erzählkunst: Zur literarischen Spiegelung eines Epochenumbruchs." *Deutsche Vierteljahrsschrift für Literaturwissenschaft und Geistesgeschichte* 59 (1985): 474–96.

———. "Kritischer Regionalismus: Zum Verhältnis von Regionalität und Modernität bei Storm." In *Theodor Storm und das 19. Jahrhundert,* edited by Karl Ernst Laage and Brian Coghlan. 120–32. Berlin: Erich Schmidt, 1989.

———. "Theodor Storm als 'Dichter-Jurist': Zum Verhältnis von juristischer, moralischer und poetischer Gerechtigkeit in den Erzählungen *Draußen im Heidedorf* und *Ein Doppelgänger.*" *Schriften der Theodor-Storm-Gesellschaft* 41 (1992): 69–82.

Seidel, Eugen, and Ingeborg Seidel-Slotty. *Sprachwandel im Dritten Reich: Eine kritische Untersuchung faschistischer Einflüsse.* Halle: VEB Verlag, 1961.

Sevin, Dieter. "Frauenschicksal und Schreibprozeß in Ost und West: Christa Wolfs *Nachdenken über Christa T.* und Peter Handkes *Wunschloses Unglück.*" In *Kulturpolitik und Politik der Kultur,* edited by Helen Fehervary and Bernd Fischer. 211–20. Frankfurt: Peter Lang, 2007.

Sheehan, James. *German History, 1770–1866.* Oxford: Clarendon, 1989.

Shuman, Amy. *Other People's Stories: Entitlement Claims and the Critique of Empathy.* Urbana: University of Illinois Press, 2005.

Silverman, Kaja. *The Threshold of the Visible World.* New York: Routledge, 1996.

Smith, Sidonie, and Julia Watson. *Reading Autobiography: Interpreting Life Narratives.* 2nd ed. Minneapolis: University of Minnesota Press, 2010.

Spaethling, Robert. "Günter Grass, *Cat and Mouse.*" *Monatshefte* 62 (1970): 141–53.

Stanton, Domna. "Autogynography: Is the Subject Different?" In *The Female Autograph: Theory and Practice of Autobiography from the Tenth to the Twentieth Century,* edited by Domna Stanton. 3–20. Chicago: University of Chicago Press, 1987.

Stanzel, Franz. *Narrative Situations in the Novel.* Translated by James P. Pusack. Bloomington: Indiana University Press, 1971.

Stefan, Verena. *Es ist reich gewesen: Bericht vom Sterben meiner Mutter.* Frankfurt: Fischer Taschenbuch, 1993.

Steinfeld, Thomas. "Die Wünschelrute in der Tasche eines Nibelungen." *Frankfurter Allgemeine Zeitung,* March 20, 2001.

Stoffel, G. M. "Antithesen in Peter Handkes Erzählung *Wunschloses Unglück.*" *Colloquia Germanica* 18, no. 1 (1985): 40–54.

Stoler, Ann Laura. *Carnal Knowledge and Imperial Power: Race and the Intimate in Colonial Rule.* Berkeley: University of California Press, 2002.

Storm, Theodor. *Sämtliche Werke.* Edited by Karl Ernst Laage. Vol. 3, *Novellen: 1881–1888.* Frankfurt: Deutscher Klassiker, 1988.

StoryCorps. "About Us." storycorps.org/about/.

Strawson, Galen. "Against Narrativity." *Ratio* 17, no. 4 (2004): 428–52.

Stuckert, Franz. *Theodor Storm: Sein Leben und seine Welt.* Bremen: C. Schünemann, 1955.

Taberner, Stuart. "German Nostalgia? Remembering German-Jewish Life in W. G. Sebald's *Die Ausgewanderten* and *Austerlitz.*" *Germanic Review* 79, no. 3 (2004): 181–202.

———. "'Kann schon sein, daß in jedem Buch von ihm etwas Egomäßiges rauszufinden ist': 'Political' Private Biography and 'Private' Private Biography in Günter Grass's *Die Box* (2008)." *German Quarterly* 82, no. 4 (2009): 504–21.

———. "Private Failings and Public Virtues: Günter Grass's *Beim Häuten der Zwiebel* and the Exemplary Use of Authorial Biography." *Modern Language Review* 103 (2008): 143–54.

Taylor, Charles. *Sources of the Self: The Making of the Modern Identity.* Cambridge, MA: Harvard University Press, 1989.

Teitel, Ruti. "Transitional Justice as Liberal Narrative." In *Out of and Into Authoritarian Law,* edited by András Sajó. 3–13. The Hague: Kluwer Law International, 2003.

Textor, Friedrich Ludwig. *Leben, Abentheuer und Heldentod Paul Roderichs des Democraten: Eine Geschichte aus dem gegenwärtigen Kriege von seinem aristocratischen Vetter beschrieben.* Vienna, 1794.

Thesz, Nicole. "Against a New Era in Vergangenheitsbewältigung: Grass's *Hundejahre* to *Im Krebsgang.*" *Colloquia Germanica* 37, no. 4 (2004): 291–306.

Thomas, N. L. "An Analysis of Günter Grass' *Katz und Maus* with Particular Reference to the Religious Themes." *German Life and Letters* 26 (1973): 227–38.

Thompson, Dennis, and Robert Rotberg, eds. *Truth vs. Justice: The Morality of Truth Commissions.* Princeton, NJ: Princeton University Press, 2000.

Todorov, Tzvetan. *The Poetics of Prose.* Translated by Richard Howard. Ithaca, NY: Cornell University Press, 1977.

Tschorn, Wolfgang. "Der Verfall der Familie: *Der Herr Etatsrat* und *Ein Doppelgänger* als Beispiele zu einem zentralen Darstellungsobjekt Storms." *Schriften der Theodor-Storm-Gesellschaft* 29 (1980): 44–52.

Tucker, Brian. "Wilhelm Raabe's *Stopfkuchen* and the Ground of Memory." *Monatshefte* 95, no. 4 (2003): 568–82.

Twark, Jill E. "Landscape, Seascape, Cyberscape: Narrative Strategies to Dredge Up the Past in Günter Grass's Novella *Im Krebsgang.*" *Gegenwartsliteratur* 3 (2004): 143–68.

van Alphen, Ernst. *Caught by History: Holocaust Effects in Contemporary Art, Literature, and Theory.* Stanford, CA: Stanford University Press, 1997.

Varsava, Jerry A. "Auto-Bio-Graphy as Metafiction: Peter Handke's *A Sorrow beyond Dreams.*" *CLIO* 14, no. 2 (1985): 119–35.

Vierhaus, Rudolf. "Bürgerliche Hegemonie oder proletarische Emanzipation: Der Beitrag der Bildung." In *Arbeiter und Bürger im 19. Jahrhundert: Varianten ihres Verhältnisses im europäischen Vergleich,* edited by Jürgen Kocka. 53–64. Munich: R. Oldenbourg, 1986.

Vogel, Sabine. "Literaturskandale: Dank Günter Grass erinnert das neue deutsche Nationalgefühl an das alte." *Berliner Zeitung,* December 30, 2006.

Walker, Mack. *German Home Towns: Community, State, and General Estate, 1648–1871.* Ithaca, NY: Cornell University Press, 1998.

Walter-Schneider, Margret. "Erzählen, 'als wenn man einen alten Strumpf aufriwwelt': Zu Raabes *Stopfkuchen,* Kafkas 'Sirenengeschichte' und Dürrenmatts *Sterben der Pythia.*" *Jahrbuch der Raabe-Gesellschaft* 46 (2006): 97–125.

Waters, William. *Poetry's Touch: On Lyric Address.* Ithaca, NY: Cornell University Press, 2003.

Watt, Roderick H. *An Annotated Edition of Victor Klemperer's LTI: Notizbuch eines Philologen.* Lewiston, NY: Edwin Mellen, 1997.

Wehler, Hans-Ulrich. *Deutsche Gesellschaftsgeschichte.* Vol. 3. Munich: C. H. Beck, 1995.

Weigel, Sigrid. "'Generation' as a Symbolic Form: On the Genealogical Discourse of Memory since 1945." *Germanic Review* 77, no. 4 (2002): 264–77.

Weitzel, Johann. *Lindau oder der unsichtbare Bund.* Frankfurt: Bernhard Körner, 1805.

Wertgen, Werner. *Vergangenheitsbewältigung: Interpretation und Verantwortung: ein ethischer Beitrag zu ihrer theoretischen Grundlegung.* Paderborn: Schöningh, 2001.

White, Hayden. "Historical Emplotment and the Problem of Truth." In *Probing the Limits of Representation: Nazism and the "Final Solution,"* edited by Saul Friedländer. 37–53. Cambridge, MA: Harvard University Press, 1992.

———. "The Question of Narrative in Contemporary Historical Theory." *History and Theory* 23, no. 1 (1984): 1–33.

Widmann, Arno. "Unser Wegweiser." *Berliner Zeitung,* August 15, 2006, 3.

Wildenthal, Lora. *German Women for Empire, 1884–1945.* Durham, NC: Duke University Press, 2001.

Williams, Arthur. "'Das korsakowsche Syndrom': Remembrance and Responsibility in W. G. Sebald." In *German Culture and the Uncomfortable Past: Representations of National Socialism in Contemporary Germanic Literature*, edited by Helmut Schmitz. 65–86. Aldershot, UK: Ashgate, 2001.

———. "W. G. Sebald: A Holistic Approach to Borders, Texts, and Perspectives." In *German-Language Literature Today: International and Popular?*, edited by Arthur Williams, Stuart Parks and Julian Preece. 99–118. Bern, Switzerland: Peter Lang, 2000.

Wilms, Wilfried. "Speak No Evil, Write No Evil: In Search of a Usable Language of Destruction." In *W. G. Sebald: History—Memory—Trauma*, edited by Mark McCulloh and Scott Denham. 183–204. Berlin: de Gruyter, 2006.

———. "Taboo and Repression in Sebald's *On the Natural History of Destruction*." In *W. G. Sebald: A Critical Companion*, edited by Anne Whitehead and J. J. Long. 175–89. Seattle: University of Washington Press, 2004.

Wirtz, Thomas. "Schwarze Zuckerwatte: Anmerkungen zu W. G. Sebald." *Merkur*, 2001, 530–34.

Wolf, Christa. *Kindheitsmuster*. Munich: Deutscher Taschenbuch Verlag, 1993.

———. *A Model Childhood*. Translated by Ursule Molinaro and Hedwig Rappolt. New York: Farrar, Straus & Giroux, 1980.

Wolff, Lynn L. "H. G. Adler and W. G. Sebald: From History and Literature to Literature as Historiography." *Monatshefte* 103, no. 2 (2011): 257–75.

———. *W. G. Sebald's Hybrid Poetics: Literature as Historiography*. Berlin: de Gruyter, 2014.

Zantop, Susanne. *Colonial Fantasies: Conquest, Family, and Nation in Precolonial Germany, 1770–1870*. Durham, NC: Duke University Press, 1997.

Zerweck, Bruno. "Historicizing Unreliable Narration: Unreliability and Cultural Discourse in Narrative Fiction." *Style* 35, no. 1 (2001): 151–78.

Zilcosky, John. "Lost and Found: Disorientation, Nostalgia, and Holocaust Melodrama in Sebald's *Austerlitz*." *MLN* 121, no. 3 (2006): 679–98.

Ziolskowski, Theodore. *Fictional Transfigurations of Jesus*. Princeton, NJ: Princeton University Press, 1972.

Zorach, Cecile Cazort. "Freedom and Remembrance: The Language of Biography in Peter Handke's *Wunschloses Unglück*." *German Quarterly* 52, no. 4 (1979): 486–502.

index

THEORY AND INTERPRETATION OF NARRATIVE

James Phelan, Peter J. Rabinowitz, and Robyn Warhol, Series Editors

Because the series editors believe that the most significant work in narrative studies today contributes both to our knowledge of specific narratives and to our understanding of narrative in general, studies in the series typically offer interpretations of individual narratives and address significant theoretical issues underlying those interpretations. The series does not privilege one critical perspective but is open to work from any strong theoretical position.